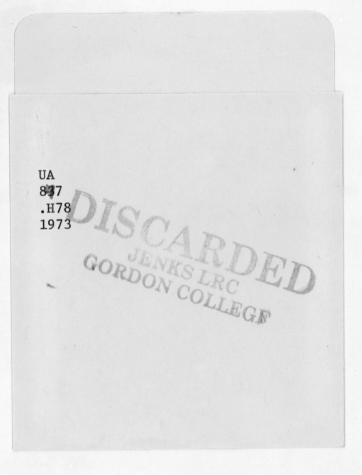

This book is presented to you with our compliments. Your comments on the compilation, collation and printing are welcome.
We would also appreciate it if you would put us on your mailing list for your publications and establish a publication exchange relationship with us.

CHUNG WU PUBLISHING CO.
33, Lane 140, Tung Hua Street
Taipei, Taiwan
Republic of China

A Brief History
of the Chinese National
Revolutionary Forces

A Brief History
of the Chinese National
Revolutionary Forces

Compiled by   Hu Pu-yu

Translated by   Wen Ha-hsiung

Revised by   Yu Po-chuan
Hsu Long-hsuen
Chang Ming-kai
Lo Han-ching
Han Tsan
Huang Hsiang-chun
Liu Han-mou
Lu Pao-ching

CHUNG WU PUBLISHING CO.
Taipei, Taiwan
Republic of China

Printed by
CHINA PRINTING, LTD.
Republic of China

Contents

MAPS

A Brief History
of the Chinese National
Revolutionary Forces

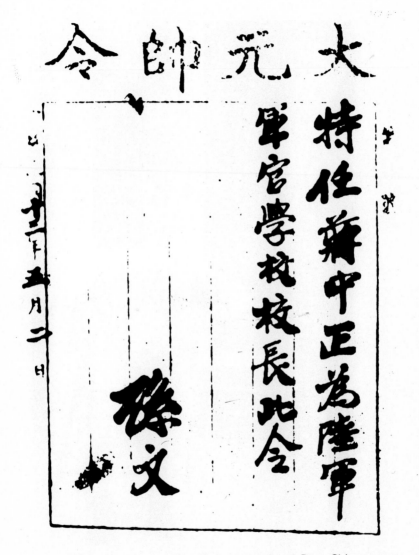

大元帥令

特任蔣中正為陸軍軍官學校校長此令

孫文

中華民國十三年五月二日

As the Generalissimo, Dr. Sun Yat-sen appointed Pres. Chiang superintendent of the Military Academy, thereby entrusting him with heavy responsibilities in the revolution. (May 2, 1924)

Dr. Sun Yat-sen posing with Pres. Chiang, then superintendent of the Military Academy. (June 16, 1924)

Commander-in-Chief Chiang at the oath-taking ceremony in Canton Prior to the Northward Expedition. (July 9, 1926)

Upon successful completion of the Northward Expedition, Chiang, leading a group of high officials and generals, pays homage to the late Dr. Sun Yat-sen in suburban Peiping in his capacity as Commander-in-Chief of the Revolutionary Forces. (July 6, 1928)

Generalissimo Chiang departing from the opening ceremony of the Lu Shan Officers' Training Corps. (May 18, 1933)

Generalissimo Chiang at a mass rally in Nanchang, Kiangsi in support of the New Life Movement. (Mar. 19, 1934)

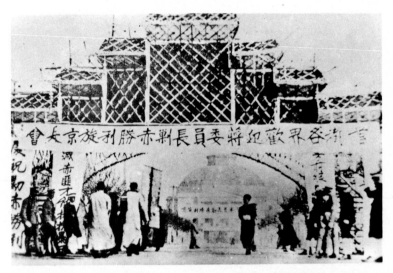

The nation's capital warmly welcoming Generalissimo's triumphant return upon suppression of the Chinese Communists. (Nov. 20, 1934)

Lukouchiao (Marco Polo Bridge) unveiling full-scale War of Resistance. (July 7, 1937)

After the outbreak of the Marco Polo Bridge Incident, President Chiang issued a statement at Lu Shan in which he considered that the critical moment had arrived, and decided to fight against Japan. (July 17, 1937)

On August 14, 1937, the Chinese Air Force shot down nine Japanese planes. The day was later proclaimed the Air Force Day (Aug. 14, 1937)

The Battle of Tai Erh Chuang in the southern part of Shantung resulted in a stunning blow to the invading Japanese forces during the anti-Japanese War. (Mar. 24, 1938)

A Chinese Air Force bomber returns from a bombing mission over Japan. (May 20, 1938)

Generalissimo Chiang reiterating his determination to fight to the end.
(December 26, 1938)

The Japanese arms and munitions captured during the Chuen-yang
battle in northern China. (Dec. 20, 1938)

President Chiang, Supreme Allied Commander, China Theater, posing with Mme. Chiang. (Jan. 3, 1942)

President Chiang inspecting Chinese Expeditionary Forces in India. (Mar. 2, 1942)

President and Mme. Chiang conferred with U.S. President Franklin D. Roosevelt and British Prime Minister Winston Churchill in Cairo. (Nov. 24, 1943)

Chinese troops cross the Irrawaddy River in Burma to rescue besieged Allied Forces. (Nov. 14, 1944)

President Chiang inspecting units of the Youth Corps. (Dec. 20, 1944)

Link-up of Chinese and American forces at Mongyu after the defeat of the Japanese forces in northern Burma. (Jan. 27, 1945)

President Chiang inspects the wartime capital of Chungking immediately after V-J Day. (Aug. 15, 1945)

On behalf of President Chiang, Gen. Ho Ying-chin, C-in-C Chinese Army, accepted the surrender text from Gen. Neiji Okamura, C-in-C Japanese forces in China, at the Central Military Academy in Nanking. (Sept. 9, 1945)

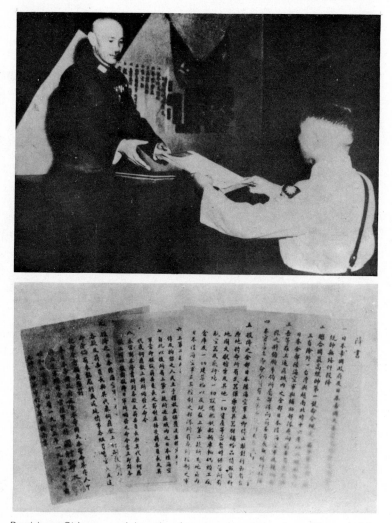

President Chiang receiving the Japanese surrender text forwarded by
Lt. Gen. Leng Hsin. (Sept. 10, 1945)

Celebrations marking the return of Taiwan to China after V-J Day. (Oct. 25, 1946)

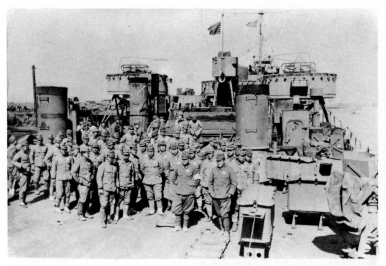

Subsequent to the Japanese surrender, Generalissimo Chiang announced the return of kindness for hatred and sent over two million Japanese troops and civilians safely to Japan. (Nov. 18, 1945)

The triumphant return to the capital city of Nanking after V-J Day. (May 5, 1946)

Russia invaded Northeast China and turned over all the equipment of the Japanese Kwangtung Army to the Chinese Communists in preparation for full-scale Communist rebellion. (May 6, 1946)

President Chiang inspects the Chinese Communist lair of Yenan captured by government forces after a mop-up operation. (Aug. 7, 1947)

President Chiang resumes presidency at the urge of the people after a brief retirement. (Mar. 1, 1950)

Gen. Lai Ming-tang, Chief of the General Staff, then chief of G-2 of the National Defense Ministry, signs document on behalf of the Chinese government to accept the 14,342 Chinese prioners of the Korean War. (Jan. 20, 1954)

Premier Chiang Ching-kuo, then director of the General Political Department of the Ministry of National Defense, welcomes the 14,000 Chinese Communist prisoners of the Korean War after they choose freedom. (Jan. 23, 1954)

Gen. Lai Ming-tang, standing beside truck, sees off the freedom fighters on their way to Taiwan. (Jan. 21, 1954)

Under the inspiring leadership of President Chiang, their commander-in-chief, the armed forces are in full preparedness for the recovery of the China mainland.

CHAPTER ONE

Founding of the Military Academy and Build-Up of Armed Forces

Section 1
Founding of the Military Academy

Danger Lurking Everywhere in the Nation

Subsequent to the establishment of the Republic of China, the remnants of the former monarchy had not been totally wiped out as the northern warlords initially controlled the central government and later occupied various areas. Meanwhile, foreign powers took advantage of the chaotic situation to reap profits. As a result, chaos and disorder reigned supreme while the nation tottered near destruction. Conscious of the difficulties involved in giving birth to the Republic and realizing that the nation's destiny was at stake, Dr. Sun Yat-sen, our National Father, reorganized the Revolutionary Government in Canton in February, 1923 and exercised the command and authority of the Generalissimo. Dr. Sun felt that the setbacks in the revolution were attributed mainly to the lack of revolutionary forces which had faith in the principles. Further, the marrying of the local forces and the revolutionary government was not one of revolutionary aspirations but one of profit and loss. As the relationship of profit and loss underwent constant changes, their actions varied greatly. Even the minority which claimed to be revolutionary forces and lacked rigid political training, fought poorly and were swayed by evil influences. As a result they frequently became turncoats thus heightening the revolutionary crises.

Meanwhile, the warlords of the various cliques courted the favor of foreign powers and competed among themselves. The influential warlords who controlled the puppet government in the north were intoxicated in the sweet dream of unifying China by force. The lesser warlords held firm in one or several provinces advocating joint, provincial autonomy. In Kwangtung Province, Chen Chiun-ming occupied Tung Chiang (East River) in the east and Teng Peng-yin was restless in the south. With the support of the British imperialists, the Canton Volunteer Corps covertly planned insurgence. The arrogant forces of Yunnan and Kwangsi created chaos. Looking into the future, the success of our revolution was hanging by the thread.

Intrigues and Infiltrations of the Communist International

In the international field, it was most noteworthy that Lenin had long recognized China's importance to the world. Hence, early in the establishment of the Republic, Lenin said: "Soviet Russia did not wish to see a strong and independent Asian republic come into being as a result of China's revolution against the Manchu Dynasty. Plans should be made to capture the newly established Republic of China as a satellite base for the expansion of Communism" (see China's Democracy and Narodism written by Lenin on 15 July, 1912). In 1920, the Communist International sent people to China to organize the Chinese Communist Party into a secret group engineering intrigues and uprisings. In order to expand its organizational basis, Chinese Communist Party members disguised as individuals joined the Kuomintang (the Nationalist Party). In reality, they still retained Communist Party membership.

In 1922 Soviet Russia sent Adolf Joffe to call on Dr. Sun in Shanghai pretending to be "sympathetic" toward the Chinese Revolution. After ten days of lengthy discussions, on 26 January, 1923 a joint declaration was issued in which the following four points were mentioned:

(1) Soviet Russia recognized that the Soviet system was not suitable to China.

(2) Soviet Russia wished to reiterate the abolition of unequal treaties.

(3) The status quo should be maintained in the operation of the Chinese Eastern Railway. Later, the two governments would consult and solve the problems of operation.

(4) Soviet Russia stated that it had no intention of practicing imperialist policies in Outer Mongolia.

Soviet Russia was forced to launch such a smiling offensive and to expand eastward as it was subjected to the encirclement and blockade of western powers. Outwardly, it pretended to be friendly to China. In reality, it permitted the Chinese Communist Party lying in hiding in the Kuomintang to engage in sabotage and division and later to realize its intrigue of capturing China.

Gen. Chiang Kai-shek's Recommendation

In the midst of these seemingly insurmountable difficulties, Dr. Sun Yat-sen deeply felt that the revolutionary task must start from scratch. Hence, he proceeded to reorganize the Kuomintang hoping to lay the foundation of the party on the youths and the people. On the other hand, he planned the establishment of revolutionary military forces in order to thoroughly implement the Three Principles of the People, unify China and save the Chinese people from destruction.

In January, 1924, in his report to Generalissimo Sun on his findings after a three-month visit to Russia, Gen. Chiang Kai-shek, Chief of Staff of the General Headquarters, stated: "Soviet Russia has never abandoned its aggressive designs on Outer Mongolia. As to assistance to China to gain independence and freedom, it has no sincerity. The Soviet political system which is an organization of despotism and terror is incompatible with the political system and the Three Principles of the People advocated by the Kuomintang. The strategy and the objective of Soviet Russia in her World Revolution program were even more dangerous to national independence movements in the Orient than the old colonialism. It is not improbable that once the Russian Communist regime becomes powerful, the political designs of the Czarist time will be reborn. The subsequent disaster befalling the Republic of China and the national revolution will be unthinkable."

This report not only saw through Soviet Russia's ambition in supporting the Chinese Communists. Later developments coincided fully with his predictions.

Fully aware of the danger lurking everywhere in the nation and the intrigues and infiltrations of the Communist International, Gen. Chiang Kai-shek formally made a recommendation to Generalissimo Sun in which he stated: "In

order to make China powerful, it is imperative that China
be unified. In order to unify China, it is imperative that the
warlords be eliminated. In order to eliminate the warlords,
it is imperative that the armed forces be organized. In order
to organize the armed forces, it is imperative that a military
academy be established." His recommendation was immediately accepted by Generalissimo Sun and submitted as
a proposal to the Kuomintang's First National Congress for
resolution. The proposal called for the establishment of the
"Kuomintang Military Academy." The establishment of the
Academy laid the cornerstone of a new China.

Founding of the Military Academy and Its Missions

On 24 January 1924, Generalissimo Sun appointed Gen.
Chiang Kai-shek chairman of the Preparatory Committee for
establishment of the Military Academy. Wang Po-ling, Teng
Yen-ta, Shen Yin-shih, Lin Chen-hsiung, Yu Fei-peng, Chang
Chia-jui and Sung Yung-chang were named members of the
Preparatory Committee. The Whampoa Island near Canton
was designated as the site of the Military Academy with
preparatory work well under way. Over 2,000 youths from
various provinces flocked to Whampoa to take the examination. 499 cadets were admitted to the Academy. On 3
May, Gen. Chiang Kai-shek was named Superintendent and
concurrently Chief of Staff of the Kwangtung Army Headquarters as well as Commander of the Chang-chou Fortress
Command. On 9 May, Liao Chung-kai was named party
representative.

On 16 June, the Military Academy held its opening ceremony which was attended by more than 500 guests. Shortly
after 9:00 A.M. on that day, Generalissimo Sun addressed

the audience and made known the objective in the establishment of the Academy and the spirit of the armed forces build-up. Excerpts of his address are as follows:

"Beginning to-day we shall re-make our revolutionary tasks. We shall use the cadet of this Academy as the basis for organizing the revolutionary forces. With such an excellent skeletal structure to organize the revolutionary forces on, we shall succeed in our revolutionary tasks. Without superior revolutionary forces, China's revolution is doomed to failure. Therefore, as we establish the Military Academy here today, our one and only hope is to organize revolutionary forces to save China from destruction.

"What are the criteria for people to become members of the Revolutionary Forces? Briefly speaking, we should follow the footsteps of our martyrs and be willing to sacrifice our lives, give up our rights and dedicate ourselves to the saving of the nation like they did. Only by so doing, can we become 'death-defying' revolutionary soldiers. I dare say that the secret of a revolutionary lies in 'death-defying' spirit. With such courage and determination, one man can fight against a hundred men. The enemy's concept is that happiness can be had from living. Our concept is that happiness can be had from dying, for a person dies for a cause. When the difference between the enemy and us concerning life and death is so great, the enemy is, of course, no match. Then, our victory will be a certainty.

"Therefore, I urge that you fear not death and follow in the footsteps of our revolutionary martyrs. What is more, I shall use these five hundred cadets as the basis on which my ideal revolutionary forces will be built. When this is done, our revolution will succeed, China will be saved and our

400 million compatriots will not perish."

Generalissimo Sun's two-hour address greatly moved the audience. It was particularly moving when he handed the official's seal of the Military Academy to the superintendent General Chiang Kai-shek, for it symbolized the turning over of the responsibilities in the revolution. Upon completion of the address, Generalissimo Sun read a prepared speech which became our national anthem to-day. Subsequently Superintendent Chiang copied the speech and had it inscribed on a tablet hung on the stone wall in Dr. Sun's Mausoleum. The title has since remained the motto of the Military Academy.

Generalissimo Sun was followed by Superintendent Chiang who described the sacred mission in establishing the Military Academy, in building up the armed forces and in entrusting the cadets with the responsibilities. Excerpts of his speech read as follows:

"The purpose of our Party's establishment of this Academy is to train us to stem the rushing tide in the midst of great difficulties, liberate our compatriots from sufferings and bring peace to mankind. This then is the objective of our Party's establishment of this Academy and the responsibility of our comrades in the Academy."

Superintendent Chiang's untiring efforts resulted in the continued improvement of the Military Academy. In November, 1924 Generalissimo Sun set out for the north via Whampoa. When he arrived at the Military Academy for an inspection, he stated: "The fact that the cadets can fight and endure such hardships is an indication that they will propagate my mission and carry out our Party's principles." His praise well reflected his expectations of Superintendent

Chiang and the Military Academy.

Organization and Education of the Military Academy

The Chinese Kuomintang Military Academy, known as the Whampoa Military Academy, had a director-general, a superintendent and a party representative who formed the Academy Headquarters. Under it there were the Office of the Superintendent, the Political Division, the Military Training Division (for military subjects), the Academic Division (for academic subjects), the Administrative Division, the Quartermaster Division, the Medical Division and the Office of the Chief Instructor. Under the Military Training Division there was a cadet corps which had four companies. Each company had three platoons.

In the personnel field, Generalissimo Sun acted concurrently as the Director-General exercising command over the Superintendent and the Party Representative in the administration of the Academy. Tai Chuan-hsien, Li Chi-shen and Wang Po-ling served respectively as the Chief of the Political, Military Training and Academic Divisions, and Ho Ying-chin was the Chief Instructor. The platoon leaders were selected from the graduates of the Kwangtung Provincial Guard Military Academy and the Kiangsi Military Academy. Outstanding personnel served as instructors and senior staff members. In addition, Hu Han-min and Tai Chuan-hsien taught as part-time political instructors.

The purpose of the Academy's education was to turn out in the shortest time revolutionary soldiers who believed in the Three Principles of the People, and to form a revolutionary force. Its educational guidelines were to imbue the cadets with the current revolutionary requirements, belief in the Three Principles of the People, establishment of the three military virtues of wisdom, kindness and courage, determination to succeed or to die, adherence to revolutionary discipline, building of strong bodies, study of revolutionary tactics and practicing of combat skills in order to undertake the sacred mission of saving the nation and the people.

Based on the above-mentioned purpose and guidelines which called for emphasis on the cadets' military knowledge and technical training, the Director-General, the Superintendent and the Party Representative constantly provided the cadets with revolutionary theories, human philosophy and inspirational talks. Additionally, a Revolutionary Military Study Group was organized at the Academy Headquarters with sub-groups organized in other localities. The group met once a month. Study outlines were divided into intelligence, current events, organization, investigation, education, armament, materials and construction. There were the following 13 topics for study:

(1) Domestic military changes which took place each week.

(2) A recording of military, political and economic orders issued by Peiping's puppet regime.

(3) Weekly political changes of the nations in the world and news of the revolution,

(4) News on the movement of the troops in the north.

(5) Study on the organizations of the combat troops in the south.

(6) An investigation on the anticipated future routes in Combat.

(7) A study on the number of personnel and of days

for cadre education after the cadets' graduation.

(8) A study on the weaknesses of the southern forces and proposed corrective measures with emphasis on the essentials.

(9) Plans for the dispatch of military topography personnel by various factions (including roads, terrain, economic situation, customs, people's practices, communications, provision capability, bivouac capability, census and population).

(10) A study on the use of old weapons.

(11) Plans for the organization of the Revolutionary Forces (number of people, duration, weapons and pay.)

(12) A study on the organization of the Revolutionary Forces.

(13) A study on the military, financial, agricultural and labor conditions in Kwangtung.

In implementing education, efforts were made to combine spirit, politics and military into one entity. Within this entity, political education provided the ends, military education the means and spiritual education the mentality or ability to recognize the ends. Spiritual education was given added emphasis. Its contents were revolutionary spirit, revolutionary thinking and fine character. Later, the slogans of "Fear no death, covet no wealth, love the nation and love the people" and the tenets of "Solidarity, responsibility and sacrifice" became the essence of the Whampoa Military Academy's spiritual training. Political education aimed at the indoctrination of the Three Principles of the People and the nurturing of the revolutionary spirit and an understanding of the world's situation and domestic social conditions.

Military education stressed the exploration of general theories and the skills required in actual combat with added emphasis on the implementation so that tactical proficiency and combat skills might be improved.

The education at the Military Academy, ranging from the purpose to the methods, was clearly defined and highly systematized. It had the form of political training of the army and paved the way for political training which in later years contributed to civil-military cooperation. Therefore, it was not only the permanent foundation in Chinese military education but also generated the Whampoa spirit in national renaissance.

As the education and training of the Military Academy had no precedents, Superintendent Chiang did much in planning and supervision. The five hundred rifles used in the early days of the training were secretly shipped by Shih Ching Arsenal at Dr. Sun's order. By Oct. when the Canton Volunteer Corps Incident instigated by the British imperialists was suppressed and over 9,000 rifles were captured, weapon replenishment became a reality. The cadets of the First Class were all infantrymen and the training duration was six months. Beginning with the Second Class, the duration was lengthened and the cadets were divided into infantry, artillery, engineer, quartermaster and military police branches.

When the Military Academy was first established, there were few weapons and funds were lacking. When the counter revolutionary forces learned of the Academy's purpose, they did everything they could to jeopardize its success. The situation then confronting the Academy was most unfavorable. Furtunately, Dr. Sun helped greatly in removing the obstacles and Superintendent Chiang was both patient and indomitable. Party Representative Liao Chung-kai spared no effort to make the funds required available. Finally they succeeded in turning out revolutionary cadres in half a year's time and laid the cornerstone in the building up of the armed forces.

The Whampoa Military Academy came into being because of the situation at that time. In less than three months after its establishment, when domestic and foreign troubles were brewing, preparations were made for war. The cadets took part in the Northward Expedition in September, 1924, leading off for Shaokuan and the suppression of the Canton Volunteer Corps[1] in October and the Eastward Expedition and the operations against Yang and Liu[2] in the following years. The courses which had been missed were made up later upon return to the Military Academy.

---

[1] Suppression of Canton Volunteer Corps Rebellion:
In August, 1924, Chen Lien-po, commander of the Canton Volunteer Corps, under the instigation of the British Imperialist Hong Kong Government, conspired with traitor Chen Chiung-ming. He attempted to turn the corps into a Fascist organization by subverting the revolutionary government. Within a period of four days, 9,000 rifles were shipped to Canton from Hong Kong. On 10 October, members of the corps shot people participating in the national day parade and forced the shops to close down. The situation in Canton was touch-and-go. Chen fled to Hong Kong when Superintendent Chiang was ordered to suppress the rebellion.

[2] Operations against Yang and Liu:
In June, 1925, under the instigation of traitor Chen Chiun-ming. Yang Hsi-ming of the Yunnan force and Liu Chen-huan of the Kwangsi force sieged Canton at a time when the party force was engaged in the Eastward Expedition. Swiftly Superintendent Chiang turned his forces and quelled the rebellion staged by Yang and Liu.

Section 2
Organizing the Academy Force

Overcoming Numerous Obstacles to Organize the Academy Force .

Shortly after the establishment of the Whampoa Military Academy, the Revolutionary Government was forced by circumstances to organize and train an elite party military force in order to protect the Constitution and to fight the traitors. Upon receipt of order, Superintendent Chiang intensified the training of the cadets and dispatched personnel to Nanking and Shanghai to recruit soldiers secretly. In September 1924 when Generalissimo Sun led the forces in the Northward Expedition and was stationed in Shaokuan, he wrote a personal letter to Superintendent Chiang in which he stated: "Troop training is the basic essential in our present task." In reply Superintendent Chiang said: "In two months, a well-trained force will be ready."

The secret recruiting work was interrupted by the warlords in various places and culminated in extreme difficulties. Even the recruiting personnel were killed. As Generalissimo Sun was anxiously awaiting the availability of the Academy force, traitor Chen Chiun-ming was laying his eyes on Canton. Indeed the Revolutionary Government found itself in a most precarious position. Fully aware of the difficult situation, Superintendent Chiang devoted himself to the organization and training of the Training Regiment. On the one hand, he led the cadres in their performance of duties. On the other hand, he indoctrinated the soldiers with the Three Principles of the People. He spared no effort in order to turn out a revolutionary force in the shortest possible time.

On 20 November, the First Training Regiment was activated. The regiment had three battalions; each battalion had three companies; and each company had three platoons. in addition, the regiment had a guard company, a reconnaissance company, a machine gun company, a signal company, a quartermaster company and a medical detachment. On 28 November, Ho Ying-chin resigned from the post of Chief Instructor to assume command of the First Training Regiment. On 26 December, the Second Training Regiment was organized, with Wang Po-ling as the regimental commander. Officers of the two regiments were selected from the instructors of the Military Academy. Platoon leaders of the cadet corps served as the company commanders of the two regiments and graduates of the Academy served as platoon leaders and squad leaders. Party representatives were installed in units from the regiment to the company and were selected from faculty members and cadets who had political knowledge. They were appointed by the Central Government. Officers and men of the two regiments shared everything and shared alike. They believed in the cause and adhered to party and military descipline. The activation of the Training Regiments led to sincerity, solidarity and flexible command, laying a firm foundation for the Party military force.

Laying a Foundation for Revolutionary Forces

The military force of the Kuomintang Military Academy was formally activated on 6 January 1925. It commanded the First and the Second Training Regiments, both of which took part in the Battle of Chaochow-Swatow and the recovery of Tung Chiang (East River).[3] On 13 April the "Academy Force" was redesignated the "Party Force," with Superintendent Chiang as the commander. On 21 April the Third Training Regiment was activated with Chien Ta-chun as the regimental commander. By the time the Yunnan and Kwangsi insurgent forces were mopped up, the "Party Force" was reorganized into a division with Ho Ying-chin as the division commander. Subsequently, the Fourth and the Fifth Training Regiments as well as the Artillery Regiment and the Military Police Regiment were activated. Hence, the strength of the "Party Force" was further increased. Since then, the Kuomintang built itself on the masses, and the National Revolutionary Forces undertook the sacred mission of historical significance.

Fully Developing Revolutionary Spirit

When the "Academy Force" was first activated, it inherited the traditional Whampoa spirit of "Fear no death, covet no wealth, love the nation and love the people; Solidarity, responsibility and sacrifice" in its organizational structure. A special party headquarters was established along the lines of the Training Regiment to strengthen military discipline with party discipline. Finances were kept open. All these measures contributed to excellent esprit de corps and harmonious civil-military relationship. Superintendent Chiang personally wrote the Revolutionary Forces Inter-

---

[3] Battle of Chaochow-Swatow and Recovery of Tungchiang:
In January, 1925, traitor Chen Chiun-ming massed a force of 100,000 to invade Canton. The Government issued orders to suppress him. Superintendent Chiang led the Whampoa Academy force as the vanguard. In three months, Chaochow, Mei Hsien, and Tungchiang were recovered.

locking Laws to enforce military discipline. Hence, satis-factory results was obtained and the revolutionary forces were invincible.

The Academy Force had a political department which not only provided deliberate political training to the military forces and the civilians, but also encouraged the military forces to sacrifice for the cause and the people. The people were taught the Three Principles of the People. They were taught that the Revolutionary Forces were the People's Military Forces so that they would assist the Revolutionary Forces in combat.

As the Revolutionary Forces had a central theme in their belief, outstanding leadership, special spirit, party-political system and strict discipline, they differed from the ordinary military forces. A spirit of sacrifice was developed which contributed to high morale in solidarity and became a force which could fight against numerical superiority and thus brought the spirit of the national revolution to a climax.

CHAPTER TWO

Eastward Expedition to Suppress Rebellion

Section 1
First Eastward Expedition (See Map 1)

Entrusting Heavy Responsibility of the National Revolution

Since the United States convened the Washington Conference in 1921 in an effort to eliminate armament competition and to strike a heavy blow against Japan's monopoly in China, the foreign powers stepped up the contest in their aggression of China under the so-called "principle of equal opportunities." Their sharp conflicts of interests led to the warlords' occupation of various areas and much fighting.

Since the death of Yuan Shih-kai, the warlords in the north were divided into the Chih (Hopei) and Huan (Anhwei) cliques. The Pei-yang Government (Government in the North) virtually collapsed. Headed by Tsao Kun and Wu Pei-fu, the Chih clique was supported by the British behind the scene. Headed by Tuan Chi-jui, the Huan clique was controlled by the Japanese. The war between the Chih and the Huan cliques[1] was a conflict of interests between

---

[1] War between Chih and Huan Cliques:
In July, 1920, the Chih clique and the Huan clique of northern warlords fought bitterly against each other ending in the defeat of the latter. As a result, Tuan Chi-jui of the Huan clique lost power.

Britain and Japan in China. This war ended in the Huan clique's defeat. Meanwhile, the Feng (Manchurian) clique headed by warlord Chang Tso-lin had already extended its influence inside the Shanhaikwan. After the defeat of the Huan clique, Japan turned to support the Feng clique warlords.

In 1922, the war between the Chih and the Feng cliques[2] broke out ending in the victory of the Chih forces. The influence of the Chih forces then spread from North China to Hupei, Hunan and Szechuan Provinces and the lower reaches of the Yangtze River. This was tantamount to extending the British aggressive influence to Central and South China. Not to be outdone, Japan finally engineered the second war between the Chih and Feng forces[3] in 1924.

At this time, Feng Yu-hsiang, a commander under the warlord Wu Pei-fu of the Chih clique, was persuaded by Kuomintang member, Yu Yu-jen to join with Hu Ching-yi and Sun Yueh in forming the National Forces. They launched converging attacks on the Chih forces and sealed the latter's fate.

The triangular coalition of the Huan clique, the Feng

---

[2] War between Chih and Feng Cliques:
In April, 1922, Wu Pei-fu of the Chih clique accused Chang Tso-lin of the Feng clique of making concessions to Japan at the Washington Conference. They resorted to war. As Chang was defeated, he retreated to north of the Shanhaikwan. Hence, the Chih clique ruled.

[3] Second War of Chih and Feng Cliques:
In October, 1924, Chang Tso-lin of the Feng clique fought the Chih clique, for he was opposed to the bribery of the Chih clique to parliament members by buying 5,061 votes to make Tsao Kun president. Feng Yu-hsiang of Tsao's clique defected and imprisoned Tsao. We Pei-fu fled to Hupei. Together, Chang Tso-lin and Feng Yu-hsiang supported Tuan Chi-jui to become the provisional premier.

clique and the National Forces resulted in Tuan Chi-jui's emergence as the provisional premier. Subsequent to the defeat of Wu Pei-fu, the Chih clique clamored for the organization of the "Protecting Constitution Military Government" thus rendering the political situation even more complicated. Later, Tuan Chi-jui, Chang Tso-lin and Feng Yu-hsiang jointly extended an invitation to Generalissimo Sun asking him to go to the North to discuss the issue of national unification.

On 10 November 1924, prior to his departure, Generalissimo Sun issued his "Northward Declaration" in which he advocated the "abolition of unequal treaties" and the "convocation of a national convention." He pointed out only a national revolution which united with the people could do away with the warlords who united with colonialism, and achieve independence, freedom, democracy and unification. This resolute move and clearcut view won the support of the people throughout the country, but was regarded with jealousy by the northern warlords. Prior to Generalissimo Sun's departure, his Russian political advisor Michael Borodin conveyed a message from Moscow inviting him to visit Russia. Generalissimo Sun asked for Superintendent Chiang's views. The latter felt that Russia's cooperation should be sought in the national revolution for the sake of China's independence and freedom. However, visiting Russia at this time would give the Chinese Communists an opportunity to spread rumors and to confuse the people, creating great obstacles to the future of the revolution. This advice ended Generalissimo Sun's plan to visit Russia.

On 12 November Generalissimo Sun wrote to Superintendent Chiang giving him full authority to handle any contingency. He further stated: "If the situation cannot be handled or is on the verge of collapse, take drastic actions without regard to success or failure." After completing the dispositions, he proceeded north stopping off for one day in Whampoa to inspect the Military Academy. Upon seeing the cadets of the First Class engaged in fortifications, he said to Superintendent Chiang: "Those who will carry out the principles of our party will be the cadets of our Academy. As I see them enduring such hardships and working so hard, I know they will propagate my life and will realize my wish." Generalissimo Sun had then clearly entrusted Superintendent Chiang with the heavy responsibility of completing the national revolution and fulfilling his unfinished wish.

First Eastward Expedition and Victory at Battle of Mien-hu

When Chen Chiun-ming was chased out of Canton, he took his remnants to the Tung Chiang (East River) region. By the time Generalissimo Sun went north, Chen took advantage of the opportunity to mass 100,000 handits in eastern Kwangtung to capture Canton. From Tung Chiang he took Tungkuan and Shihlung. Establishing contact with the Yunnan forces stationed in suburban Canton led by Yang Hsi-ming and the Kwangsi forces led by Liu Chen-huan, he covertly sought Tuan Chi-jui's support from the north. Britain also provided him support from Hong Kong.

As Superintendent Chiang had always considered the insurgent forces revolutionary obstacles, he decided to launch an eastward expedition in late January, 1925. He took the initiative before the rebel forces were massed. With a force of 3,000 which was composed of the First and the Second Training Regiments (organized by graduates of the First Class of the Military Academy) and the cadets of the Second and the Third Classes, he formed the Whampoa Military Academy force. This force and the Kwangtung force became elements of the Right Route force under Superintendent Chiang's command. In addition, the Kwangsi force and Yunnan force were designated respectively the Central Route Force and the Left Route Force ready to move out.

On 1 February, the mobilization order was issued. On 4 February, the inexperienced and poorly equipped right wing Academy force under the personal command of Superintendent Chiang took Tungkuan to score the first victory. In his personal order, Superintendent Chiang urged his officers and men: "The survival or destruction of our nation and the success or failure of our principles will depend on the outcome of this battle, I call upon you to combine your efforts, advance gallantly and destroy the rebels so as to fulfill the desire of our Generalissimo." By the 15th, Shihlung, Changping and Tamsui were captured with Huichow only 70 li's away (each li is one third of a mile), At noon on the 16th, a cable was sent to Generalissimo Sun in Peiping announcing the victory. Meanwhile, Generalissimo Sun's liver illness recurred as a result of his long journey to the north, inadequate diet, severe weather, Tuan Chi-jui's acting on his own to recognize the unequal treaties and to please foreign powers in exchange of their recognition of his regime and his violation of the "convocation of national convention." Nevertheless, in his sick bed, Generalissimo Sun found the news most gratifying and answered the cable with his commendation.

At this time, as the Yunnan and Kwangsi forces in the Left and Central Route Forces have already collaborated with the rebel forces, they stayed put thus isolating the Academy Force. During his stopover at the Chang-ping Station, Superintendent Chiang wrote a poem which reads as follows:

"Leading a force three thousand,
To take part in the Eastward Expedition,
Brandishing my sword with tears abound,
An insolated force fighting desperately for the revolution."

To decide on the subsequent strategy, a military conference was held. During the conference, it was noted that the Left and Central Route forces had not moved. It was then decided not to advance too rapidly but to employ a portion of the strength to guard Haifeng and Lufeng. The main strength would be used to capture Huichow and to control the estuary of the Tung Chiang (East River) thus facilitating both offense and defense. Superintendent Chiang felt that it was dangerous to move a lone force deeply and to dissipate our strength attacking fortified positions. Instead he felt that an absolute offensive to strike at the enemy's left flank, conduct defeat in detail, move right into the enemy's heartland, force the enemy's right flank to fall back, and to destroy a numerically superior enemy was the right course of action. On 20 February, he decided to continue the advance.

Under aggressive leadership, the Whampoa Academy Force advanced boldly to attack the enemy flanks and rear. On 22 February, in spite of heavy rain, it took Ping Shan and broke Hung Chao-lin's main strength in the vicinity of Santochu. Continuing the pursuit, it captured Haifeng on the 27th. On 7 March, it continued the rapid advance gathering momentum in a series of actions which resulted in the capture of Chaoan and Swatow. Realizing that the situation was gone, Chen Chiun-ming fled from Swawei to Hong Kong.

At this time the enemy Right Wing Force commanded by Lin Hu saw the danger to the Left Wing Force. It immediately joined force with the units led by Liu Chih-lu and Huang Jen-huan to turn eastward and to collect the 20,000 routed remnants in an attempt to attack the flank and the rear of the Whampoa Academy Force. When informed of this in Chiehyang Superintendent Chiang ordered his troops to meet the attack.

On 12 March, the Academy Force moved out from Chiehyang, divided into three routes with the Second Training Regiment on the left, the Kwangtung force on the right and the First Training Regiment in the center, the entire force headed toward Mienhu to engage the enemy.

On 13 March, the First Training Regiment encountered the rebel force at Mienhu. From morning until noon, an exhausted force of over 1,000 fought valiantly against an enemy several times its strength resulting in heavy casualties. Later, the rebel combined the strength of two forces to attack the First Training Regiment. The situation then was most critical. Nevertheless, the regiment fought hard and was determined to stand firm. After a number of counterattacks, the regiment had used up all its reserves. At this critical moment, Superintendent Chiang arrived at the frontline areas to take personal command. He ordered the 7th Brigade of the right route Kwangtung Force to attack the enemy's left flank. Morale was greatly boosted, and the revolutionary forces gallantly fought against an enemy who outnumbered them ten times. Meanwhile the Second Training Regiment, upon arrival in Li Hu (Carp Lake), found no trace of the enemy but heard gunshots from the direction of Mienhu. Knowing there must be heavy fighting there, it immediately turned to Mienhu to attack the enemy from the rear. In one day's time, the rebel forces were routed. In the midst of great danger, the hitherto untested Academy fighters received their baptism of fire and proved themselves in the Battle of Mienhu which decided the success or failure of the revolution.

Following their defeat in the Battle of Mienhu, Lin Hu's rebel forces fell back to Wuhua and Hsingning. On 15 March, the Academy Force employed mobile units to stage a long-distance turning movement and in a surprise attack captured Wuhua and on 25 March took Hsingning ending in the complete rout of Lin Hu's remnants.

Generalissimo Sun's Death in Peiping

Soon after the successful conclusion of the First Eastward Expedition, news was received at 5:00 P.M., 21 March that Generalissimo Sun had passed away in Peiping. All officers and men of the Revolutionary Force mourned the passing of their beloved commander-in-chief. Generalissimo Sun passed away at 9:00 A.M., 12 March at a time when heavy fighting was underway in the Eastward Expedition. It was feared that his death might have an impact on troop morale. Hence, the news of his death was not released until a later time after a series of victories had been effected. On 22 March, Superintendent Chiang led the Academy Force in a week-long service mourning the Generalissimo's death. At noon, 27 March, the Academy Force was assembled outside the East Gate of Hsingning City in a memorial service at which Superintendent Chiang issued the following statement to all the members of the Academy Force:

"In memorium. Our Generalissimo had devoted his whole life in the struggle for our cause. The Three Principles of the People was his second life. He sought only its implementation. To us our Generalissimo is still very much living. On the shoulders of our officers and men rest the responsibility of carrying out his will. Indeed our nation's plight is difficult and our people's conditions destitute. With our Generalissimo's death, our officers and men should be conscious of our added responsibility so that we may be united in our struggle to eliminate the evil influences of the warlords and the imperialists and to carry out the Three Principles of the People. Only by so doing can we live up to his expectations. Although we have broken the main strength of the rebels in Tung Chiang (East River), we have not destroyed them nor have we captured their leader. We must be more determined than ever to continue our advance, destroy the enemy and annihilate the remnants so that we may remove the disgrace our party has suffered and fulfill our responsibility as members of the Party Force. Thus, our Generalissimo will lie in peace in Heaven and we shall not fail our Generalissimo's expectation in training the Party Force, implementing the Three Principles of the People and propagating his life. I urge all of you to do your utmost."

As a result of the Eastward Expedition, the Whampoa Academy Force had achieved great distinction and had grown in stature. The Kuomintang Central Executive Committee sent its commendation and passed a resolution on 29 April to comply with the late Generalissimo's wish in "redesignating the New Force as the Party Force." Consequently, the Academy's First and Second Training Regiments together with the Third Training Regiment which was only activated on 21 April were redesignated the First Brigade of the Party Force with Ho Ying-chin acting concurrently as the brigade commander. Superintendent Chiang was appointed the commander of the Party Force. Officers and men were elated upon hearing the appointment and were determined to fight for national revolution.

Section 2
Returning to Suppress the Rebellion (See Map 2)

Suppressing the Rebel Forces of Yunnan and Kwangsi

Upon recovery of Hsingning, the Whampoa Academy Force seized in the rebel headquarters the coded messages between rebels Yang Hsi-ming and Liu Chen-huan of the Yunnan and Kwangsi forces. It was further learned that Liu had been to Yunnan asking Tang Chi-yao to send his forces through Kwangsi to attack Kwangtung and that Yang had been to Hong Kong seeking British support and contact with Tuan Chi-jui in Peking.

Meanwhile, knowing their intrigues had leaked out, Yang and Liu moved the Yunnan and Kwangsi forces to the vicinity of Canton ready to engage in open rebellion.

On 15 May, 1925, the senior officers of the various forces met in Swatow to discuss the plans leading to the return of the forces to suppress the rebellion. Superintendent Chiang candidly made the following remarks: "I need 8,000 rifles and am willing to take charge of the forces to destroy the counter-revolutionary forces in Canton. The rest of the enemy forces in Chaochow and Meihsien can be left alone." At the conference, it was decided to abandon the attack on Chaochow and Meihsien; concentrate on the mop-up of revolutionary obstacles — Yang and Liu; and consolidate our revolutionary bases. Superintendent Chiang was elected the commander-in-chief of the forces returning to suppress the rebellion.

On 21 May, commander-in Chief Chiang led the Party Force, the Guard Force, the 4th Division of the Kwangtung Force and the 1st Brigade; a Naval detachment of 11 ships "Chung Shan," "Fei Ying," "Pao Pi," "Chiang Han," "Chiang Ta," "Kwang Hua," "Chiang Chen," "Chiang Ku," "Kwang An," "An Nan," and "Pu An;" an air detachment and an air cover detachment returning from Chaochow and Swatow to coordinate with the Hunan and Honan forces in Peichiang (North River), the Yunnan force in the Hsi Chiang (West River) and the Kwangtung force in Southern Kwangtung to effect an envelopment. Arrangements were made for railroad workers of Canton-Hankow Railroad, Canton-Kowloon Railroad and Canton-Sanshui Railroad to stage strikes in order to cut off the liaison between the Yunnan and Kwangsi rebel forces. Academy cadets remaining in Whampoa received orders to be on full alert ready to respond to the returning forces. On 12 June, the high grounds in the vicinity of Canton including the White Cloud Mountain were captured. A general offensive was launched on 13 June. In less than a day, the so-called 60,000 strong rebel forces were completely wiped out. On 15 June, elements of the rebel forces in Tsengcheng attempted to attack Canton in a final struggle. Their encounter with the Revolutionary Force lasted less than two hours, as they collapsed in the presence of the combat ready Party Force. Rebel remnants who had been mistreating the local populace in their 2-yr. occupation of Canton were seized and killed by the angry masses.

As the rebel forces of Yunnan and Kwangsi toppled over, Tang Chi-yao lost his capability to invade eastward. Canton then became the revolutionary base. At a time when the Revolutionary Government was putting things in order in the household, British designs to increase internal disturbances in China did not cease and led to the outbreak of the "Shaki Incident." Earlier, the Japanese in the Japanese mills in Shanghai killed Chinese workers, resulting in the workers' strikes. As students sought donation to help the workers, British Municipality in Shanghai blindly arrested them. The local people in Shanghai were greatly enraged. Parades and demonstrations which took place in Shanghai on 30 May led to the shooting and killing of several thousand people by the military forces and police of the International Settlement in Shanghai. This was known as the "May 30 Incident." Strong reactions through the nation were aroused. On 23 June, a parade was held by the various circles in Canton responding to the Shanghai Incident. At 2:00 P.M. when the parade moved to Shaki, British soldiers from Shamen suddenly opened fire. The French warships in White Goose Lake also opened fire to respond to the British. In the Shaki Incident, some 600 people were wounded or killed. In an effort to maintain security and restore order in Canton, the Revolutionary Government appointed Superintendent Chiang Garrison Commander of Canton. It lodged strong protest with the British and French Governments and severed economic relationships with them.

Establishing the National Government

In January 1924, in the convocation of the First National Congress resulting from the reorganization of the Kuomintang, the proposal on the "Organization of the National Government" was passed. It was intended to reorganize the Generalissimo's Headquarters into the National Government. However, the occupation of such areas by rebels like Yang and Liu under the name of revolution delayed the reorganization. By the time of Generalissimo Sun's death in Peking, this problem needed to be resolved more than ever. By early June 1925, the Central Executive Committee continued its discussion and decided to reorganize military activities. First was military unification. All forces were required to receive the Party's political training before seeking civil and financial unification thus laying the foundation for the establishment of the National Government. By the time the rebellion of Yang and Liu were suppressed, the revolutionary obstacles had been removed. The successive outbreaks of Shanghai's "May 30 Incident" and Canton's "Shaki Incident" met with parades and opposition throughout the nation. The northern warlords continued to betray the nation and acted at will. In order to resist foreign aggression the Canton Revolutionary Government issued the reorganization declaration on 25 June. On 1 July, the National Government[4] was formally

---

[4] Establishment of the National Government:
On 1 July, 1925, the National Government was established. Wang Chaoming, Hu Han-min, Chang Jen-chieh, Tan Yen-kai, Hsu Chung-chih, Yu Yu-jen, Chang Chi, Hsu Chien, Lin Sen, Liao Chung-kai, Tai Chuan-hsien, Wu Chao-shu, Ku Ying-fen, Chu Pei-teh, Sun Fo, and Cheng Chien were appointed members of the National Government. The bicameral government was headed by Chairman Wang Ching-wei (also known as Wang Chao-ming).

established on a bicameral basis. There were a total of 16 members with Wang Ching-wei as the chairman. Hu Han-min was appointed the minister of foreign affairs, Hsu Chung-chih the minister of war, and Liao Chung-kai the minister of finance. The National Military Council was formed with Superintendent Chiang as its chairman.

On 26 July, the National Military Council held a meeting to discuss the problem of military-political unification. The proposal was made by Chairman Chiang who stated: "The unification of military-political efforts must begin with the unification of names. For example, the former Hunan force, Yunnan force, Kwangsi force and Kwangtung force should be abolished and replaced by unified designations." Three designations were proposed, namely (1) National Force, (2) Revolutionary Force and (3) National Revolutionary Force. The idea was to provide a name which indicated that the force was organized by fine citizens who had the revolution at heart. Hence, the "National Revolutionary Force" was the most proper name. The purpose for the formation of the National Revolutionary Force was also explained as follows: "What is National Revolutionary Force? The word 'national' represents the people, and in this case our 400 million people, specifically the 400 million oppressed people. Our force is the people's force belonging to the 400 million people, particularly the 400 million oppressed people. In the revolution, whose lives will be terminated? We intend to end the lives of the imperialists, warlords and bureaucrats, as well as some of our own people. The responsibility of the National Revolutionary Force is to bring the downfall of the warlords and the imperialists. The objective of the National Revolutionary Force is to seek freedom and equality for China and China's people. The position of the National Revolutionary Force is to stand before the people, and seek their welfare and liberation."

This proposal was adopted. On 26 August, the National Revolutionary Force was formally organized. Already on 15 June, the First Brigade of the Party Force had been reorganized into the First Division of the Party Force. On 1 August, the Second Division of the Party Force was activated. The First Division and the Second Division were brought under the First Corps with Gen. Chiang as its corps commander. Military efforts were gradually unified. For the formation and the subsequent development of the revolutionary strength, see appended Chart.

Communist Designs of Division and Intrigues

Despite the elimination of rebels Yang and Liu and the formal organization of National Revolutionary Force, Communist designs of intrigue and division became active. Communist instigations led to the creation of the "left" and "right" factions. Hu Han-min, Tai Chi-tao and a number of Kuomintang members were called "rightists," while Wang Ching-wei, Liao Chung-kai and a number of pro-Communist Kuomintang members were called "leftists." They fanned the mutual suspicion and conflicts between Hu Han-min and Wang Ching-wei and took advantage of the feudal thinking of such ambitious militarists and bureaucrats as Hu Yi-sheng, Wei Pang-ping, Liang Hung-kai, Chao Kuei-chang, Tan Chi-hsiu and Mo Hsiung to openly advance the slogan of "Local force dispelling outside force" to increase the confusion. The situation became more aggravating. On 20 August when

Liao Chung-kai was on his way to a conference at the Kuo-mintang Central Headquarters, he was assasinated at the gate thus endangering the already precarious situation. Later, the careful investigations of the Canton Garrison Headquar-ters and fair handling of the case led the Communists to step up their surrounding of Wang Ching-wei in their so-called struggles agianst the "rightists." Eventually Wang was de-ceived. Under Communist pressure and claiming that suspect of the Liao Chung-kai's assasination was Hu Han-min's brother, they forced Hu to leave Kwangtung in the name of making an inspection in Russia. As a result of the success of this intrigue, the Communists applied the same trickeries they used in driving a wedge between Hu and Wang to create confusion and undermine national revolution.

Section 3
Second Eastward Expedition (See Map 3)

Capturing Well-Fortified City to Secure East River

Following the First Eastward Expedition to suppress Chaochow and Swatow, the Yang-Liu rebellion necessitated the return of the National Revolutionary Force to Canton with only a small force left for garrison. Hence, the rem-nants of Chen Chiun-ming's force headed by Hung Chao-lin in Chaoan and Meihsien became restless. Massing a force of 30,000 at a time when the defense of Tung Chiang (East River) was weak, they undertook rebellious activities. On 1 September, they invaded Chaochow and Swatow. Later, they occupied Haifeng, Hopo, Meihsien, Wuhua and Hsingning. Further, they collaborated with Hsiung Ke-wu's Szechuan force and Teng Peng-yin's force in Hainan Island numbering over 10,000 to invade Canton. The situation was most critical.

On 28 September, 1925, Superintendent Chiang become the commander-in-chief of the Eastward Expeditionary Force. With the First and the Fourth Corps of the National Revolutionary Force as the nucleus, he was ready for the second Eastward Expedition.

On 1 October, prior to the Eastward Expedition Hsiung Ke-wu who was visiting Canton and his corps commander Yu Chi-tang were detained. Immediately forces were dispatched to subdue the Szechuan forces in Lienhsien, northern Kwangtung Province. On 8 October, the Eastward Expeditionary Force was assembled in Tsengcheng and Shihlung. Having been divided into three columns, it proceeded to capture Huichow in accordance with prearranged plans.

As the largest fortress on the Pearl River and guarding the entrance and exit of the Tung Chiang (East River), Huichow was surrounded by water on three sides with high ramparts and critical terrain. It was the first fortified city in Kwangtung which had never fallen. This was a saying to the effect that "Iron chains tying lonely boat; flying geese float on water. Despite chaos reign supreme; this place has no fear." Rebel forces under Yang Kun-ju defended Huichow heavily, and the defense works were well-constructed. On 10 October, as the Eastward Expeditionary Forces approached the suburbs of Huichow, they occupied Flying Goose Ridge on the outskirts.

At 10:00 A.M. 13 October, Commander-in-Chief Chiang arrived at the frontline areas to inspect the dispositions.

Immediately afterwards, orders were issued to lay siege to the city. At Flying Goose Ridge, he directed the artillery to fire at the towers of Huichow's city gates. Liu Yao-chen, commander of the 4th Regiment, personally climbed a bamboo ladder to lead the death-defying detachment in the assault on the North Gate under the cover of artillery. Unfortunately he was stopped by nailed cross-bar and was killed by enemy machine gun fired from the city.

By the morning of 14 October when renewed efforts were made in the assault of the city, the 4th Regiment nevertheless requested permission to lead the assault. Smilingly Commander-in-Chief Chiang said: "The morale of the regiment did not suffer despite heavy casualties. It is indeed a revolutionary force." At 2:00 P.M. he ordered the 7th Regiment and the Replacement Regiment to approach the West Gate and the 4th and 8th Regiments to attack the North Gate at the same time. The artillery provided fire support in the assault on the North Gate. As the machine guns of the rebel forces were concealed in the straw huts to the right of the North Gate, it was difficult to knock them out. At this time, artillery commander Chen Cheng moved a battery of pack howitzers near the civilian houses outside the North Gate to conduct direct fire. As the first round scored a direct hit, infantry took advantage of the opportunity to climb the ladders and to throw hand grenades. Almost immediately, hand-to-hand fighting took place. By the same evening, the first fortified city in Kwangtung which had not fallen for more than 1,000 years was taken in less than 40 hours. This marked the first time that victory was achieved in an attack of fortified positions, since the National Revolutionary Forces scored successes in mobile warfare and meeting engagement in the First Eastward Expedition.

After the fall of Huichow, Commander-in-Chief Chiang divided the Eastward Expeditionary Forces into three columns. The first column headed for Haifeng; the second column for Tzuchin; and the third column for Hoyuan to continue the attack.

On 4 November, the first column recaptured Chaochow and Swatow. On 7 November, the second column took Yaoping. Meanwhile, the third column captured Wuhua on 28 October and Hsingning on 31 October. It also mopped up the enemy in Meihsien and Tapu pursuing the enemy to Yungting on the Fukien border. Enemy remnants had been totally destroyed and Tung Chiang (East River) was at last secured.

When the Eastward Expeditionary Forces were scoring a series of victories, rebel Teng Peng-yin was getting ready to move in from the south and was threatening Chiangmen in containing actions. Elements of the Eastward Expeditionary Forces turned back for the rescue and broke enemy resistance. By 7 November, when Teng retreated to Hainan Island, he was completely helpless when December arrived, enemy remnants were wiped out and Kwangtung was secured.

Foregoing Military Command and Streamlining Military Administration

With the fall of Tung Chiang (East River), Commander-in-Chief Chiang thought that peace had come to Kwangtung. In the light of military men's past arrogance and bad practices, he cabled the Central Government requesting that he be removed of military command so as to set an example for a model, revolutionary soldier. The Central Government considered his modesty most commendable; however, it turned down his request as the reactionary forces were not eliminated and the future of the revolution was laden with obstacles. A citation was published commending the officers and men of the Eastward Expeditionary Forces.

Commander-in-Chief Chiang considered that the successful conclusion of the Eastward Expedition was merely the first step in the National Revolution. It was essential that the fulfillment of the Northward Expedition in Generalissimo Sun's will be expedited. However, the power of the northern warlords far surpassed that of the Tung Chiang (East River) rebels. In order to seek victory in the Northward Expedition, the revolutionary combat effectiveness had to be vastly greater. In other words, there must be uniformed military administration. The training of the forces and various military preparations must be stepped up before undertaking the heavy responsibility of the Northward Expedition. On 15 December, the "Military Administration Reform Program" was proposed to the National Military Council. The highlights of the proposed reform are as follows:

(1) Abolition of military titles — In order to prevent the seizure of military power, the title of corps commander be abolished placing all the divisions under the command and control of the National Military Council.

(2) Formulation of province-wide military system — In accordance with financial receipts, and future military requirements, it is expected that regular forces maintain 15—18 divisions. It is advocated that self-defense forces be organized by agricultural and labor organizations. In addition, the stationing areas of the various

divisions be determined.

(3) Implementation of quartermaster independence — The pay, clothing and provisions should be drawn from the Quartermaster Bureau of the National Military Council. Various units must not obtain funds from their stationing areas. It is hoped that medical and quartermaster activities be carried out satis- factorily.

(4) Unification of military education — Military educa- tional institutions must be unified. Various troop units must not establish their own educational institutions. Special attention should be given to the elevation of military educational standards. Establish- ment of military institutions of higher learning should be planned.

(5) Revamping of arsenals — This is an important problem which must not be overlooked in the Northward Expedition. Improvements should be made and expansion planned. Firstly, machinery for the pro- duction of ammunition should be augmented. Secondly, arsenals for the manufacture of guns should be increased. Thirdly, steel mills should be increased.

(6) Restriction on absorption and reorganization of troop units — In order to forestall the secret augmentation of the various units, should such augmentation be discovered, the units concerned will be punished for insubordination. In addition to the drafting of punishment regulations for promulgation, careful checks are made from time to time.

Apart from the above-mentioned six points, the proposal

also included preventive measures governing military men's interference with politics, and the standardization of military flags. This proposal was adopted by the Central Government. Since then, the administrative system of the National Revolutionary Forces had been molded and the basis for the development of the forces laid.

CHAPTER THREE

Northward Expedition and Unification of China

Section 1
Overcoming Numerous Obstacles in Preparation for the Northward Expedition

Russian Communist Intrigues to Undermine the Northward Expedition

During the Second Eastward Expedition of the National Revolutionary Forces, Commander-in-Chief Chiang felt strongly that "We should unify Kwangtung-Kwangsi in one year and China in three years." By January 1926, in his military report at the Second National Congress, he stated that "Presently the National Revolutionary Forces are completely under the control of the Government. An order will be able to mobilize 85,000 men. A budget has been prepared for the pay of military personnel and the soldiers' living conditions have been improved. In addition, the 6,000 cadets of the Military Academy will be equivalent to one division. With this spirit to undertake positive revamping measures, it will not be difficult to achieve unification of China." This advocacy of the late Generalissimo Sun's will to undertake the Northward Expedition received the unanimous approval of the Congress. Michael Borodin, the Soviet political advisor, did not demur. However, immediately after the conclusion of the Congress, he was recalled to Russia for consultation and left hurriedly. After Borodin's return, Kissanka, the chief of the Soviet Military Mission who had been in China for less than one month, advanced the view in a conference at the Military Academy that the Northward Expedition could not possibly succeed. In the successive issues since the 161st issue of the "Guide Weekly," Communists continued to write articles ridiculing the Northward Expedition as a military venture. Later, they published their declaration on the current situation openly opposing the Northward Expedition. Additionally, they distributed leaflets in the City of Canton distorting facts and undermining plans for the Northward Expedition. In the meantime, the Communists had organized the so-called "Farmers' Self-Defense Force" in various hsiens in Kwangtung exercising control over the civil organizations. Militarily, however, they had no decided influence. Undertaking the Northward Expedition at this time would, of course, heighten the people's expectations of the National Revolutionary Forces. A successful Northward Expedition would mean a successful national revolution. It would also mean that the poisons of Communism would not be able to spread. In the interests of the Communists, they felt it would be advantageous to restrict the strength of our national revolution to Kwangtung, while they waited for the opportunity to expand and profit. By 8 February, Superintendent Chiang had clearly known the Soviet efforts to interrupt the Northward Expedition. However, the circumstances were such that he was unable to continue as the inspector-general of the National Revolutionary Forces. On the 9 February, he tendered his resignation from the posts of member of the National Military Council and the garrison commander of Canton. Since Liao Chung-kai's assassination and the expulsion of elder statesman Hu Han-min, Chairman Wang Ching-wei of the National Government had collaborated with the Russians for quite sometime. As late as 14 March, he had not accepted Superintendent Chiang's resignation, yet he hinted that the latter should soon leave Kwangtung. On the one hand, he made known that something unexpected would happen. On the other hand, if it should happen he could accuse Superintendent Chiang of desertion. Since then Kissanka and the Communists became even more boisterous. To thoroughly undermine the Northward Expedition, they were actively engaged in struggles against the convocation of the Hsi Shan (West Hills) Conference hoping to divert the attention from the Northward Expedition. They called all those who expressed slight dissatisfaction with the Communists as members of the Hsi Shan clique and attacked them maliciously. Much damage resulted both at home and abroad. Further, they planned for the assassination of Superintendent Chiang implementing the so-called "Coup d'etat" plan and attempting to eliminate the only obstacle in the so-called proletarian rule under the name of national revolution.

Crushing the C.N.S. Chung Shan Incident

On 19 March, Soviet advisor instigated Li Chin-lung (a Communist Party member), acting director of the Naval Bureau, into issuing an order instructing the C.N.S. Chung Shan to sail to Whampoa. They had hoped to kidnap Superintendent Chiang while he was on his way back to Whampoa from Canton and take him on board the ship to

sail to Vladivostok. The plot was known to Superintendent
Chiang. Early in the morning of the 20 March, Superintendent Chiang took drastic actions by having the Canton
Garrison Headquarters declare martial law. Li Chih-lung and
Communists among the party representatives in various forces
were arrested and the weapons in the hands of the Communist-controlled Canton's Port Strike Committee[1] were
confiscated. Moreover, the C.N.S. Chung Shan was brought
back. Knowing that their actions were unjustified, the Soviet
Consulate in Canton ordered Kissanka to return to Russia.
Once again, the Russian Communist attempt to undermine
the Northward Expedition failed.

Mobilization for the Northward Expedition and Oath-Taking at Canton

Since the Communists failed in both attempts to seize
the base at Canton and to undermine the Northward Expedition, Superintendent Chiang recommended to the Central
Government that the military forces be revamped, the party
be purged and forces be dispatched for the Northward
Expedition. On 30, April, he personally requested that the
Kuomintang Central Executive Committee and the Supervisory Committee discuss the plans for the Northward
Expedition. The essentials of the request indicated that "The

---

[1] Canton's Port Strike Committee:

In June, 1925, protesting over the British killing of Chinese people at Shaki
in Canton, the Canton Labor Union staged strikes against Hong Kong. In
name the union was led by Liao Chung-kai, however, the union was in the
hands of the Communists. The labor pickets even carried weapons. The Communists considered these men equivalent to the "labor, farmer, soldier soviets"
in the February Revolution in Russia in 1917. These labor pickets were
similar to the Russian "Red Guards," and were intended to serve as the basis
in the establishment of "proletarian rule."

balance of power in China has undergone changes. The National Forces of Feng Yu-hsiang which were fighting against warlord Chang Tso-lin's (Feng-Manchurian) clique had withdrawn from Peking in order to hold the Peiping-Suiyuan Railroad. It was anticipated that Japan would provide Chang Tso-lin with financial and military assistance in order to destroy Feng's National Forces. Meanwhile it was possible that Britain and Japan would support warlord Wu Pei-fu so that he would attack the National Revolutionary Force in Kwangtung. Similarly, warlord Tang Chi-yao in Yunnan would also receive foreign assistance and would dispatch forces to disrupt the Northward Expedition. Under these circumstances, Kuomintang's proper strategy was to seek Feng Yu-hsiang's cooperation persuading him to withdraw to the northwest, and to align with Yen Hsi-shan's Shansi's forces in order to check Chang Tso-lin's Feng clique forces from expanding southward. Meanwhile, efforts were made to win over Kweichow and Szechuan local forces in order to prevent Tang Chi-yao from disrupting the Northward Expedition. Additional efforts were made to win over Tang Sheng-chih's Hunan forces and Kiangsi local forces so that they may join the camp of the National Revolutionary Forces. Warlord Sun Chuan-fang's forces occupying the five provinces of Kiangsu, Chekiang, Kiangsi, Anhwei and Fukien should be neutralized. If the above efforts had proceeded smoothly, then the preparations for the national revolution would have been completed in three months. It was believed that the Northward Expedition would lead to the capture of Wuchang-Hankow and the wiping out of the first obstacle in the national revolution — Chih clique warlord Wu Pei-fu's influence."

Another proposal pertained to the reorganization of the military forces. In order to insure that Communist inability to engage in division in the military forces, it was felt that party representatives must not be fence-riding elements. It was also proposed that the Kuomintang Central Party Headquarters undergo complete reorganization in order to prevent Communists from occupying key political positions like they did at the Second National Congress.

On 15 May, the Second Plenary Meeting of the Second Central Executive Committee unanimously passed the above plans. Communists who had formerly served as ministers were expelled and were replaced by Kuomintang members. Superintendent Chiang was elected chairman of the Standing Committee of the Central Executive Committee and concurrently minister of organization. However, he was completely taken up with the preparations for the Northward Expedition and therefore asked Chen Kuo-fu to act as the acting minister and Chang Ching-chiang as the acting chairman of the Standing Committee. In the midst of great difficulties, the preparations for the Northward Expedition were gradually completed.

On 4 June 1926, the Extraordinary Session of the Central Executive Committee decided to accept the request of our people at home and abroad to initiate the Northward Expedition and to fulfill the late Generalissimo Sun's desire to unify the nation and to complete national revolution. On 5 June, a special appointment of the National Government made Superintendent Chiang Commander-in-Chief of the National Military Council exercising command over the Army, Navy and Air Force and undertaking the Northward Expedition.

On 1 July, the following mobilization order of the North-ward Expedition was published by the National Military Council:

"In fulfilling the will of our late Generalissimo, the National Revolutionary Forces considered that, in order to carry out our revolutionary aims and to safeguard our people's interests, all the warlords must be brought down and reactionary influences purged before the Three Principles of the People may be implemented and our national revolution completed. We therefore mass our forces to recover Hunan and Hupei and recapture Wuchang-Hankow in order to link up with our friendly forces — the National Forces so as to achieve unification of China and national renaissance. Apart from the 4th and the 7th Corps which had already moved out in conjunction with the 8th Corps, the assembly plans and various maps and charts are hereby distributed to the 1st, 2nd, 3rd, 5th and 6th Corps."

On 9 July, the Commander-in-Chief of the National Revolutionary Forces took command. An oath-taking ceremony and an inspection were held at Tungchiao Parade Ground in Canton. Over 50,000 citizens observed the solemn ceremony, Chairman Tan Yen-kai of the National Government and Wu Ching-heng representing the Central Party Headquarters and member of the National Government Sun Fo respectively turned over the official seal, flag and Generalissimo Sun's photograph to the Commander-in-Chief adding special significance to the occasion. Commander-in-Chief took his oath, issued a statement and dispatched cables announcing his assumption of command. In his statement, he pointed out that "The objective of the revolutionary war is to establish an independent nation on the basis of the

Three Principles of the People and having in mind the interests of the nation's people." He called upon the soldiers and the people to share the responsibility in the national revolution and to fight for a nation practicing Three Principles of the People. He further stated: "Upon my assumption of command to-day, I wish to impress our people with the following three points: Firstly, we must continue to struggle against imperialists and their instruments. There can be no room for compromise. Secondly, we urge all our military personnel to fight against outside intruders and for the revolution in order to fulfill the Three Principles of the People at an early date. Thirdly, we must weld our military personnel and our people so that our military forces become the people's military forces. Furthermore, we hope our people will share the responsibility of the re-volution. All in all, national revolution, unlike the warlords' dreams of armed unification, relies heavily on principles. The success or failure of our Three Principles of the People will determine my own survival or death. Adherence to or violation of the Principles will determine our friends or foes. Everything else is secondary."

Section 2
Oath-Taking for the Northward Expedition and Naming of Nanking as the Nation's Capital
(See Maps 4 and 5)

Defeating Numerically Superior Forces by Breaking the Wu Forces

At the time of the initiation of the Northward Expedition by the National Revolutionary Forces, among the northern warlords, Wu Pei-fu, Sun Chuan-fang and Chang Tso-lin were the strongest. Wu Pei-fu's forces of some 250,000 controlled the traffic communications centers of the nation by occupying Hupei, Honan, Hunan, Shensi and southern Hopei. He had remote control of Szechuan and Kweichow, and aligned with the Kwangtung-Kwangsi rebel remnants. Sun Chuan-feng's forces of another 250,000 occupied the five provinces of Kiangsu, Chekiang, Fukien, Anhwei and Kiangsi where the wealth of southeast China was. Chang Tso-lin's forces plus the Hopei forces under Chu Yu-pu and the Shantung forces under Chang Tsung-chang totalling approximately 500,000 who occupied Fengtien, Chirin, Hei-lungchiang, Shantung and northern Hopei with the coastal areas of the northeast and Po Hai under their control were geographically more favorable. The warlords whose forces totalled one million were restless. The size of the National Revolutionary Forces rose from the Academy Force of 3,000 during the Eastward Expedition to 100,000 (The 1st through the 8th Corps, the four Cadet Regiments of the Military Academy, 8 naval ships and 3 planes) with many youths joining the military service.

Nevertheless, these were only one tenth of the strength of the warlords' forces. Furthermore, the equipment of the National Revolutionary Forces was poor and inadequate. One could well imagine the arduous tasks facing our revolutionary fighters.

Despite the sharp disparity in strength as well as in equipment, there were a number of factors which insured our success in the Northward Expedition:

(1) Outstanding Operational Guidance — The operational

guidance of Commander-in-Chief Chiang was the defeat of the enemy in detail. Wu Pei-fu, Sun Chuan-fang and Chang Tso-lin were respectively the first, second and third targets. In the initial phase of the operations, the slogan was "Down with Wu Pei-fu, align with Sun Chuan-fang and ignore Chang Tso-lin." It was hoped to divide the enemy and to achieve individual defeat in detail. The plan was to mop up Wu's forces in Central China, break Sun's forces in the southeast, finish off Chang's forces in the northeast and achieve unification of China. With the initiative in our hands, we were certain to achieve success.

(2) Developing the Spirit of Armed Forces Buildup

Under the distinguished leadership of Commander-in-Chief Chiang, officers and men of the National Revolutionary Forces displayed love, sincerity, solidarity, unparalleled morale as well as the spirit of initiative, responsibility, bravery and sacrifice. Such will-to-fight generated from solidarity, responsibility and sacrifice led to such prerequisites as aggressiveness, initiative, seizing opportune moment, defeating a numerically superior enemy and overcoming the enemy to achieve victory.

(3) Inclination of the People — Under the double oppression of the warlords and the foreign powers, the people fully realized that only the Three Principles of the People could liberate them. The reputation of "fearing no death, seeking no wealth, love the nation and love the people" displayed by the National Revolutionary Forces during the Eastward Expedition had made the people long for them.

With these factors contributing to victory, the Northward Expeditionary Forces moved out of Canton on 9 July. In one stroke, they broke through Lienshui to score the first victory. Divided into three columns, they took Changsha on 11 July and continued the pursuit toward Milo River. In succession they recaptured Hsiangyin, Yiyang, Liuyang and Yuehchow. After 14 days of blooding war, they forced Wu Pei-fu's forces to fall back to Tingsze Bridge awaiting reinforcements. Meanwhile, Wu was leading his forces to link up with Chang Tso-lin's Feng forces to attack the National Forces at Nanko. When he was informed of the situation, he turned his forces southward in an attempt to reverse the worsening situation in Hunan and Hupei.

Giving the enemy remnants no time to complete reorganization, Commander-in-Chief Chiang moved his forces along the Changsha-Wuchang Railroad to press the enemy. A portion of his forces detoured to the upper stream of the Yangtze River crossing the river to take Hanyang and Hankow. Simultaneously, he ordered the 6th Corps to advance toward Tungcheng and to be prepared to cross the river for the capture of Huangpi. The 9th and 10th Corps (reorganized from the former Kweichow forces shortly after the initiation of the Northward Expedition) were ordered to move east to Chingmen and Shashih linking up with the 6th at an appropriate time. Later, they would move in the area west of the Peiping-Hankow Railroad in a converging attack on Wusheng Pass thereby cutting off the retreat of Wu's southbound forces and forcing his main force to fight a decisive battle so as to destroy his forces in toto.

On 27 August 1926, the positions of Wu's forces at Tingsze Bridge were attacked. After three days of heavy fighting, thousands of Wu's forces were destroyed with the remnants holding Hosheng Bridge. At this time, Wu's main force had moved south to the main battlefield. Nine of Wu's brigade and regimental commanders who were held responsible for the fall of Tingsze Bridge were executed by Wu's order. Wu personally led his Ta Tao (Large Blade) detachment to stage a counterattack at Hosheng Bridge. The fierce battle raged for four days and nights with charges and countercharges and hand-to-hand fighting. The fighting was most intense. The morale of the Northward Expeditionary Forces was never higher as they fought against great odds and proved themselves invincible. Despite Wu's execution of a number of his officers for having retreated, he was unsuccessful in his last ditch efforts to turn the tide of battle and to stop his forces from collapse. Wu's forces suffered an overwhelming defeat as they fled to Wuchang. The pursuit took the Northward Expeditionary Forces to the outskirts of Wuchang-Hankow. On 5 September, Wuchang was surrounded. On 6 October, the National Revolutionary Forces made a turning movement to capture Hanyang. On the 7th, Hankow was taken and so was Wusheng Pass. After a siege of 39 days, the fortress of Wuchang fell on 10 October. Some 30,000 enemy soldiers were captured including their commanders Chen Chia-mo and Liu Yu-chun. Wu barely managed to take a small group of remnants and fled to Honan. Subsequently, his forces collapsed altogether, as our national flag of blue sky, white sun and crimson background flew majestically over the Yellow Stork Tower.

Pacifying the Southeast and Establishing the Capital in Nanking

As the National Revolutionary Forces were fighting Wu Pei-fu, warlord Sun Chuan-fang was watching carefully hoping to profit from it. It was not until Wu's forces had suffered defeat at Tingsze Bridge that Sun threw the entire forces of the five provinces totalling five divisions and eight brigades for the invasion westward. To seize the initiative, Commander-in-Chief Chiang left only small forces to continue the siege of Wuchang and turned his main force to the east. On 6 September, he began the general offensive. On 7 September, Kiangsi forces under Lai Shih-huang who was favorably inclined toward revolution defected in southern Kiangsi. His forces were reorganized into the 14th Corps to recover Kanchow heading for Chian. On 5 October, the 14th Corps took Changshu, Yichun, Kaoan, Hsiushui and Tungku. On 25 September, it had taken Nanchang, then withdrew to seek and destroy the enemy forces along the Nanhsun Railroad. The corps was divided into two columns to attack from the south and the north. On 1 November, a general offensive was launched along the entire front. Commander-in-Chief Chiang personally directed the operations at Niuhsing RR Station in the attack on Nanchang. He led his forces in spite of heavy enemy fire and was nearly killed. On 7 November, once again Nanchang was captured. Sun Chuan-fang fled from Chiuchiang to Nanking in a warship. On 9 November, upon hearing the operational results of the various forces, Commander-in-Chief Chiang said: "With the exception of Meng Chao-yueh's brigade, none of rebel Sun's main forces was spared. We suffered 20,000 casualties against the enemy's 60,000 casualties. Our heavy casualties resulted in the elimination of our major concern in Southeast China."

When Sun found his forces in great danger on Nan Hsun Railroad, he ordered Chou Yin-jen in Fukien to throw three divisions against our revolutionary base in Kwangtung. Ho Ying-chin who had orders to stay out in Chaochow and Mei-had only a portion of the 1st Corps totalling 6,000 men and 8 guns. In the face of the enemy's three powerful divisions (30,000 rifles and 12 guns), Ho wisely decided on offense instead of defense. On 9 October, he conducted a turning movement to effect a surprise attack on Sungko. With the collaboration of the enemy's two brigade commanders, he took Yungting in one stroke and continued his bold pursuit. On 8 and 23 November, he recovered Changchow and Chuanchow respectively. Commander-in-Chief Chiang redesignated Ho's forces as the East Route Army with Ho as its Commander-in-Chief. The 14th Corps under the command of Lai Shih-huang in southern Kiangsi was ordered to move eastward in order to join the battle to recover Fukien and later Chekiang and Shanghai. Another Kiangsi force on the right flank was ordered to move to eastern Kiangsi, Chuchow and Yenchow in western Chekiang. In early February, 1927, Chiehteh, Tunglu and Fuyang were recaptured. On 19 February, the East Route Army entered Hangchow and pursued the enemy along the Hangchow-Shanghai Railroad. Subsequently, the entire province of Chekiang was secured.

Fleeing to Nanking, Sun Chuan-fang found his fate sealed and sought Chang Tso-lin's help. He asked Chang to serve as the Commander-in-Chief of the An Kuo (National Pacification) Forces, while he, Chang Tsung-chang and Chu Yu-pu served as the Deputy Commanders-in-Chief. He turned over his broken realm of Kiangsu and Anhwei to Chang Tsung-chang and Chu Yu-pu. Thus, the joint Chi (Hopei)-Lu

(Shantung) force was able to move southward along the Tientsin-Pukow Railroad to control Nanking and Shanghai.

On 14 March, the Yangtze River naval commander Yang Shu-chuang defected and became the Commander-in-Chief of Navy of the National Revolutionary Forces. His ships helped the East Route Army in the recapture of Shanghai. He further sent three ships along the Yangtze River to go west to Chiuchiang to assist in the recovery of Nanking.

On 15 March, Commander-in-Chief Chiang ordered the Central Route Army in Kiangsi to take Nanking in ten days. The army was divided into the River Left and River Right forces moving along both banks of the Yangtze River toward Nanking. As Chen Tiao-yuan and Wang Pu's forces in Anhwei successively surrendered, the situation in Anhwei Province was brought under control, and the National Revolutionary Forces headed toward Nanking. On 19 March, the East Route Army defeated Chang Tsung-chang's forces and recovered Shanghai. On 21 March, the Central Route Army reached the outskirts of Nanking. On 23 March, the siege began. Commander-in-Chief Chiang sailed in C.N.S. Chu Tung to direct the operations near Tsaishihchi. The East Route Army moved westward from Shanghai to fall on Chenchiang in a converging attack resulting in the hurried retreat of the Chih-Lu force across the Yangtze River to the north. On 24 March, Nanking was captured.

Noticing that the rapid progress in the Northward Expedition was extremely unfavorable to them, the Chinese Communists ordered Lin Tsu-han, (a Communist) director of the Political Department, 6th Corps, to incite the officers and men of the 6th Corps into killing and plundering of the British and American diplomatic personnel in Nanking.

Such a move was intended to undermine the Northward Expedition by means of a diplomatic incident. Fortunately, Commander-in-Chief Chiang handled the incident through diplomatic channels and disarmed the troops involved in the incident. Meanwhile, Lin Tsu-han had fled to Chiuchiang. In order to forestall Communist repetition of a similar incident in Shanghai, Commander-in-Chief Chiang personally went to Shanghai on 26 March to supervise the various activities. The demonstration that the Communists had planned to stage in Shanghai turned out to be victory rally welcoming Commander-in-Chief Chiang. Through cooperation with the National Revolutionary Forces, labor unions and chamber of commerce, the armed labor pickets were disarmed and disbanded on 12 April. Thus, peace was restored in Shanghai. On 9 April 1927, Commander-in-Chief Chiang returned to Nanking. On 18 April, the National Government proclaimed Nanking the nation's capital. Shortly after the Northward Expedition began, in less then ten months, half of the nation was restored, and Generalissimo Sun's will to establish the capital in Nanking was fulfilled. Indeed, it was a historical miracle.

Section 3
General Purge of Communists and Unification of China

General Purge of Communists and Quelling of Uprisings

Just when military operations were progressing smoothly, Communist intrigues of division led to great political disturbances.

In November, 1926, the Seventh Communist International Enlarged Executive Committee in Moscow, adopted a resolution on China. The military progress in China's Northward Expedition and the response of the nation's people were regarded as "the third stage of the Communist revolutionary movement." At this stage, the Chinese Communists were to utilize government organs for making contacts with farmers to start a "farmers' revolution" in fulfillment of their so-called "agrarian program," establishment of Communist regime and realization of a "democratic dictatorship of the workers, farmers and the petite bourgeoisie." This was the blueprint which led to Stalin's manufacture of the "people's democratic dictatorship" in Eastern Europe and China upon termination of World War II. To thoroughly implement this program, Moscow dispatched M. N. Roy and Tan Pingshan to China to provide the direction.

To carry out the Communist International's resolution, the Chinese Communists took advantage of the progress of the Revolutionary Forces to work through the Kuomintang's mass movement activities and to collect all the riffraff and vagabonds. They put them in control of labor unions and farmers' associations, and organized armed terrorist gangs. On the other hand, they sought to create disunity within the Kuomintang and to foster ill feeling and conflicts among our armed forces so as to facilitate infiltration and to extend their sphere of control.

On 13 December, Borodin saw that the time was ripe and called an authorized meeting in Wuhan of some members of the Kuomintang Central Executive Committee and of the National Government. They decided to set up a "Joint Conference," usurp party power and issue orders. By 24

December, they openly called the Wuhan Party Plenary Meeting and held the so-called "Rally in Celebration of the Removal of the Central Party Headquarters and the National Government to Hupei and in Support of Shanghai's Grand Strikes and Demonstrations." Subsequently, the Communists engaged in Russian-style struggles to arrest and kill people and to confiscate properties resulting in social disorder and fear among the people.

On 10 March, 1927, the Third Plenary Session which was controlled by the Communists nullified the ruling of the Second Plenary Session which forbade the appointment of dual-party members as heads of departments in the Kuomintang. They also disregarded the earlier agreement on the submission by the Chinese Communist Party to the Kuomintang Central Executive Committee of a complete roster of dual-party members, and on the formation of a two party conference to review the Communist orders. Under the name of "party power above all," they deliberately held up supplies and munitions urgently needed by the National Revolutionary Forces fighting in Nanking and Shanghai and obstructed the movement of our reinforcements in order to help instigate riots in Nanking and Shanghai. On 1 April, at a special meeting of the Kuomintang Central Supervisory Committee held in Shanghai, more evidences were reported by Wu Ching-heng. The committee unanimously resolved to request the Central Executive Committee to adopt emergency measures. At this time, Wang Ching-wei suddenly returned from abroad. Commander-in-Chief Chiang and members of the Central Executive Committee in Nanking and Shanghai urged him to adopt a positive position so as to end the disputes. Wang pretended to show his willingness, yet on 4 April he issued a joint statement with Chen Tu-hsiu openly proclaiming "the cooperation between the Kuomintang and the Chinese Communist Party." When he left Shanghai for Hankow, the Communists became more boisterous, the Wuhan Government headed by Wang and dominated by the Communists openly opposed the Central Government in Nanking leading to the Communist-engineered "Nanking-Hankow Split." On 17 April, the Communist-controlled Wuhan Government ordered Tang Sheng-chih to organize the "Eastward Expeditionary Forces," clamoring for an invasion of Nanking. Elements of Tang's forces headed by Liu Hsing entered Anhwei, while Chang Fa-kuei's forces were deployed in western Hupei. Meanwhile, Commander-in-Chief Chiang was taking the National Revolutionary Forces across the Yangtze River advancing along the Tientsin-Pukow Railroad in the Northward Expedition. Pangpu was taken on 14 May 1927, followed by Hsuchow on 16 May. When the forces were heading toward southern Shantung, this unexpected incident occurred disrupting the Northward Expedition. The National Expeditionary Forces were compelled to fall back to the area south of the Yangtze River to redeploy and protect Nanking.

At this time, the Kuomintang Central Party Headquarters, realizing the gravity of the situation, began the purge of the Communists. Earlier, members of the Kuomintang Central Supervisory Committee such as Teng Tse-ju, Wu Ching-heng, Li Shih-tseng, Tsai Yuan-pei, Ku Ying-fen, Chang Ching-chiang and Chen Kuo-fu, having uncovered evidences of Communist insurgence, requested the Central Executive Committee to adopt emergency measures. On 6 April, northern warlord Chang Tso-lin uncovered Communist

International documents of intrigues from a search[2] he conducted at the Russian Embassy in Peking thus indirectly proved the Communist crimes. On 5 May, the basic principles for enforcing a party purge were approved by members of the Party Central Standing Committee and heads of departments in the Party at a joint session. Since then, positive actions had been taken to purge the Communist elements.

Heart-broken over the internal split and hoping to achieve solidarity in the wake of disruption of the Northward Expedition, Commander-in-Chief Chiang voluntarily resigned on 12 August, 1927. Once again, the warlord remnants took advantage of this opportunity to rise up. Chang Tsung-chang's Chih-Lu forces occupied Hsuchow and Pangpu, while Sun Chuan-fang led his forces southward across the river taking Chihsia Mountain and Lungtan. Nanking was shaken and so was the entire nation. Indeed, the monumental task of National Revolution was at stake. Fortunately, the National Revolutionary Forces, conscious of Commander-in-Chief Chiang's determination and imbued with his revolutionary spirit, resolutely fought against a 60,000 enemy force with a force which was only half the size. In the vicinity of Lungtan they fought bitterly for five days and nights and fully displayed the traditional revolutionary spirit. Though greatly outnumbered, they made use of revolu-

---

[2] Search of the Russian Embassy in Peiking:
On 6 April, 1927, Peiking's armed police and the military police of the Feng forces obtained prior consent of the diplomatic corps before surrounding and searching the Russian Embassy and its affiliated Far Eastern Bank and the office of the Chinese Eastern Railway. A total of 60 Chinese and Russian Communists including Li Ta-chao were arrested. Many important documents pertaining to Russia's communication in China were uncovered.

tionary tactics, persisted in the offensive and conducted turning movement to attack the enemy on the flank. As they were successful in annihilating the invading enemy near the bank of the Yangtze River, they restored security to the nation's capital.

Commander-in-Chief Chiang's spiritual inspiration enabled the political situation to move from separation to solidarity. Another factor contributing to solidarity was the alertness caused by the Communist-inspired disturbances.

Ever since the Communists dominated the Wuhan Government, they became more arrogant than ever. Armed labor pickets appeared on streets day and night to interfere with local politics and arrest innocent people. Armed farmers' 'Red guards were everywhere liquidating landlords, confiscating land and pooling provision to seriously undermine social organizations. The situation was most serious in Hunan where the Communists killed people at will. People found life under Communist control intolerable. As the forces under the Wuhan Government were mostly composed of the sons of Hunan and Hupei Provinces, they were greatly disturbed by the miserable conditions they saw in their homes. Hence, the Equine Day Incident took place.

The Equine Day Incident was started by the 33rd Regiment of the Hunan Province Defense Force under the command of Hsu Ke-hsiang stationed in Changsha. Having witnessed the Communist atrocities in Hunan and the terror that the Communists had generated together with the information that 75,000 Red troops would be organized to stage large-scale uprisings, the regiment, after acquiescence with friendly forces took actions to get rid of all the Communists in the night of 21 May. 70 some organizations in

Changsha were ordered closed and all the labor pickets and farmers' Red defense detachments were disarmed and integrated into the Party Saving Committee. A cable was sent to all parts of the country proclaiming fight against Communism. Equine Day was the telegraphic code for the 21st day in any month. Hence, the incident was so named.

Since the Equine Day Incident broke out, farmers in various places rose against the Communist control, and troop units under Hsia To-yin responded immediately. On 29 June, Ho Chien, commander of the 35th Corps, openly denounced the Communists of their crimes, expressed his support of the Three Principles of the People, implemented the Three Principles of the People and eliminated the riffraff who deceived the farmers and the workers. Though named Commander-in-Chief by the Wuhan Government, Feng Yu-hsiang issued a statement on 21 June reiterating his determination to fight for the realization of the Three Principles of the People and to accomplish the mission of overthrowing the warlords. His final note to the Wuhan Government included the following points:

(1) The stable elements in the Wuhan Government should work with the Nanking Government to fight against the public enemy in the north.

(2) Expel Borodin and all his Russian assistants.

(3) All the Communist leaders should be dismissed from the Kuomintang.

This development raised the anti-Communist feelings of the Wuhan Government. What agitated the Wuhan Government most was the instructions given by Stalin to the Chinese Communists in a telegram on 1 June, 1927, which reads as follows:

(1) Land should be confiscated upon orders of local authorities only and not those of the "National Government" (meaning the one set up by the "leftists" and the Communists in Wuhan).

(2) The Party should check excesses on the part of the farmers.

(3) All unreliable military officers should be removed, 20,000 Communist members armed, and a new army of 50,000 men formed of selected and farmers in Hunan and Hupei Provinces.

(4) New elements from among workers and farmers should replace the older members on the Kuomintang Central Committee.

(5) Revolutionary courts for the trial of reactionary military officers should be set up with well-known Kuomintang members sitting in judgement.

When Stalin's telegram reached Wuhan, Borodin suggested that it be kept from Wang Ching-wei. But without Borodin's knowledge, Roy showed it to Wang. Only then did the "leftists" at Wuhan finally wake up to the fact that Moscow was using our National Revolution to communize China. As a result, they, too, decided to break away from the Chinese Communist Party. On 3 July, they further decided to send Roy back to Russia. On 13 July, when the Chinese Communists received instructions from Moscow, they announced their split with the Kuomintang. On 15 July, Communists all resigned, while Borodin and Teng Yen-ta were sent to Russia.

The Wuhan regime's rupture with the Communists forced Stalin to adopt Trotsky's ideas of setting up a separate sovietized regime in China. He sent Heinz Neumann and

Besso Lominadse to bring it about. The first target chosen was Nanchang. The uprising was planned by Besso Lominadse and carried out by Yeh Ting, commander of the 25th Division and Ho Lung, commander of the 20th Corps (both were Communists). It began in the night of 31 July, with a force of 30,000, Chu Teh, commander of the Training Regiment, 3rd Corps and concurrently chief of police in Nanchang responded resulting in the Nanchang Uprising of 1 August. Banks were robbed, properties ransacked and Kuomintang members arrested, a bogus "Revolutionary Committee of the Kuomintang" posted a public notice. But in less than four days' time, local forces moved against the rebels forcing them to break the sieze and flee toward Kwangtung.

Subsequent to the failure in the Nanchang Uprising Neumann directed the Communists to call an emergency meeting in Wuhan on 7 August known as the "August Seventh Meeting" Chen Tu-hsiu was denounced as an "opportunist" and lost his position as secretary-general of the Chinese Communist Party. Chu Chiu-pai, Hsiang Chung-fa and Li Li-san were elevated to members of its Standing Committee. Their policy turned to one of uprisings. Since September, a succession of uprisings such as the "Hunan-Hupei Autumn Crop Uprising[3]", "Weihua Uprising[4]", "Hailufeng Uprising[5]", "Canton Uprising[6]" took place but were soon quelled.

---

[3] Hunan-Hupei Autumn Crop Uprising:
   In early September, 1927, the Chinese Communist Party designated Hsiang Ying to take the Wuhan labor pickets and unemployed workers to stage uprisings in Tung Shan, Chungyang and Puchi in Hupei Province. Mao Tse-tung merged two regiments of farmers and miners into the First Division of the Labor and Farmer Red Army in Pingchiang, Liuyang, and Liling in Hunan Province and in Hsuishui, Tungku, Pinghsiang, and Anyuan in Kiangsi Prov-

Mao's remnants who had started the "Huan-Hupei Autumn Crop Uprising" fled to Ching-kang Shan on the Hunan-Kiangsi border where they became bandits.

On 11 December, Neumann again directed the Communists to stage a major uprising in Canton leading to the burning of more than 10,000 houses and killing and wounding of 15,000 citizens. There was much killing and plundering. As a result, Canton was in complete ruins. The Communists took advantage of the confusion to organize a Red Government. Ho wever, in less than three days, the death-defying detachments organized by more than 10,000 workers of Canton helped the government put down the uprising, A Russian vice-consul and his assistant actively participated in the Canton Uprising and were caught red-handed on the scene, secret documents unearthed in subse-

---

ince. This division attacked Changsha on 15 September. Due to internal confusion, the attack failed, 700 remnants, led by Mao, fled to Chingkang Shan at the Hunan-Kiangsi border.

[4] Weihua Uprising:

In the spring of 1928, Shensi Communists Liu Tzu-chou, Kao Kang and Hsieh Hao-ju, using the local bandits and farmers as the backbone, organized the 20th Corps of the Red Army. This corps staged the Huayin Uprising in Weinan, Shensi Province and was routed by Feng Yu-hsiang's forces, Liu and Kao barely escaped alive.

[5] Hailufeng Uprising:

On 7 November, 1927, Communist Peng Pai at Lufeng in Kwangtung Province massed several thousand bandits and riffraff of Tungchiang to establish a "Soviet Government" in Lufeng and Haifeng. The 11th Corps of the Red Army was organized. Many people were massacred. In one month, the uprising was put down.

[6] Canton Uprising:

In the morning of 11 February, 1927, Communist Party secretary in Kwangtung Province Chang Tai-lei engineered the Canton Uprising by employing the labor pickets under his control, Yeh Chien-ying's unit in the Training Regiment and Liang Pin-shu's unit in the Guard Regiment. There was much burning, killing and looting. In three days, the uprising was quelled.

quent investigations proved that the Soviet Consulate and Soviet Commercial establishments in Canton were the espionage and subversive organs where the insurrection was planned. This brought matters to a head, and on December 14, the National Government severed its diplomatic relations with Russia and ordered the immediate closure of all Russian diplomatic missions and commercial establishments in China.

Northeast Changing Flags and Unification of China

The Nanking-Hankow Split not only destroyed the fruits of the Northward Expedition which Commander-in-Chief Chiang fought so hard to bring about, it also subjected the people living in areas south of the Yangtze River to the torments of war. The people and the servicemen of the nation unanimously requested that Commander-in-Chief Chiang reassume command to save the nation from still greater catastrophe. On 14 August, 1927, newspapers throughout the nation reported the messages from various organizations requesting his reassumption of command. On 17 August, the representatives of the Kuomintang jointly requested Commander-in-Chief Chiang to take the leadership and complete the Northward Expedition. On 3 September, the citizens of Shanghai voluntarily staged the largest mass movement for the same reason. Meanwhile, Wang Ching-wei also expressed his regret and went to Shanghai to persuade Commander-in-Chief Chiang to accede to the request. On 2 December, a conference was called in Shanghai at which a resolution was passed requesting Commander-in-Chief Chiang to reassume command and continue the Northward Expedition.

On 4 January, 1928, upon request of the nation's people,

Commander-in-Chief Chiang returned to Nanking and was sworn in on 18 January as the Commander-in-Chief of the Northward Expedition. To achieve unified command, he organized the forces into three Army Groups with himself in command of the First Army Group advancing north along the Tientsin-Pukow Railroad. The Second and the Third Army Groups advanced along the Peiping-Hankow Railroad and the Peiping-Suiyuan Railroad respectively in a converging attack on Peking and Tientsin. Later, the Fourth Army Group was organized moving along the Peiping-Hankow Railroad as the general reserves.

Meanwhile, northern warlord Chang Tso-lin's operational guidance was to take advantage of the political confusion in the south by concentrating his main forces in an attack on Shansi Province in order to control the key terrain, consolidate his bases in Northern China before moving south. In anticipation of the enemy's next move, Commander-in-Chief Chiang wisely ordered the Third Army Group to hold at all costs Ching Ching and Lady's Pass-gateways to Shansi so as to tie down most of Chang's forces. While the First and the Third Army Groups moved north along the Tientsin-Pukow Railroad and the Peiping-Hankow Railroad, the Third Army Group waited for an opportunity to shift the offensive. Eventually attacking the enemy from three directions the Revolutionary Forces sieged Peiping and Tientsin.

On 31 March, the First Army Group began its advance to the north. On 10 April, Taierhchuang was captured. On 12 and 13 April, Tsaochuang and Linchen were recovered. By 21 April, Teng Hsien, Chufu, Yuehchow and Tsou Hsien were successively captured to effect a link-up the Second Army Group at Chining.

Immediately before the Northward Expedition, Commander-in-Chief Chiang, in a farewell message to his comrades remaining in the rear, stated the following:

"We have failed in our Party's two northward expeditions. The underlying reason was not the fierceness of the enemy but the lack of solidarity and mutual trust of our comrades in the rear. We were taken advantage by the counter-revolutionaries. Consequently, our frontline troops were deprived of what they depended upon the most, and our revolutionary tasks came to a stand still. Thus, we were unable to eliminate the warlords in the nation, nor were we able to forestall international aggression. The situation in the rear to-day is most serious with the Communists creating chaos and instigating people to harass the society. Corrupt elements also were brought into our Party in an attempt to create disunity among our party members. It is essential that our comrades maintain vigilance, realize our Party's policy so as to thwart the Communist intrigues, and believe in our comrades so as to forestall the division attempted by counter-revolutionaries." On the same day, he also sent a message to the troops and the compatriots of North China in which he said:

"(1) Our revolutionary discipline has always been strict. It is our duty to love the people but not to trouble them. The customs of our northern compatriots will be respected.

(2) Knowing too well the northern people have long been oppressed by the warlords and cannot sustain additional burdens, the Revolutionary Forces will not draw their pay from them and will abolish the harsh taxes levied by the Feng and Lu forces.

Reports can be made by people on disturbances made by undisciplined troop units. Those in the rear areas of the warlords who defected prior to the arrival of the Revolutionary Forces will retain their original positions. Those who come over on the battlefield will be given fair and equitable treatment accorded to members of the Revolutionary Forces. If at all possible, the Revolutionary Forces will not kill one more person, fight one more battle or hand out one bit of pain so as to maintain the nation's strength. The same attitude is taken toward the people as well as toward the belligerent enemy forces."

Such powerful political calls led to the wholehearted support of the people wherever the Revolutionary Forces went.

On 1 May, 1928, the National Revolutionary Forces captured Chinan. Seeing that the warlords they exploited were unable to resist the Northward Expeditionary Forces, the Japanese imperialists openly sent troops to Shantung, to disrupt the military development of the Northward Expedition. On 3 May, the Japanese killed Tsai Kung-shih, Chinese commissioner in Chinan, and slaughtered 11,000 people and troops there resulting in the May Third Incident. The feelings throughout the nation were boiling.

As Commander-in-Chief Chiang knew the Japanese treachery only too well, he did not alter in his determination to proceed with the Northward Expedition despite the Japanese interference. On the one hand, negotiations were made with the Japanese forces through diplomatic channels. On the other hand, he secretly ordered large forces to make a bypass and cross the Yellow River in order to continue the

Northward Expedition. Japanese attempt to interfere with the Northward Expedition fell through. To the enraged troops, he delivered the following message to them:

"In order to take revenge, remove national disgrace and deliver China from imperialist oppression so as to achieve true independence and freedom, it is imperative that we tolerate insults, suffer hardships and follow the footsteps of our fore-fathers. I am convinced our lost territories will be recovered and our national disgrace removed."

On 6 May, Commander-in-Chief Chiang moved his headquarters to Tangchiachuang to direct his forces in the northward advance. On 12 May, he directed the operations along the Peiping-Hankow Railroad. On 17 May, he directed the operations along the Tientsin-Pukow Railroad resulting in the capture of Tehchow. When the triumphant news was spread throughout the nation, even Japan had to admit its rashness in sending troops and the failure of its plans. On 31 May, the Second and the Third Army Groups jointly took Paoting to complete the envelopment of Peiping and Tientsin. Seeing that the situation was too far gone after the fall of Tsang-chow, Chang Tso-lin headed north in his retreat despite the Japanese attempt to stop him. Greatly enraged over Chang's retreat, the Japanese laid mines at Wangkutun Station and killed him. Hurriedly, Chang Hsueh-liang took his remnants back to Manchuria to meet the contingency. On 8 June, the National Revolutionary Forces entered Peiping. With the capture of Tientsin on 11 June, the revolutionary situation was well under control. On 23 September, remnants of warlords Chang Tsung-chang and Chu Yu-pu were completely mopped up. On 8 October the Central Standing Committee reorganized the National Government in accordance with the organization law of the National Government. With reorganization the Executive Yuan, the Legislative Yuan, the Judicial Yuan, the Examination Yuan and the Control Yuan were established. Commander-in-Chief Chiang was elected Chairman of the National Government. On 29 December, greatly inspired by Commander-in-Chief Chiang, Chang sent a cable pledging his allegiance to the National Government. Thus, Manchuria officially came under the rule of the National Government bringing an end to the Northward Expedition, and the realization of the nation's unification.

CHAPTER FOUR

Internal Pacification and Suppression of Communists

Section 1
Reorganizing Armed Forces and Strengthening National Defense

Tang Shan Reorganization Conference

In June, 1928, with the completion of the Northward Expedition and the subsequent unification of China, the common desire of the Chinese people was the post-war reconstruction of a new China practicing the Three Principles of the People. In view of the tremendous size of the Army which stood at 2,200,000 with different cliques complicated organizations, scattered military power and vast military expenses which took 92% of the nation's total income, Commander-in-Chief Chiang knew where the obstacles to the nation's reconstruction lay. It was imperative that the armed forces be reorganized and national defense strengthened. Consequently, a conference was called in June at Tang Shan in suburban Peiping to study the military reorganization proposals. It was decided that the highest military authority rest with the National Government and that the peacetime major military unit be the division. A reorganization and discharge committee which was composed of the commanders-in-chief of the National Revolutionary Forces, the Navy, and the various Army Groups, the chief and the deputy chiefs of the general staff and members of the Central Committee was organized to take charge of the reorganization and discharge as well as to select the elite and battle-proven units. The first step was to organize a national defense force of 50–60 divisions which would be reduced at a later date. Officers and men of the deactivated units would first be organized into a 200,000 man military police force with a sizeable number to be organized into the police and peace preservation units. The remainder of the officers and men in the deactivated units would be trained to engage in road repair, river dredging, land reclamation, forest building, dam building, mining and economic reconstruction in order to realize the Principle of Livelihood. Additionally, concrete measures were prepared for the supreme military command, air force, navy, arsenals, military schools and the education of the reorganized units. The drafted proposals were submitted to the Central Government for implementation.

In early August, 1928, the Fifth Plenary Meeting of the Central Executive Committee reviewed and passed the various military reorganization proposals. The meeting also decided on the following five major principles in the military reorganization:

(1) Military administration and military operations must be combined. The military forces must be adequate. Conscription should be gradually implemented.

(2) Reduced the number of military units so that the military budget would not exceed 50% of the nation's total income.

(3) Unified military education in order to complete the basis of military build-up.

(4) Reduced the number of officers and men so as to implement the policy of properly utilizing the manpower of the armed forces.

(5) Developed the navy and built up the air force.

The five major principles and the reorganization proposals were turned over to Commander-in-Chief Chiang, Commanders-in-Chief Feng, Yen, Li and Yang and Chief of the General Staff Li for detailed planning before submission to the National Government for approval and later implementation.

On 10 October, Commander-in-Chief Chiang was elected Chairman of the National Government. In accordance with the Outline of National Reconstruction five yuans, eight ministries and the four commissions on Reconstruction, Planning, Overseas Affairs, and Mongolian and Tibetan Affairs were established to form an all-around government. The period of military tutelage ended as China entered into the period of political tutelage. Domestically, efforts were made to synchronize the nation's political, economic and educational activities, reduce internal revenues, abolish harsh measures, straighten provincial administration, establish hsien administration and practice local government in order to have a good start in the fulfillment of the Principle of Democracy (Principle of People's Rights). Externally, China took back her custom rights and foreign concessions, and signed new treaties with foreign powers so that she could march toward independence, freedom and equality for the realization of the Principle of Nationalism. However, economic reconstruction depended largely on military reorganization. Based on the principles and the programs passed by the Central Executive Committee, Chairman Chiang ascertained the military organization of the Central Government, terminated the National Military Council reorganizing it into the General Staff, the Ministry of Training and the Ministry of War. The organizational rules of these three organizations were promulgated. The General Staff was responsible for military operations and land survey. The Ministry of Training was charged with the education and training of the nation's military forces, military schools as well as military training of the people. The Ministry of War was responsible for the administration of the army, navy and air force. In addition, a Military Advisory Council was established, as the highest body to provide advice and recommendations, handle inspections and exercises and cultivate the command and leadership ability of senior cadres in time of war. The Reorganization and Discharge Committee was organized to prepare and promulgate the outline of reorganization and discharge, army organizations, measures for the settlement of discharged officers and men, and control and payscale of the army, navy and air force so that adequate organizations and systems for the build-up of the armed forces could be made available.

Implementing Reorganization and Strengthening National Defense

In early January, 1929, approval was granted by the National Government after submission by the Reorganization and Discharge Committee that the total strength of the Nation's army should not exceed 85 infantry divisions, 8 cavalry brigades, 16 artillery regiments and 8 engineer regiments totalling 800,000 men. All the war-time organizations were abolished. In accordance with the approved reorganization, the division, was the largest unit. There were three types of division; namely, Type A, Type B, Type C. A Type A division was built around two infantry brigades with three regiments in each brigade. A Type B division was built around three infantry brigades with two regiments in each brigade. A Type C division was built around two infantry brigades with two regiments in each brigade. Each division was assigned a number of special troops and had a strength of 14,000. Those units which had not been assigned missions in the suppression of the Communists were reorganized in accordance with their individual characteristics. The nation was divided into six reorganization and discharge areas with the headquarters of the Central and First Areas in Nanking, the Second Area in Kaifeng, the Third Area in Peiping, the Fourth Area in Hankow, and the Fifth Area in Mukden (the location of the headquarters of the Sixth Area was undecided) respectively in charge of reorganization and discharge.

Army: According to the decisions of the Tang Shan Conference, beginning July, 1928, the forces directly under the Central government and the First Army Group included 4 armies, 20 corps, 4 independent divisions, general reserves, rear area garrison units and the forces in Hopei, northern Anhwei, Shantung and Fukien totalling 500,000 men. They were reduced by 260,000 officers and men in strength and reorganized into 26 divisions, 4 brigades and 18 regiments. Three divisions were ordered to Kansu Province in the northwest for land reclamation and border defense. The Third Army Group which commanded 5 armies, 13 infantry corps, 5 independent brigades, 7 artillery brigades, 3 engineer regiments and miscellaneous units had a total strength of 300,000 men. Apart from turning over to the Central Government the 7 divisions and 3 brigades which were reorganized in Peiping and Tientsin, the remaining units were reorganized into 13 divisions, 6 infantry brigades, 2 independent regiments, 6 cavalry divisions, 1 independent brigade, 2 independent artillery regiment, 1 training regiment and 17 independent artillery, engineer, transportation and quartermaster battalions with a strength of 230,000 men. The Fourth Army Group which had 16 corps, 9 independent divisions and miscellaneous units totalling 300,000 men were reorganized into 13 divisions, 2 independent brigades and 1 cavalry brigade. The Third and the Fourth Armies in Manchuria which had 38 infantry brigades and 4 cavalry brigades deactivated 23 infanry brigades, 2 cavalry brigades, special troops and various corps headquarters. Some 200,000 officers and men from the deactivated units were engaged in land reclamation in border areas to strengthen national defense. After the Whampoa Military Academy, the Central Military Academy was established in Nanking and the Army War College was resumed to synchronize the education of army cadres. Gradually the academies in various places were designated the sub-academies of the Central Military Academy.

Navy: In view of the importance in the development of sea power and in national defense, Chairman Chiang advocated the buildup of the new Navy. He said: "Our National Father, in his lifetime, had already recognized the need to develop sea power. In his Outline of Ten Year National Defense Planning, he listed naval reconstruction as most important." "In accordance with our National Father's teachings, I strongly feel that we can have no national defense. to speak of if we do not strengthen our navy. In our planning, I have always emphasized the provisions for the navy and' have had high hopes for the navy." Consequently, the Bureau of the Navy was organized in the Ministry of War. With the reorganization and discharge of the armed forces, the General Headquarters of the Navy was deactivated and was replaced by the Navy Reorganization and Discharge Division. On 12 April, 1929, the Bureau of Navy was expanded and was redesignated the Ministry of Navy with Yang Shu-chuang as the minister (Yang was then governor of Fukien Province, Chen Shao-kuan was the acting minister). The Navy's 6-year reconstruction program in the period of political tutelege was prepared dividing the various activities into the six departments of naval administration, shipbuilding, ordnance, engineering, naval science and quartermaster. The Navy was organized into the First, Second, Training, Torpedo, Survey and Patrol Squadrons totalling 53 vessels of various sizes and a total displacement of 34,1951 tons. The marines had 2 brigades. To standardize naval education, the Medical School was deactivated while the Tientsin Navy Medical School was retained. The Yentai Naval Academy was integrated into the Foochow Naval Academy. The Canton Naval Academy was renamed the Whampoa Naval Academy. Similarly, the Tsingtao Naval Academy was redesignated the Hulutao Naval Academy. Indeed, the naval build-up of the National Revolutionary Forces had made remarkable progress.

Air Force: Upon completion of the Northward Expedition the Air Forces of the National Revolutionary Forces had only the First and the Second Squadrons which came under the Division of Aeronautics. In view of the equal importance of air power and sea power in national defence, and Dr. Sun Yat-sen's advocacy of building a strong air force in his Outline of Ten Year Program in National Defense, Chairman Chiang decided to expand the Division of Aeronautics into the Directorate of Aeronautics under the Ministry of War at the time of the reorganization and discharge. The directorate would be in charge of all aeronautical activities, civil and military. Subsequently, the Aeronautical Class was established at the Central Military Academy in Nanking in 1929 to train air force personnel. This marked the beginning of the air force of the National Revolutionary Forces.

In March, 1929, the offices of the various Reorganization and Discharge Areas began their activities. However, at this time Li Tsung-jen and Feng Yu-hsiang successively staged rebellions as they wanted to divide and rule. For the sake of consolidating the nation's unification and thoroughly implementing the military reorganization program, the Central Government decided to take military actions against them by moving the military forces toward Wuhan. The Kwansi forces in Hupei and Hunan and the Rebel Suppression Forces were organized into 9 divisions. For the suppression of rebellion in Central China, the Shansi forces were reorganized into 4 corps; the Northwest forces into 1 corps and 2 divisions. By the winter of 1930, apart from 180,000 men in Szechuan and Sikang and 20,000 men in Kweichow, 9 brigades in Kirin, 2 brigades in Heilungchiang and 17 brigades in Liaoning which were awaiting reorganization, the first phase reorganization of 100 divisions was completed. In order to turn out elite national defense forces, Commander-in-Chief Chiang approved the revised organization changing the original Type A divisions into Type B divisions, and the original Type B divisions into Type C divisions. The organization of the independent brigade was also decided. It was planned to further reduce the size of the forces to 60 divisions and 15 independent brigades. The number of air squadrons was increased to 6.

General military education was conducted in accordance with the troop education directive promulgated by the Min-- istry of Training with emphasis on Dr. Sun's spiritual training, the Three Principles of the People, political subjects, recognition of words; and tactical and technical training. For cadre training, the Central Military Academy, the various service schools and the Army War College provided the education in different phases. Simultaneously various training classes and study classes were organized to provide the specialized training. Additionally, the Military Police and Police Training Class was established in the Central Military Academy. Together with the already established Aeronautical Class all these training organizations shouldered the education and training of the army, navy (including marines) air force, military police and police under the direction of Superintendent Chiang. All the personnel were united in the military reconstruction of national defense. In reorganizing the arsenals, all the small arsenals were deactivated and the facilities were used for industrial reconstruction. The six major arsenals in Hangyang, Shanghai, Nanking, Chinan, Ku Hsien and Huayin as well as the Shanghai Steel Mill and the Kaifeng Nitrite Plant were retained. The Ho Shan Dynamite Plant was established. Munitions production was standardized in the manufacture of rifles, light machine guns, mortars, pack howitzers and field guns. The equipment of the units were improved. Incendiary bombs, chemical weapons, 75mm howitzers were tested. The ordnance development and industrial reconstruction proceeded smoothly. National defense, national economy and communications showed remarkable progress.

Section 2
Suppression Operations, Consolidation and Unification

Westward Expedition toward Wuhan

In January, 1929, when the reorganization and discharge of the armed forces began, Li Tsung-jen refused to abide by the programs and principles passed at the Tang Shan Conference and the Central Executive Committee. Against the wish of the people, he betrayed the Party and the nation. With the Kwangsi forces under his command, he attempted to control Kwangtung, Kwangsi and Hunan by committing two divisions in the invasion of Changsha thereby forcing the 18th Division and the 50th Division to fall back into Kiangsi Province. When efforts made by the Central Government to check him had failed, it was necessary to take military actions against him. The military forces taking part in the westward expedition toward Wuhan was divided into the river left and river right forces. The Navy's Second Squadron moved west along the Yangtze River to respond to the Army's operations. Air stations were established in Chiuchiang and Nanchang to support the Army and Navy operations. Commander-in-Chief Chiang personally went to

Huangchow to direct the operations. As the rebel forces defected in large numbers, the entire front collapsed leading to the enemy's general retreat toward western Hupei Province. On 5 January, the Westward Expeditionary Forces recovered Wuhan without bloodshed. On 20 January, the entire rebel forces surrendered. Subsequently, they were assembled at Chiangling and were reorganized.

Capturing the Southwest

When the situation in Wuhan was stabilized, rebel Li Tsung-jen enlarged his rebellious activities despite messages from the Central Government and various circles urging him against such actions. Li named himself the commander-in-chief and directed the Kwangsi rebel forces in the invasion of Kwangtung. On 8 May, 1929, the rebel forces neared Sanshui and Tungchiang seriously threatening Canton. Commander-in-Chief Chiang ordered Ho Chien's Fourth Route Army to enter Kwangsi from Chuanchow in order to trail Li's rebel forces. Meanwhile, the cadets of the Whampoa Military Academy and the Revolutionary Forces in Kwangtung were massed to protect Canton. Additional forces were sent to Kwangtung from Wuhan as reinforcements. Li Tsung-jen, having been defeated, fled to Lungchow. In reorganizing the Kwangsi Provincial Government, the Central Government replaced Yu Tso-po with Li Ming-jui. Under Communist influence, Yu attempted rebellion. The Central Government dispatched forces which entered Kwangsi to attack Hsun and Kwei in three columns. The rebel forces surrendered in large numbers as the National Revolutionary Forces entered Kweiping pressing against Nanning. As Yu Tso-po and Li Tsung-jen fled to Lungchow, the situation in

Kwangsi became stable. In November, 1929, when Feng Yu-hsiang's rebel forces invaded Central China, the new and old Kwangsi cliques once again took advantage of the opportunity to harass Kwangtung. Thus, the National Revolutionary Forces withdrew to defend Pei Chiang (North River). Commander-in-Chief Chiang ordered the 4th Corps to enter Kwangtung from Pin and the 6th Route Army and the Navy's Second Squadron to head south in an effort to draw and destroy the rebel forces on the east bank of Pei Chiang (North River). In December, Hua Hsien and Wuchow were captured. In the spring of 1930, the situation in Kwangsi was once again stable.

Pacifying Central China

In April, 1929 when the Kwangsi clique began the rebellion, Feng Yu-hsiang was restless with his Northwest forces. In spite of Chairman Chiang's messages to the contrary, Feng continued actively in his military preparations. However, Feng's major subordinate commander Han Fu-chu was displeased with Feng's betrayal and cabled the Central Government declaring his allegiance. Thus, Feng was forced to announce his retirement leaving his subordinates such as Sun Liang-cheng, Sung Che-yuan and Liu Yu-fang to lead the Northwest forces. Wang Ching-wei who was then touring Europe issued a statement calling for the reorganization of the government. This led the rebel forces to enlarge the rebellions. Once again, Feng Yu-hsiang was prevailed to mass 200,000 troops in an attempt to capture Wuhan in a seven-pronged attack. The Central National Affairs Conference decided to chastise the rebels. On 5 November, Commander-in-Chief Chiang called a military conference on the battlefield in Hsuchang at which he gave his instructions. The next day, he went to Yu Hsien to make an inspection. At this time, the National Revolutionary Forces launched the general offensive. On 29 November, Loyang and Tzushing Pass were recovered. With the capture of Shanchow on 1 December, the rebel forces retreated to Shensi. Meanwhile, Shih Yu-san's forces mutinied at Pukow; Tang Shengchih responded at Chengchow. Ho Chien, Yang Chieh, Hsu Yuan-chuan, Yen Hsi-shan, Chang Hsueh-liang and Han Fuchu cabled to the Central Government declaring their allegiance. When military forces were dispatched to fight Tang, he suffered a heavy defeat and fled abroad. Later, Shih Yu-san defected to the Central Government. Thus, the suppression of the first rebellion in Central China was brought to an end.

In February, 1930, upon his return from Europe Wang Ching-wei, under the pretext of dissatisfaction with the Third National Congress, instigated Li Tsung-jen and Feng Yu-hsiang to form the puppet Republic of China Forces composed of 700,000 Shansi troops and Northwest troops. The puppet forces moved southward along the Tientsin-Pukow Railroad and the Peiping-Hankow Railroad. Additionally, the remnants of the Kwangsi clique entered Hunan from Kwangsi in an effort to capture Wuhan and Nanking. The Central Government cabled in vain urging ceasefire and maintenance of peace and unification. The National Affairs Conference decided to use military force. The disarmament movement staged by the nation's civil bodies and public opinion frightened the rebel leaders. With a force of 300,000, Commander-in-Chief Chiang successfully applied the strategy of defeat in detail. He ordered the National

Revolutionary Forces in Kwangtung to enter Hunan in order to intercept the Kwangsi forces. Elements of the National Revolutionary Forces halted the Northwest forces north of Hsuchang and west of Liuho concentrating first on the destruction of the Shansi forces along the Tientsin-Pukow Railroad and then shifting the main forces to Lung Hai (Haichow to Paochi) Railroad and Peiping-Hankow Railroad to effect mobile envelopment and destruction of the enemy. Chang Hsueh-liang's forces were ordered to attack Peiping. These moves shuddered the rebel leaders and developed the full effectiveness of psychological warfare. By the latter part of September the rebel forces along the Tientsin-Pukow Railroad, Lung Hai Railroad, Peiping-Hankow Railroad were all individually defeated, retreated and surrendered. Meanwhile, the forces that had entered Shanhaikwan captured Peiping. Wang Shu-chang was appointed the governor of Hupei Province and Yu Hsueh-chung the Peiping-Tientsin garrison commander by the National Government. On 27 September, Commander-in-Chief Chiang made public his "Message to the Officers and Men of the Second and the Third Army Groups" urging their immediate defection. Subsequently, the forces under Pang Ping-hsun, Chang Hsiang-yin, Shih Chen-ching, Hsueh Chuan-feng and Chang Tze-chung defected. The total collapse of the rebel forces came two days later. On 3 October, the National Revolutionary Forces recovered Kaifeng. Chengchow and Loyang were captured on 6 and 9 October respectively. Later, the key localities in North China and Central China were successively taken. On 13 October, Chairman Chiang issued his message, "Consolidation and Unification to Insure Peace." With Wang Ching-wei fleeing abroad, the rebel forces underwent reorganization and were assigned border defense missions. The wartime organizations of the rebel-suppressing Revolutionary Forces were abolished and the forces returned to their home stations. Thus ended the rebel-suppressing operations.

Section 3
Four Sieges and Fighting on Both Sides

Judicial Decision of the Supreme Command

In 1929, Chairman Chiang led the nation's people to enter from the period of military tutelege to the period of political tutelege. Centering on national defense, improvements were made in government, economics, communications, social conditions, education, cultural reconstruction and synchronization of military administration and military operation. In external relations, treaties were signed with Germany, Norway, Belgium, Italy, Denmark, Holland, Portugal, England, France, Sweden, Spain and Greece. Gradually, foreign concessions in Hankow, Chiuchiang, Chenchiang, Tientsin and Weihaiwei were returned. China exercised control over her custom duties. Throughout the nation, people were greatly inspired. However, the Japanese imperialists were intent in their aggressive designs of "Conquering China before conquering the world, and conquering Manchuria and Mongolia before conquering China." Japan was actively engaged in political and economic aggression on China. Meanwhile, having been stopped in Central and South China, British influence turned to Tibet. Although the Soviet influence was withdrawn from Manchuria for the time being, Russia continued to execute Lenin's strategy of communizing the world which was "the shortest route from Moscow to Paris is via Peiping and Calcutta." On the one hand, Russia engineered the seeking of independence by Outer Mongolia. On the other hand, Russia helped the Chinese Communist Party to grow. In 1928, when the Sixth National Congress was held in Moscow, the following guiding principles were laid: "Seize the political and industrial centers of several provinces" and "seek an early victory in one or several provinces" so as to undermine China's unification and social organizations. Obstruct the practice of the Three Principles of the People and the conduct of national defense reconstruction in the border areas of Honan, Hupei, Anhwei, Kiangsi, Chekiang, Fukien and Hunan Provinces. Coerce the people, confiscate the land, develop guerrilla activities, and enlarge rebellious activities. Efforts would be made to further communize the people living along the strategically important Chinese Eastern Railway. On 27 May, 1929, Soviet Communist leaders convened the Third Communist International Propaganda Conference at the Soviet Consulate in Harbin. The commissioner of the Northeast Special District uncovered many secret Soviet documents attempting to undermine China's unification, propagandize Communism, conduct assassinations and instigate internal disturbances. Since such Soviet subversive activities violated the Sino-Russian Pact, orders were issued to take over the Chinese Eastern Railway. When the National Government began the suppression operations, Russia dispatched 80,000 army, navy and air force troops to invade Tungan, Fuching (Manchouli) and Hulun (Hailal) in Manchuria using the Chinese Eastern Railway Incident as a pretext. The Chinese Communist even advanced such slogans as "Support Soviet Union" and "Take up Arms to Protect Soviet Union." Chinese Communists receiving training in Russia at the time such as Liu Po-cheng, Yeh Chien-ying and Chou En-lai were given 300,000 rubles by the Soviet Union each month, wore Soviet uniforms and went to Manchuria to organize the International Red Army. Indeed, they were traitors fighting with the Russians in their aggressions of China.

In view of the situation in which both Japan and Russia had aggressive designs on China, Chairman Chiang was concerned over the Fifth Columnists that Soviet Russia had in China which would subject China to subversion from within in war against Japan or Russia. Based on the basic policy of "seeking independence in external affairs and unification in internal affairs," he sought solution to problems through diplomatic channels against the aggressive actions of Japan and Russia. Successively, China signed the Nine-Power Pact and No-War Pact in order to restrain the aggressive actions of Japan and Russia. Decisions were made to lay siege to the insurgent Communists so as to destroy them once for all and to consolidate the nation's foundation.

From the First to the Fourth Sieges

In the fall of 1930, the Chinese Communists took advantage of the suppression campaigns being waged by the National Revolutionary Forces against the rebels and threatened Nanchang and Chiuchiang after the capture of Chian and Hukou in an attempt to harass the Yangtze River and envelop Wuhan under the operational guidance of "having the cities lead the villages." Later, when the Communist forces were defeated, Mao advanced the strategy of "surrounding the cities with villages." His forces fled to southern Kiangsi, Kiangsi-Hupei-Hunan border areas, Honan-Hupei-Anhwei border areas and Hunan-Hupei-Szechuan border areas claiming to have a force of 121,000 organized into 11 corps. They took advantage of the terrain in the mountain areas and the vast potentials of the farm villages to exercise a policy of terror, confiscate land, coerce the people and step up the rebellion. They achieved internal control by means of slaughtering the innocent people. Some 14,300 people in the Soviet zone of southern Kiangsi and 40,000 people in western Fukien were slaughtered surpassing the brutality of any previous tyrants. Meanwhile, Japan stepped up its design on China by moving armed colonists to Manchuria and created tension. Chairman Chiang adopted a policy of resisting foreign aggression and pacification after the conclusion of the suppression operations. National defense was strengthened to resist Japanese aggression while adopting the strategy of isolation, blockade, envelopment and annihilation. In December, forces were dispatched to conduct suppression and mop-up. Air force units were stationed in Hankow, Nanchang and Changshu to support the ground operations. Naval units were ordered to effect the blockade of the Yangtze River, the Kan River and the southeastern coastal areas, cut off outside support of the Communists and coordinate with the army units in ground operations. Unfortunately, the vast areas, necessary troop dispositions against the Japanese, relatively weak army forces, lack of coordination between troop units, and lack of security consciousness failed to bring about an effective suppression of the first and the second sieges in southern Kiangsi and the mop-up of the Honan-Hupei-Anhwei border areas. However, the siege of the Hupei-Hunan border areas was successful as efforts were made to take advantage of swamps and make up the strength deficiency by effecting gradual phased blockade. After the Communists were encircled and destroyed in the Hung Lake area, forces were shifted to link up with Hunan forces and naval forces in the destruction of the enemy in the vicinity of Huayung. As to the other remaining areas, our forces were only able to isolate and block the Communists in the barren regions. This strategy was partly successful.

In May, 1931, the National Government convened the National Convention at which regulations were prepared and a Communist suppression declaration issued calling upon the people to jointly destroy the Communists. Efforts were made to increase the strength of the forces participating in the suppression campaigns. Plans were made to block the enemy in the east with the reserves from Chian, Tai Hsien, Wanan, and Kanchow. The main force was divided into the Left and the Right Army Group[1] to launch a converging attack on southern Kiangsi. The main force would make a "seeking the heart movement" against the enemy. Just when the encirclement was getting satisfactorily smaller, the Kwangtung Incident broke out. Under the pretext of protecting the constitution[2], Wang Ching-wei and Li

---

[1] Left and Right Army Groups:
  The Left Army Group commanded 7 divisions and the Right Army Group 8 divisions. The strength of each division was 10,000 to 15,000 men. The average divisions were 10% to 30% understrength.

[2] Battle over Protecting of Regulations:
  In May, 1931, the National Government called the National Congress to formulate the regulations of the Republic of China during the period of political tutelege. The regulations were revised by the National Congress. Prior to the implementation of the Constitution, these regulations were com-

Tsung-jen conspired in an invasion of Hunan and Kiangsi. The Chinese Communists conducted the so-called "strategic withdrawal" and fled westward to Hsingkuo. Later, with the Manchurian Incident (The September 18 Incident of 1931), Japanese forces invaded Manchuria. As the Government forces were moved to the north, the third siege was interrupted.

Subsequent to the Manchurian Incident, Japan continued her aggression on China. Taking advantage of the Chinese people's hatred of Japan, the Chinese Communists launched political offensive by instigating student strikes, driving a wedge between local governments and the Central Government, and manufacturing political disunity. Hoping to rouse the Chinese people into national solidarity, Chairman Chiang tendered his resignation. When repeated attempts of the Central Government failed to make Chairman Chiang withdraw his resignation, Mr. Lin Sen was elected Acting Chairman. When the Shanghai Incident broke out on 28 January, 1932, elements of the National Revolutionary Forces were drawn and deployed in Kiangsu, Chekiang and Anhwei. Seeing that the National Government was pre-occupied with external affairs, the Communists encircled Wuhan, threatened Nanking and attacked the flank and rear of the Government forces then fighting against the Japanese. However, they were routed by the Government forces at Kanchow, Kiangsi Province and Chengyang Pass in Anhwei Province. Realizing the danger of fighting on two sides, the National Government decided to establish the National Military Council and

---

parable to the Constitution. In an attempt to realize his personal ambition, Wang Ching-wei refused to abide by the regulations. He conspired with Li Tsung-jen and sent forces to invade Hunan and Kiangsi.

appointed Commander-in-Chief Chiang as its Chairman to exercise command over the armed forces and to save the nation from impending disaster. After the cessation of hostilities in Shanghai, Chairman Chiang, on 1 June, standardized the organizations of the divisions stipulating the corps as the direct subordinate unit and the provision that corps commanders did not act concurrently as division commanders. The nation had 48 corps and 96 divisions. Each division had additional special troops such as engineer, quartermaster and signal battalions so as to strengthen their combat effectiveness. Communist intrigues were exposed and the policy of giving prior attention to internal pacification as a prerequisite to resisting foreign aggression was announced. The guiding principle of "combined employment of political and military efforts" in the suppression of Communists was advanced dividing the country into six areas for suppression and mop-up operations. On 18 June, Generalissimo Chiang convened the Five Province (Honan, Hupei, Anhwei, Kiangsi and Hunan) Communist Suppression Conference at which it was decided to mop up the Communists in Honan, Hupei and Anhwei first. It was found necessary to eliminate bad local practices, put in order local finances and economy and establish "pao chia" (A system of mutual assistance and security, dating back nine centuries) and self-defense organizations. Later in early July, suppression operations began in accordance with prearranged strategy of isolation, blockade, encirclement and destruction. The successful maneuver of two flanking forces resulted in the destruction of many Communist troops. Concurrently, political activities kept pace with military progress. "Permanent Tiller" licenses were issued, land rent reduction effected and relief funds and edible salt distributed. People were encouraged to work for their livings instead of depending on relief, and improvements in traffic communications were made. The combined efforts of Generalissimo Chiang and the party-political-military-civil organizations led to the annihilation of 100,000 Communists in Honan, Hupei and Anhwei Provinces in less than three months. Some 20,000 Communists fled to the west. Further operations conducted by the National Revolutionary Forces in the Honan-Shensi border areas forced such Communist commanders as Hsu Hsiang-chien and Ho Lung to barely escape to northern Szechuan and Ho Feng in western Hupei where they planned further development. Meanwhile, Communists in the Kiangsi-Kwangtung-Fukien-Hunan border areas had been driven back and sealed in the vicinity of Lichuan and Tzuhsi. The National Revolutionary Forces were ready for the fourth siege. However, shortly after the operations began, Japanese invasion of Yukuan and Jehol forced the abandonment of the successful fourth siege.

Section 4
The Fifth Siege and A New Type of Total War
(See Map 6)

Communist Suppression Conference

In May, 1933, Generalissimo Chiang arrived in Nanchang to preside over a Communist suppression conference at which gains and losses in previous suppression campaigns were reviewed and the plans of the fifth siege was formulated. Under the policy of "internal pacification as a prerequisite to resisting foreign aggression" and the guiding principle of "30% military effort and 70% political effort," the national strategy of management (organizational warfare), education (cultural warfare), maintenance (economic warfare) and defense (military warfare) was carried out. The Nanchang Headquarters of Chairman, National Military Council was established. The Party Political Committee was organized for the waging of a new type of total war which emphasized party-political-military joint operations. The eight provinces of Szechuan, Shensi, Honan, Hupei, Kiangsi, Hunan, Kwangtung and Fukien were mobilized and forces were massed for a converging attack from four different directions. Apart from the 3rd and 4th Squadrons of the Air Force, the 1st, the 2nd and the 5th Squadrons were also added to the order of battle. The main force was disposed in the north in order to isolate, block, encircle and destroy the enemy forces. With regard to the enemy forces in southern Kiangsi, Kiangsi-Anhwei-Fukien border areas, Kiangsi-Hupei-Hunan border areas and western Kiangsi, a number of sieges were laid. In the meantime, Russia intended to sell the Chinese Eastern Railway to Japan thereby encouraging the Japanese forces in their aggression of China and to invade Sinkiang. Russia also dispatched Chey[3] to the so-called "Soviet Zone" in southern Kiangsi via Fukien directing the Chinese Communists to comply with Russia's supreme strategic guidance

---

[3] Chey:
Chey was a German sent to the Kiangsi Soviet Zone by the Communist International to guide the Chinese Communists in their rebellion. Upon termination of World War I, he went from Germany to Russia to join the Communist International. In late August, 1933, he was sent to China via Yangko near Hsunchang in Fukien Province. He found his way into the Kiangsi Soviet Zone to undertake planning, reorganize the Communist forces and formulate the so-called "counter-suppression plans."

in the operations against the Government Forces. Again on 28 May, Generalissimo Chiang called a conference at Kuling in which personnel from the Executive Yuan, the Legislative Yuan and the Foreign Ministry participated. Apart from appealing to the League of Nations for the return of sovereignty to China the conference decided to sign the Tangku Agreement with Japan, resume diplomatic relationships with Russia and negotiate the return of the Chinese Eastern Railway in order to ease the aggressive attempts of Japan and Russia. On the domestic side, the Conscription Laws were promulgated, division and regimental control areas divided, conscription system implemented, construction of the seven-province highway net expedited, Lushan Training Corps established, party-political-military cadres trained, revolutionary spirit streamlined, tactical doctrines unified and battlefield psychology fortified. In addition, the three-year Air Force build-up program was formulated, administrative outline for Communist-suppression areas promulgated, Communities and village farms revived, schools in the recovered areas established, the Three Principles of the People publicized, poisonous thinking of Communism eliminated, "pao chia" system enforced, local organizations tightened, local military forces strengthened and rear area security maintained. Cable orders were dispatched setting target dates for the completion of the five major highways, namely the Kiangsi-Chekiang Highway, the Kiangsi-Hupei Highway, the Kiangsi-Hunan Highway, the Kiangsi-Kwangtung Highway and the Kiangsi-Fukien Highway. The flow of materials, traffic communications and news leading into Communist-occupied territories was sealed, and combat readiness was stepped up. These measure laid the cornerstone of a superior posture in the new type of total war.

Putting Down Mutiny in Fukien

In the latter part of September, 1933, the Communist forces were expanded to a strength of 150,000. Prior to the massing of our main force, the North Route Army Group, the Communist 1st and 5th Armies were organized into the West Area Force which was left in the areas south of Yihuang in order to block the advance of our North Route Army. Their 3rd Army together with other newly organized units formed the East Area Force ready to grow in northern Fukien. Fortunately, the North Route Army Group dispatched the 8th Column in a swift, surprise attack on Lichuan to separate the Communist East and West Area Forces and broke the liaison between the Communist forces in northeastern Kiangsi and those in southern Kiangsi. Communist attempt to recapture Lichuan in a coordinated attack failed when the attack was frustrated by the Government North Route Army. Group. In October, our intelligence agencies learned of the Communist conspiracy with Li Chi-shen and Chen Ming-shu to have the 19th Route Army stage a coup in Fukien and the signing of the so-called "Resist Japan Operational Agreement." Communists urgently cabled Soviet Russia for the shipping of large quantities of army equipment and aircraft to the interior via Amoy in order to supply the Communist forces in Kiangsi. This cable, when intercepted and decoded, was interpreted by us to be an attempt designed to save their crisis by means of political intrigues. On 20 November, the Fukien coup started with the Communist forces of Peng Teh-huai and Lo Ping-wen entering Fukien to lend support and attack the flank of the North Route Army Group so as to enlarge the political impact. Fully aware of the enemy's plot, Generalissimo Chiang went from Hangchow to Yenping in order to direct the operations in Fukien. He ordered a number of units to move to the border of Fukien in order to check the Communist forces in southern Kiangsi and to respond to the Government Forces fighting in Fukien. Representatives were sent to Fukien to point the way to the rebel division commanders and urge their defections. Sixteen Air Force planes assisted in the operations, while marines headed for Foochow and Amoy by water in order to make landings and converging attacks, Army made long drives in two routes to recover key localities. In less than two months, the Fukien Coup was quelled.

Destroying the Communist Hideout

By 11 December, 1933, Generalissimo Chiang's guiding principle of "30% military effort and 70% political effort," enforcement of "pao-chia" system, implementation of the pillbox policy of "strategic offensive and tactical defensive," and "economic blockade and material cut-off" led to the construction of pillbox groups in the twenty hsiens located along the perimeter of the Communist-controlled areas. By 26 January, 1934, in addition to the pillboxes guarding the highways, the various forces had built a total of 2,900 pillboxes, thus completing a tight blockade on the Communists. On 17 February, Generalissimo Chiang initiated the "New Life Movement" in Nanchang to restore China's traditional virtues and uplift the morale of the people. As the entire nation responded favorably, a new atmosphere prevailed. Further, promulgation of "Outline Measures for the Relief of People by the Communist Suppression Forces" promoted civil-military cooperation; farmers living in the Communist suppression areas were provided loans; and economy of the villages in the Communist-troubled areas and recovered areas were rebuilt. A total of 3,600 mutual assistance associations and 5,900 cooperatives were established. In addition, excessive revenues and taxes were abolished. All these led to the people's gratitude to the Government and, in turn, our absolute political superiority. Meanwhile, Party-political offices representing the North, East, West, South Route Army Groups were set up to coordinate with the provincial governments and the provincial party headquarters concerned and to dispose of party and political affairs in the Communist suppression areas. Similar offices were set up by the various Route and Column Headquarters to be responsible for the handling of party-political matters in the recovered areas in coordination with the special party headquarters and political training departments of the various divisions. The various Route Armies were organized into suppression forces, garrison forces and reserve forces in order to constitute a flexible party-political-military entity in offense or defense capable of effecting strategic deployment of deeply disposed double envelopment. Nanchang, Changsha, Chuchiang and Foochow became strategic bases to support the operations of the North, East, West and South Route Army Groups. The gradual implementation of reforms in the political, economic and cultural fields not only eased the people's anxieties and boosted morale but also shattered and crippled the Communist-controlled areas resulting in our favorable political and military postures. Economically, Communists organized food spot check detachments to grab the foods of the people as their own provisions. Politically, they organized the old and the young, the male and the female declaring curfews, sabotaging traffic communications, conducting scorched earth policy, suppressing the wealthy farmers, allocating land and forcing productions. Militarily, they expanded raid activities and stepped up military defections. Despite all these efforts, they were unable to break the blockade of the Government Forces.

In mid-February, 1934, in a converging attack the East and the North Route Army Groups of the Government Forces gradually moved against southern Kiangsi. As the participating forces effected a penetration in depth on a narrow front, mobile advancing guerilla units were dispatched on both flanks to align with the main force and to carry out the attack thoroughly. As Generalissimo Chiang directed that the six principles of reconnaissance, patrol, security, liaison, cover and observation be emphasized, the East and the North Route Army Groups swiftly completed a blockade by means of the pillboxes in the various hsiens. The 3rd and the 6th Route Armies provided mutual cover to each other and advanced in bounds. Furthermore, the organization of each combat unit was such that it was capable of conducting independent operations and achieving the superior strategy of capturing key localities and luring enemy main forces. On 1 April, in the attack on Kwangchang and Shuiko, enemy main force was broken and the gateway to the Communist areas in southern Kiangsi opened. Simultaneously, the East Route Army Group recovered in succession a number of key localities in the Communist-controlled areas and completed local administrative organizations and pillbox blockade making steady progress. With the support of our Air Force, the North Route Army Group captured the key localities in the vicinity of Kwangchang to effect the pillbox blockade between the East and the North Route Army Groups. Later, Lungkang was recovered. By this time Communist-controlled areas gradually felt the pressure on them. Kung Ho-lung, a Communist commander surrendered with Liu Hsueh-wu, his director of Political Department and Chang Yi, his division commander. Communist remnants headed by Hsiao Ke fled south. The phased construction of highways and pillboxes as well as political work proceeded in accordance with military progress. Local administrative organizations were reestablished, "pao-chia" system enforced, relief funds distributed, census checked, displaced persons comforted, masses organized, business resumed, schools established, land registered and the New Life Movement promoted in order to reach the state in which "the roads are void of Communists; the pillboxes insure the security of the people; the schools educate the people and the bountiful food draws the support of the people." The impact was so great that the people in the recovered areas voluntraily organized volunteer corps to eliminate Communists and to assist the Government Forces in the suppression campaigns. As morale was high and people eager, the resulting effect was beyond expectations.

In an a tempt to save the rapidly deteriorating situation, the Communists continued to carry out the Russian instruction of a "pillbox against pillbox" policy. In addition, they fell back to the line along Yichien-Ningtu-Kulungkang-Hsingkuo-Changting to construct the so-called "fortress zone" where they intended to offer stubdorn resistance. Generalissimo Chiang then redeployed his forces to continue the operations southward. In October, with the support of the Air Force, the North Route Army Group was divided into three columns to penetrate into the Communist fortress zones and to tighten the ring of encirclement. Knowing they were on the brink of total collapse and that the South Route Army Group had not completed the lateral line of pillboxes in accordance with the pre-arranged schedule, the Communist remnants fled westward through the gap between Kanchow and Hsinfeng. A total of over 30,000 Communist troops were killed, 74,000 wounded and 28,000 captured. Over 20,000 rifles were also captured. The Soviet Zone in which the Communists had stayed for six years, was completely recovered. Meanwhile, keeping pace with military progress in the Communist suppression campaigns, reconstruction in national defense, government, economics, education, military affairs, traffic communications and society in Central and South China proceeded satisfactorily.

This siege fully reflected the full effectiveness of Generalissimo Chiang's new type of total war in which maximum joint party-political-military efforts were developed to wrest the initiative in war. The strategy of isolation, blockade, encirclement and destruction was most successful.

Section 5
25,000 Li Pursuit (See Map 7)

Suppression Operations in Hunan-Kwangsi Border Areas

In the fall of 1934, after the fifth siege laid by the Chinese Government Forces, the Communists broke the siege and fled to the west. The hot pursuit of the West Route Army

Group resulted in 1,000 remnants of Hsiao Ke's forces fleeing to Tayung and Sangchih in western Hunan. Though linked up with Ho Lung's forces fleeing southward form Ho Feng (Crane Peak) in western Hupei, these remnants were routed after subsequent siege and were scattered in the border area of Lungshan and Yungshun. With some 100,000 people under their coercion, the Communist remnants began the long westward track on 16 October.

Generalissimo Chiang then terminated the Nanchang headquarters of the Chairman, National Military Council and set up similar headquarters in Wuchang, Ichang and Chungking. A staff corps was organized and sent to Szechuan to separately direct the Communist suppression operation in Hunan, Hupei and Anhwei and to plan the military operations in Szechuan, Sikang, Yunnan and Kweichow. The 6th Route Army was reorganized into the Pursuit Army and was divided into the 1st through the 5th Route Corps. With the 2nd and the 3rd Squadrons of the Air Force stationed in Hengyang, this army was to give chase. The Yunnan and Kwangsi forces were ordered to intercept the enemy at the Hunan-Kweichow and Hunan-Kwangsi border areas. As the Communist forces fled through Hunan and Kwangsi, Government Forces gave chase along the way. Half of the enemy forces became stragglers or casualties with the remnants heading for the Kweichow-Kwangsi border. Meanwhile, the Pursuit Army had been redeployed and reorganized into the 1st and the 2nd Armies continuing the chase to the west. Two divisions were sent to intercept the enemy at the Wukang area.

Suppression Operations in Kweichow-Yunnan Border Areas

On 24 December, 1934, the Communist forces fled north

to Sansui via Licheng. Meanwhile, Communist forces led by Hsiao Ke and Ho Lung darted to Taoyuan. In the pursuit, our 1st, 2nd and 3rd Route Armies advanced to Sansui and Chengyuan. On 22 December, the enemy forces fled to Chengyuan and were broken into two columns fleeing westward. Again, our 2nd and 3rd Route Armies gave chase. In January, 1935, the Communist main force and portions of their forces moved northward respectively from Hsifeng and Tanan to Tsunyi and Suiyang. Later, Government Forces entered northern Kweichow from Szechuan to form a converging attack with elements of the Government's 25th Corps. Communist remnants, therefore, fled to and harassed the Yunnan-Kweichow border areas. On 2 February, Generalissimo Chiang organized the Pursuit Army and the Yunnan-Kweichow Forces into two routes. The 1st Route Force commanded the 5th through the 8th Columns which jointly laid siege to the Communists in western Hunan. The 2nd Route Force commanded the 1st through the 4th Columns laying siege to the Communist forces in the Yunnan-Kweichow border areas. Szechuan and Hunan Provinces were ordered to repair and build the Hunan-Kweichow and Szechuan-Kweichow Highways. The 5th Squadron of the Air Force was moved to Kweiyang. Between mid-February and late March, Communist forces were intercepted by the Government's 3rd Column in northern Yunnan and were attacked by the 1st, 2nd and 4th Columns in the Yunnan-Kweichow border areas. Thus, the Communist forces crossed the Wu River and fled southward to Yunnan via Kweiyang and Lungli. Generalissimo Chiang left Chungking for Kweiyang to direct the military operations there. He also initiated the "National Economic Reconstruction Movement" and the "New Life Movement" which would be carried out on a parallel basis. The response from the nation's people was spontaneous. Meanwhile, the Communist forces under Hsu Hsiang-chien had fled to Tung-chiang and Pachung. Having been attacked by the Government Forces in Szechuan and Shensi, Communist forces fled through the gap at Langchung to cross the Chialing River. Government forces had a strength of four corps to fight the Communists in areas southeast of Mao Hsien, Lifan, and Maokung. When the Communist forces were heading toward Chinsha River (Golden Sand River), Government Forces were already defending Huili, Hsichang and the banks of Chinsha River. Government Forces in Shensi rushed to Szechuan with the main force of the Second Route Army driving into Yunnan. On 3 May, Communist forces secretly crossed the Chinsha River to flee to Maokung. The 3rd and the 4th Squadrons of the Air Force moved to Kunming from Kweiyang. On 10 May, Generalissimo Chiang flew to Kunming to direct the Army and Air Force efforts in pursuit of the enemy. On 24 May, he flew to Chengtu via Chungking to exercise unified command of the Szechuan Forces in the pursuit. The Szechuan-Shensi-Kansu Border Area Communist Suppression General Headquarters was established to contain and destroy the enemy.

Suppression Operations in Szechuan-Sikang-Kansu-Shensi Border Areas

On 14 June, 1935, pursued by Government Forces, Communist forces fled to Maokung where they joined force with Communist Hsu Hsiang-chien's forces. Generalissimo Chiang then ordered the 2nd Route Army to push toward Yaan and the 4th Route Army toward Maokung. Additionally, the 3rd and the 6th Squadrons of the Air Force moved to Chengtu, Yaan and Yungching airfields to support the ground operations. On 20 June, Hsu's main force moved toward Lifan to confront the 1st Route Army of the Government forces, while other Communist forces fought bitterly against the 2nd Route Army. Meanwhile, portions of Communist forces had fled to Chunghua and Wupien. Having been routed by the Government's 95th Division, Communist forces under Hsu Hai-tung in Liang-tang fled to southern Shensi in the hope of responding to the Communist forces in Shensi and northern Szechuan. In an effort to consolidate central Szechuan, Generalissimo Chiang ordered Government forces to intercept and contain the enemy in Shensi and Kansu. By early August, the Communist forces under Chu, Mao and Hsu were surrounded by the Government Forces at Maoerhkai. Supply difficulties led to starvation, cold and many deaths. Furthermore, internal dissensions were about to bring total collapse to the Chinese Communists. In order to save the Chinese Communists from complete destruction, Russia took it upon herself to sell the Chinese Eastern Railway to Japan and instigated Japanese aggression to check the Government Forces. She went further to call the Communist International's Seventh Congress directing the Chinese Communists to propose the "Anti-Japanese People's United Front," incite anti-Japanese organizations, sow the seed of disaccord between the local forces and the Government forces, adopt neutral tactics and undermined the policy of "internal pacification as a prerequisite to resisting foreign aggression" in the hope of making a last ditch fight. Generalissimo Chiang established Omei Officers' Training Corps to train cadres of local forces briefing them on the importance of the policy of "internal pacification as a prerequisite to resisting foreign aggression." The Szechuan forces were reorganized for unity in the Communist suppression campaigns. Realizing his intrigues had failed, Mao led the 10,000 remnants of his 1st and 3rd Armies in a northward flight. They were intercepted by Government forces at Tienshui and Huan Hsien. Again, the enemy remnants were routed and fled to northern Shensi where they joined force with the Communist forces under Hsu Hai-tung in southern Shensi for the northward flight. By the time they joined the local Communist forces led by Liu Tzu-tan, their exhausted force of 2,000-3,000 men were completely helpless. The Government forces, therefore, completed the unprecedented long distance campaign to press and annihilate the enemy. At last, the administrations of the southwestern provinces were unified.

Section 6
Laying Siege in the Northwest and
Communists Suing for Surrender (See Map 8)

Laying Siege in Northern Shensi and Western Shansi

Between September and October, 1935, Communist remnants successively entered northern Shensi to link up with the local Communist forces headed by Liu Tzu-tan attempting to take advantage of the special circumstances of the northwest to revive their activities in communization. In order to put an end to Communist troubles, and to consolidate the northwest frontier so as to maintain the defense, communications and economic reconstructions of the northwest in the past few years, Generalissimo Chiang established the Northwest Communist Suppression General Headquarters in Sian. Generalissimo Chiang acted concurrently as its commander-in-chief and Chang Hsueh-liang the deputy commander-in-chief. However, Chang was the acting commander-in-chief directing the military operations in Shansi, Shensi, Kansu and Ninghsia.

In mid-October, the Northwest Communist Suppression General Headquarters, based on the experiences obtained in the fifth siege in Kiangsi, the guiding principle of "30% military effort and 70% political effort," the annihilation strategy of "isolation, blockade and encirclement," and the principle of "strategic offensive and tactical defensive," prepared plans for the suppression compaign. However, it was at a time when water was frozen and traffic communication was congested. Furthermore, the Japanese forces repeatedly provoked incidents in Suiyuan as excuses for invasion, Government forces were limited to blockade activities. The Communists then advanced the slogan of "joint actions against Japan" to plot disunity in the Government forces, gain time, and augment their strength. By late January, 1936, their strength was increased to 50,000. Due to tight blockade effected by the Government forces, the cut-off of material resources and supply difficulties, Communist forces attempted to flee to the east. Meanwhile, the Taiyuan Pacification Headquarters employed four divisions and three independent brigades for the defense of northern, western and southern Shansi.

On 20 February, 1936, Mao decided to keep a portion of his forces to hold their lairs in northern Shensi, while moving his main force across the Yellow River in the eastward direction toward western Shansi. The Taiyuan Pacification Headquarters ordered the 33rd corps to cross the Yellow River and to contain the enemy in conjunction with the 1st through the 4th Columns reorganized from the Shansi forces. A cable report was submitted to Generalissimo Chiang to dispatch the 32nd Corps, the 13th Corps and the 25th Division as reinforcements converging from Chungyang, Hsiaoyi, Homa and Hsiangning in a three-pronged attack. As a result, the Communists suffered heavy casualties. In early May, the Communist forces crossed the Yellow River turning westward toward northern Shensi.

Laying Siege in the Shensi-Kansu Border Areas

On 2 May, 1936, Mao's forces fled to northern Shensi after being defeated in western Shansi. Cornered and incapable of taking another risk, Mao instigated the Third Party and anti-Japanese organizations, and conducted reactionary propaganda. On the one hand he conducted infiltration and division in the ranks of the Northeast forces and attempted to undermine the siege of the Government forces. On the other hand, he conducted political breakout. Fully aware of the Communist plots in the united front, Generalissimo Chiang established the Four Provinces (Shansi, Shensi, Suiyuan and Ninghsia) Border Area Communist Suppression Command on 1 June to exercise unified command of these areas and to quell the Communist disturbances. Already the Communists found themselves in great difficulties. However, the Pailing Temple Incident and the Kwangtung-Kwangsi Incident broke out and gave the Communists an opportunity to create disturbances. Fortunately, the military operations in Suiyuan were successful. Subsequently, the military forces of Kwangtung-Kwangsi cabled to pledge their support of the Central Government. The Kwangtung-Kwangsi Incident[4] ended after the entire Kwangtung-Kwangsi air force defected and flew the planes to Nanchang. Thus, the Communist suppression campaign in Shensi-Kansu border areas was able to continue.

On 16 August, 1936, some 40,000 Communist troops under Chu, Hsu, Hsiao and Ho moved north to attack Min Hsien, but their attempt ended in failure. Again, they invaded Hui Hsien, Linhui and Linchao and were routed. Remnants fled to Chingyuan and Chingning for rest and replenishment. The Northwest Communist Suppression Command redeployed the forces and attacked the enemy from Lanchow, Huining and Ninghsia. On 16 October, the surrounded Communist forces broke out, crossed the Yellow River and fled westward toward Wuwei and Yungchang. After being intercepted by the Government forces, large numbers of enemy were destroyed.

Sian Incident and Communists Suing for Surrender

In November, 1936, Mao's forces suffered heavy losses in the vicinity of Huan Hsien where they were defeated by the Government forces. Eight long years of military opera-

---

[4] Kwangtung-Kwangsi Incident:
In late June, 1936, taking advantage of the fact that the National Forces were occupied in the northwest fighting the Communists and in North China fighting the Japanese, the local authorities in Kwangtung and Kwangsi organized the puppet National Military Council ready to engage in insurrection. However, most of their subordinates knew what was right. In early July, they sent a message to the Central Government pledging their allegiance. Members of their air force flew 49 of their airplanes to Nanchang deserting the puppet organization. In the end the Kwangtung-Kwangsi Incident was solved through peaceful means.

tions against the Communists were about to end in total victory. To save themselves from their military predicament, the Communists started the "peace" political propaganda offensive taking Shensi as their No. 1 target. Communist front organizations, namely, the "Third Party," the "National Salvation Association" and the "Students' Federation" carried out the initial reactionary propaganda to instigate rebellious actions by Chang Hsueh-liang and Yang Hu-cheng. They even subjected Chang Hsueh-liang and his troops to intensive propaganda, and they kept on provoking Chang, who, being torn between "suppression of the Communists" and "resistance against Japan," finally succumbed to this incessant offensive by the neutralists.

When he was informed that certain units engaged in Communist suppression conspired with the Communists and retreated at will and that there were indications of a plot and rebellion, Generalissimo Chiang entered Shensi from Loyang on 4 December to interview and confer with the local commanders. He advised them that the military campaign against the Communist was on the verged of success and urged them to make continued efforts. He had planned to call a military conference at the end of the year in order to announce the Government's policy in the suppression of the Communists and resistance against Japan. He had wanted to let them know where the nation's interests lay so that they would not be deceived by the Communist rumors and lies.

Unfortunately, Chang Hsueh-liang, Yang Hu-cheng and their troops had already been influenced by Communist instigations and had fallen into the Communist intrigue willing to be used by the Communists. On 12 December, they started the world-shaking Sian Incident in which the nation's

Supreme Commander was detained. They completely disregarded the fatal blow they had dealt to the nation's future.

When Chang went to see Generalissimo Chiang in the quarters where the latter was detained, Generalissimo Chiang sternly admonished him by saying: "Either for your own sake or for the sake of the nation, the only thing for you to do is to repent at once and escort me back to Nanking. You must not fall into the trap set by the Communists. Repent now before it is too late." Chang withdrew in shame.

On 14 December, Chang saw Generalissimo Chiang again and presented absurd demands requesting the latter to sign them. Unmoved, Generalissimo Chiang reprimanded him by saying: "Regardless of any significance your advocacy may have and any attractiveness in your speech, the absurdity of your actions will most certainly not be forgiven, much less supported by anyone," Chang still wished to continue his explanation, but Generalissimo Chiang cut him short. He told Chang resolutely: "I have decided to sacrifice my life in order to uphold the spirit of righteousness. I have given this matter deliberate considerations. You can deprive me of the freedom of action of my body, but you can never deprive me of my will. I will not accommodate myself to you. Unless I am in Nanking, I will not listen to a word of your explanation on this." He remained resolute in his refusal to discuss political terms with the rebels. In the meantime, the Government in Nanking ignored the rebels' preposterous demand and launched a punitive expedition against them.

On 22 December, Mme. Chiang suddenly arrived in Sian. The first thing Generalissimo Chiang said to her when they met was: "For the past ten days the rebels have been putting varied and persistent pressure on me. If I accepted their terms, they would escort me back to Nanking. You have come to share my peril. I believe you have done this out of consideration for our national interests and not for personal reasons alone. National interests must come first. If the rebels should ask you to persuade me to accept any of their terms, they must be resolutely refused. We would rather die than accede to their demands." Her determination was equally resolute. She replied that she too held his integrity above his life, that she would not ask him to compromise his principles, and that she had come to share his fate.

By 25 December, rebel Chang Hsueh-liang was so greatly inspired by Generalissimo Chiang's personal integrity that he begged forgiveness and escorted the latter to Nanking. The entire nation rejoiced over and celebrated its leader's safe return.

The nation's united voice urging punitive actions against the rebels and the people's enthusiastic support of their leader at the Sian Incident reflected the fact that Generalissimo Chiang had become the nucleus in the leadership, as the nation's security hinged on him. Communist International knew only too well that if the Chinese Communists did not alter their measures, they would be destroyed by the people. On January, 1937, it sent Petrov to Yenan instructing the Chinese Communists to surrender to the National Government and to seek development in other areas. Based on these instructions, the Chinese Communists brought up the five demands and four guarantees to the National Government in an attempt to set up a special district government. On 21 February 1937, the Government passed the

"Proposal on the Elimination of Red Peril" pointing out to the nation's people that the Communists' demands obstructed the nation's solidarity and unification. However, to show its sincerity in peace, the Government would withhold preparations for the attack on northern Shensi in the hope of achieving Communists' total repentence. On 7 July, the Marco Polo Bridge Incident broke out. Generalissimo Chiang issued a statement at Lushan on our resistance against Japan. As the Chinese people were united against Japan, the Communists who had always faked "unity for resistance against Japan" had to give up their demand for the establishment of a "special district government" and to temporarily fulfill their four promises by surrendering to the National Government. In accordance with the "Proposal on the Elimination of the Red Peril," the National Military Council began to reorganize the surrendered Communist forces. At this time, the policy of "internal pacification as a prerequisite to resisting foreign aggression" was eventually implemented leading eventually to final victory in the eight-year War of Resistance.

CHAPTER FIVE

The Sino-Japanese War

Section 1
Beginning of the Sino-Japanese War (See Map 9)

The Manchurian Incident[1]

As the Chinese Communists made use of the Japanese war-lords to subvert China by means of aggression, the Japanese warlords made use of the Communist armed rebellions to invade China. From the outbreak of the Manchurian Incident in 1931 to the Japanese unconditional surrender on 14 August, 1945, the Chinese Government, being sandwiched in the 14-yr. period, fought against great odds.

Between 1930 and 1931, fighting[2] was most intense when Government forces began military operations against the Communists. Communist International did its best to instigate the Japanese invasion of China in order to respond

---

[1] The Manchurian Incident:
On 18 September, 1931 the Japanese fabricated an incident by detonating the Liutiaokou Railroad. They staged a night attack on the Chinese 7th Brigade at Peitaying in Mukden and imprisoned Governor Tsang Shih-yi of Liaoning. One week later, Japanese forces occupied Liaoning and Kirin generating a well-planned, large-scale aggression.

[2] Massive Campaign against the Communists:
In the autum of 1930, Chinese Communist forces captured Changsha, Chian and Hukou operating in the Yangtze River area and engineering a nationwide uprising. On 16 December, the National Government began the first siege.

to the Chinese Communists' counter siege. In April, 1931, the Japanese Kuangtung Army slaughtered many Chinese farmers in the Wanpao Shan Incident in which the Japanese forced the renting of farm land. In June, Japan fabricated the disappearance of Capt. Nakamura at the reclamation land in Hsinganling and began to pour reinforcements along the Southern Manchuria Railroad. On 18 September, the Japanese bombed the Liutiaoko Bridge and used the bombing as an excuse to stage a night attack on Peitayin in Mukden.

Chang Hsueh-liang who was then the Northeast Border Defense commander and chairman of the Northeast Political Affairs Committee was stationed in Peiping. At first, he had thought that the incident was accidental and did his best to seek a peaceful solution. As he ordered his troops to fall back gradually, the Japanese forces attacked and captured over twenty cities of Liaoning and Kirin Provinces including Mukden.

The National Government negotiated with the Japanese Government urging the withdrawal of its forces on the one hand and appealed to the League of Nations and the signatories to the Nine Power Pact urging the upholding of the justice on the other. Subsequently, repeated resolutions of the League of Nations urged the withdrawal of the Japanese forces and called upon the Chinese and the Japanese Governments to refrain from taking any actions which might further increase seriousness of the situation. The United States, in a note to Japan, also referred to the Nine Power Pact calling on her obligations to international laws. Meanwhile, the Japanese Government stated that it had no territorial ambition on the Northeast; that it would not aggravate the situation; and that Japanese forces were gradually being withdrawn. Nevertheless, Japanese Army authorities informally stated that international laws were no longer applicable and refused to accept the mediations of the League of Nations nor the restrictions of the Japanese Government. Meanwhile, Japanese Army took active measures in accordance with their pre-scheduled invasion plans. On 19 November, Japanese forces overcame the heroic resistance of the Chinese forces led by Heilungchiang Governor Ma Chan-shan to occupy Tsitsihar. On 3 January 1932 Japanese forces occupied Chingchow.

When the third siege of the Government forces was progressing satisfactorily with the encircled main strength of the Communist forces in Kiangsi about to be destroyed, the Manchurian Incident broke out. Taking full advantage of this opportunity, the Chinese Communists instigated the students in Peiping, Shanghai and Nanking to stage mass demonstrations in the national capital on the pretext of petitioning to the Government. Actually they were out to embarrass it. They also sought to undermine the Government's relations with local authorities. This compelled the Government to interrupt the siege and to divert its forces to North China. Finally, Generalissimo Chiang felt it incumbent to resign all his positions in the National Government. On 15 December, he retired[3] from public life. The Communists were thus given another chance to grow in strength.

Battle of Shanghai

The Japanese Army's bloodless northward invasion of the

---

[3] Generalissimo Chiang's Retirement:
This marked Generalissimo Chiang's second retirement. His first retirement took place on 12 August, 1927.

Northeast Provinces aroused the Japanese Navy's desire to move southward for parallel development. The Chinese Communists took advantage of the agitated sentiments of the merchants and people in Shanghai to add fuel to fire and gave the Japanese forces an excuse to take military actions.

On 20 January, 1932, Japan sent spies disguised as monks to set fire to the main plant San Yu Industries in Shanghai and killed the Chinese policemen who went there to maintain order. In the afternoon, overseas Japanese in Shanghai paraded, demonstrated and smashed Chinese stores. Under the pretext that two Japanese had been wounded, the Japanese consul-general in Shanghai advanced strong demands [4] on the Shanghai Municipal Government and demanded a reply by 28 January. In compliance with the instructions of the Central Government, the Shanghai Municipal Government tried to avoid an escalation and conceded in the interest of peace. The Japanese expressed satisfaction when their demands were accepted in the afternoon of 28 Januray. Under the pretext of protecting the overseas Japanese and in the hope of realizing their pre-determined invasion plans, Japanese marines started an unprovoked attack on the local forces. Finding this intolerable, our forces rose in resistance. Thus, began the Battle of Shanghai.

The Japanese warlords had hoped that with superior equip-

---

[4] Japan's Strong Demands:
   Japan's strong demands were as follows:
   (1) That the mayor make a formal apology.
   (2) That the culprit who killed the Japanese monk be apprehended immediately.
   (3) That gratuity and medical expenses be paid.
   (4) That anti-Japanese movement be properly handled.
   (5) That all organizations which encourage hostilities, riots and discriminations against Japan be dissolved.

ment they would be able to occupy Shanghai, threaten Nanking and force the Chinese Government to seek peace. Elements of the 5th Corps resisted and fought gallantly for more than thirty days. As repeated Japanese attacks were frustrated, the Japanese changed commanders on four occasions and poured in reinforcements. They suffered heavy losses at Chapei, Wentsaopin, Wusung, Tsaochiachao and Miaohsing. On 29 February, the Japanese sent in more reinforcements and conducted frontal attacks. Another Japanese division made a forced landing at Liuho. Without waiting for the arrival of reinforcements, the 19th Route Corps withdrew leaving the flank of the 5th Corps fully exposed. This led to heavy losses on our side. On 1 March, our forces withdrew to the second line of defense in the vicinity of Nanhsiang to continue the resistance.

When the war broke out, the National Government still appealed to the League of Nations through diplomatic channels for the stopping of outrageous Japanese aggression of China. The Japanese had thought at first that they were certain to win. It was not until they met with repeated setbacks that they complied with the resolution of the League of Nations for a ceasefire. On 5 May, the Sino-Japanese Shanghai Ceasefire Agreement[5] and the Japanese Forces Withdrawal Agreement[6] were signed.

---

[5] Shanghai Ceasefire Agreement:
The Shanghai Ceasefire Agreement was signed on 5 May, 1932. The main text was divided into 5 portions. Annexes 1-3 covered the restoration of Chinese and Japanese forces to their original positions before the Incident. The areas from which the Japanese forces were withdrawn should be taken over by the Chinese police and that a joint committee (with representatives of friendly nations participating) be set up.

[6] Japanese Forces Withdrawal Agreement:
The Japanese Forces Withdrawal Agreement was signed on 5 May, 1932.

During the Battle of Shanghai, the Communists established the so-called "Soviet Provisional Central Government" at Juichin, Kiangsi Province. They ruled the Honan-Hupei-Anhwei area, the central Hupei area, the western and southern Hupei areas. There was much turmoil and people were restless. It seemed that the situation would get out of hand at any time. Realizing that the nation was confronted with the crisis of two wars, the entire nation requested that Generalissimo Chiang resume office. In compliance with the people's unanimous wish, Generalissimo Chiang took office again on 17 March and announced the policy of "internal pacification as a pre-requisite to resisting foreign aggression."

Battle of the Great Wall[7]

On 4 March, 1932, the Battle of Shanghai ended. On 9 March, the establishment of the puppet Manchukuo was proclaimed under the tutelege of the Japanese Kuangtung Army. In April, the League of Nations Investigation Team arrived in the Northeast for investigations. On 12 July, the

---

Its contents included the following:

(1) That beginning 5 May, 1932, forces of both nations cease hostilities.

(2) That Chinese forces remain in their present locations before conditions in the vicinity of Shanghai return to normal. That the Japanese forces withdraw to the same areas in the International Settlement and Hungkou as before the January 28 Incident.

[7] Battle of the Great Wall:

Immediately after the termination of the Battle of Shanghai, the Japanese Kuangtung Army helped set up the puppet Manchukuo on 4 March, 1932. On 12 July, the League of Nations Investigation Team stated that the independence of Manchuria was tantamount to the rupture of Chinese territory and in violation of the Nine Power Pact. However, Japan paid no heed. Soviet Russia proposed the signing of a Russo-Japanese Non-Aggression Pact and instigated the Japanese invasion of Yukuan, Jehol and the various passes of the Great Wall.

team formally stated: "The independence of Manchuria is tantamount to carving up China's territories and violates the Nine Power Pact." On 5 September, the Japanese Government openly recognized the puppet Manchukuo and appointed the Kuangtung Army commander Shingi Muto concurrently commander of the Manchukuo National Defense Force. Our Government immediately lodged a strong protest with the Japanese Government. At this time, Soviet Russia proposed the signing of the Russo-Japanese Non-Aggression Pact to abet active Japanese aggression of China. On 2 October, the League of Nations Investigation Team published its report denouncing Japan as an aggressor nation and Manchukuo the product of Japanese creation and proposing measures, ways and procedures to solve the problems. On 24 February, 1933 the League of Nations conference passed the proposal with a 42-1 majority. In complete disregard of the resolution, Japan, in a statement, withdrew from the League of Nations.

Since April, 1932, Japanese forces had reinforced their troops between Yukwan and Suiyuan. On 15 May, Japanese Prime Minister Taxeshi Inukai was assassinated by members of the Ketsumeidan. Since then, the Japanese warlord's aggressive actions against China became more outrageous than ever. In early December, Japanese forces shelled Yukwan. On 1 January, 1933, they attacked and captured it two days later. On 13 January, Chiumengko had to be abandoned. Thus, Japanese forces occupied the key locality between Hopei and Liaoning threatening eastern Hopei and consolidating the left-turning pivoting point in the attack on Jehol.

On 21 January, Japanese foreign minister made the following statement:

"The boundary between Manchukuo-Mongolia and China is the Great Wall. Furthermore, Jehol Province is a part of Manchukuo."

In the name of puppet Manchukuo, Japan issued a statement on the use of military force against Jehol. The following day, Chinese Acting Premier T.V. Soong stated: "If the Japanese forces should attack Jehol, such an attack will be tantamount to an attack on the nation's capital. We shall fight against it with all our power." On 19 January, Chinese military commanders jointly sent a cable message vowing to fight against the Japanese.

On 23 January, Japanese Foreign Ministry sent a memorandum demanding that the area on either side of the Great Wall be delineated as the neutral zone. The Chinese Foreign Ministry immediately repudiated such a demand. Meanwhile, Japanese forces began to advance toward and attack Jehol. The military and administrative efforts of Jehol were not yet normal. Despite a seven-year rule in Jehol, Tang Yu-ling's forces were timid refusing first the entry of the Government forces into Jehol and later abandoning fighting altogether and taking public and private belongings with them in their flight. Units of the Government forces separately fought in the vicinity of Chihfeng and Lingyuan. Later, they were forced to fall back to the Jehol-Chahar border mountain areas and the areas inside the Great Wall. On 4 March, the Japanese forces took Chengteh and continued the attacks on the various passes of the Great Wall. The situation was most critical. Generalissimo Chiang arrived in Peiping for an inspection and replaced Chang Hsueh-liang with Minister of War Ho Ying-chin. Thus, Ho became the acting chairman of the National Military Council in Peiping. He redeployed the forces, occupied positions in depth and conducted sustained resistance. For two months his force fought against the Japanese and achieved excellent combat results, in particular the gallantry of the 29th Corps at Hsifengko and the 17th Corps at Kupeiko. The holding actions of the Communists in Kiangsi prevented the Government from pulling elite forces to reinforce the forces in the north in order to shift the offensive. The impact of this failure at the decisive moment of the fourth siege enabled the Japanese 6th Division to break through our junction at Lengko and to launch a drive along the Peiping-Yukwan Highway. In early May, our forces withdrew to the line along Pai Ho (White River) ready to continue fighting. By the time the Japanese forces arrived at the lines along the Canal in Hopei Province, Peiping and Tientsin were threatened. With the enlargement of the theater, the Japanese who found their strength insufficient and their objective of invading Jehol attained then proposed a ceasefire. With forces checked by the Communists, military build-up unfinished and the "policy of internal pacification as a pre-requisite to resisting foreign aggression" not yet implemented, the Government decided to negotiate peace with the Japanese through the good office of British Minister Lampson. On 31 May, the Tangku Armistice Agreement[8] was signed. Thus, Japan

---

[8] Tangku Armistice Agreement:

The Tangku Armistice Agreement included the following:

(1) That the Chinese forces be withdrawn to the areas south and west of the line extending from Yenching-Changping-Kaoliying-Lintingchen-Ningho-Lutai and that the Japanese forces be withdrawn to the line along the Great Wall.

(2) That the Chinese police be held responsible for the security of the areas north and east of the lines mentioned in the above agreement.

(3) That the agreement become effective upon signing on 31 May, 1933.

annexed Jehol, a key area in North China, into the puppet Manchukuo.

Special Status on Hopei and Chahar Provinces

Since 1933, our Government did all it could to withstand Japanese provocations in order to gain time, mop up the Communists, engage in reconstruction and strengthen combat readiness. As a result of marked improvements in combat readiness, the Fukien Coup[9] was suppressed in no time. In 1934, the Communists' lairs in southern Kiangsi were wiped out. As the Communists fled westward, their remnants were cornered in northern Shensi. Thus, the Government's crisis of attacks by the enemy from within and without was removed. In the autumn of 1934, Generalissimo Chiang, in a pamphlet entitled, "Friend or Foe?"[10] advising the Japanese authorities to awaken and recognize the Chinese and the Russian Communists as the common enemies in East Asia and the world. However, the Japanese warlords refused to pay heed to this advice. In March, 1935, despite our Government's protest, Soviet Russia sold the Chinese Eastern Railway to the puppet Manchukuo encouraging the Japanese in their invasion on China. On 29 May, under the pretext of the killing of the head of a pro-Japanese news service, the Japanese forces stationed along the Peiping-Liaoning Railroad brought up six unreasonable demands[11] to the National

---

[9] Suppression of Fukien Coup:
   See Section 4, Chapter Four of this book.

[10] "Friend or Foe?" This article was written by Hsu Tao-lin and appeared in Takungpao in Tien-tsin in the fall of 1934.

[11] Six Unreasonable Demands:
   The six unreasonable demands advanced by the Japanese forces stationed along the Peiping-Liaoning Railroad included the following:
   (1) That Yu Hsueh-chung retire and that the capital of Hopei Province be

Military Council in Peiping. Our Government therefore, instructed our ambassador in Japan to negotiate with the Japanese Government through diplomatic channels. However, the Japanese Government was incapable of restraining the actions of the military. Despite Foreign Minister Hirota's promise to forward our Government's views to the Japanese military authorities, the repeated negotiations between our National Military Council in Peiping and the local Japanese forces were unable to overcome the pomposity of the Japanese military. Using the relief of units as an excuse, the Japanese augmented the forces and stated that they would take drastic actions if their demands were not accepted altogether. Not wanting to start the war hastily, our National Government exercised extreme patience in accepting their six demands. Government forces were withdrawn from Hopei.

On 10 June, after the signing of the Ho-Umezu Agreement, Ho left Peiping. Later, with the special status of Hopei-Chahar in the making, our Government was forced to establish the Peiping Administrative Reorganization Committee. In July, Communist International advanced the "united front" slogan to save the Communists from a crisis and to

---

     moved to Paoting.

(2) That the Central Forces withdraw from Hopei.

(3) That Mayor Chang Ting-ao of Tientsin and Police Commissioner Li Chun-hsiang be replaced. That Commander of Third MP Regiment Chiang Hsiao-hsien and Director of Political Training Tseng Kuang-ching be relieved.

(4) That Hopei provincial and city KMT headquarters and Political Department of the National Military Council in Peiping end their activities and that all anti-Japanese organizations be dissolved.

(5) That persons responsible for the assassination of pro-Japanese news service director be apprehended and punished and that indemnity be paid to the victim's family.

(6) That anti-Japanese publications be suspended.

subvert the National Government by turning the Communist suppression campaign into an anti-Japanese war. In November, our Ministry of Finance introduced the new monetary system[12] to stabilize the currency. In presenting his report on foreign affairs at the Kuomintang Fifth Plenary Session, Generalissimo Chiang stated: "We will not abandon peace until peace is hopeless. We will not mention sacrifice until the critical moment when we must make sacrifice." Doehara, chief of the Japanese intelligence, went so far as to set up the "Eastern Hopei Anti-Communist Self-Rule Committee" and occupy the 22 hsiens in eastern Hopei. By this time, the Japanese design to divide eastern Hopei and encroach upon North China was fully exposed.

Fight A Two-Front Diplomatic War

On 26 February, 1936, a coup d'etat broke out in Tokyo. It led to the seizure of political power by the militarists, increased military budgets, and resulted in Army-Navy parallel development and fanatic advance to the north and to the south. Subsequently to the formation of the Hirota cabinet, their plans for the aggression against China were consolidated into a conglomerate policy embracing three demands of "neighborly friendship, joint defense against Communism, and economic cooperation." Again, negotiations were made with the National Government. On 12 March, Soviet Russia published the "Russo-Mongolian Mutual Assistance Pact" and sought to appease Japan. Through their front organization, the so-called "Anti-Japanese Na-

---

[12] New Monetary System:
The new monetary system was intended to end the circulation of silver dollars and to bring in the bank notes known as "fah-pi" issued by the Central Bank, the Bank of China, the Bank of Farmers and the Bank of Communications.

tional Salvation Alliance," the Communists demanded the National Government to end the military campaigns against them, join force against Japanese and advocate the alignment with Russia movement. Fully aware of the real motives of Japan and Russia which were anything but alignment with us but were to force us into separation from the west, isolation and division. Generalissimo Chiang established our foreign policy, promoted the cooperation of democratic nations in the League of Nations and sternly refused Japan's unreasonable demands. Within the realm of the above-mentioned policy, efforts were made to promote relationships with Soviet Russia. On 25 November, Japan made known the German-Japanese Anti-Communist Pact.

In the spring of 1935, the Japanese Kuangtung Army invaded the six hsiens of northern Chahar and instigated Prince Teh, deputy chief of the Hsi Meng tribe to organize the Mongolian Autonomous Government. Military administration was, of course, in the hands of the Japanese advisors. On the one hand, they took in the bandits to organize the puppet forces. On the other hand, they set up intelligence agencies in such big cities in Chahar, Suiyuan and Shansi Provinces to harass our rear areas and to lend moral support to the puppet forces. In early November, Japanese planes reconnoitered Suiyuan. On 16 November, a four-pronged attack began. Our local forces in Suiyuan resisted bravely and counter-attacked at the opportune time. In one stroke, our forces captured the enemy's main base at Pailing Temple. As the puppet forces defected in large groups, enemy remnants fell back to the six hsiens in northern Chahar.

When Japan's unreasonable demands were turned down and her Suiyuan invasion plans failed, she was afraid that there might not be an opportunity for her to engage in aggression. Furthermore, Generalissimo Chiang's safe return from Sian[13] detonated a series of spontaneous celebrations on the part of the people who lit fire-crackers night after night. All these reflected that there was no division. Instead, unification prevailed and defense preparations were stepped up. In view of the above, Japan initiated large-scale armed aggression against China. Thus, China began heroic resistance along the entire front. As China's military build-up was not completed, international aid was not forthcoming, and the nation and its people were exhausted after years of Communist suppression activities, the disparity in strength between the Japanese and our forces was great indeed. (Ratios: Army—3:1, Air Forces—9:1, Navy—32:1, replacements—54:1.)

Section 2
First Phase Operatons: (See Map 10)

July 7 Incident

On 7 July, 1937 elements of the Japanese forces stationed at Fengtai along the Peiping-Liaoning Railroad staged a night attack on Lukouchiao (Marco Polo Bridge) under the pretext of conducting an exercise. One regiment of the 29th Corps under Colonel Chi Hsing-wen resisted bravely and frustrated the Japanese attempt. On 8 July, additional Japanese reinforcements arrived from Tientsin. Soon the Japanese were threatening Peiping and Tientsin.

---

[13] For the safe return of Generalissimo Chiang after being kidnapped at Sian, see Sec. 6, Chapter Four of this book.

Realizing the seriousness of the situation even as far back as the outbreak of hostilities, Generalissimo Chiang, in a cable on 9 July, instructed that "peace negotiations be conducted without neglecting combat readiness." The 26th Route Corps was ordered to move two divisions by rail to Paoting and Shichiachung. On 17 July, he indicated the following essentials at Lushan:

"(1) The Lukouchiao (Marco Polo Bridge) Incident involves not only the survival or destruction of China but also has a bearing on the fortune or misfortune of mankind in the world.

(2) China's foreign policy has always aimed at peaceful co-existence. However, when the critical moment comes, she has no alternative but to fight with everything she has.

(3) The Lukouchiao (Marco Polo Bridge) Incident is one of the enemy's habitual plots. The arrival of the critical moment will determine whether or not the incident will be brought to an end.

(4) In the event we are confronted with the critical moment, we fight by necessity but not by choice. Once the war begins, we must make every sacrifice for the sake of victory.

(5) The basic position of the Government in ending the Lukouchiao Incident has been as follows:

  1. Any solution must not infringe upon the sovereignty and the territorial integrity of China.

  2. No unlawful change of the Hopei-Chahar administrative organizations will be made.

  3. No demand will be made to replace such local officials appointed by the Central Government

such as Chairman of the Hopei-Chahar Adminis-
strations Committee Sung Che-yuan.

4. No restrictions will be imposed upon the areas
in which the 29th Corps is stationed."

The above statement aimed to awaken the Japanese militarists before it is too late. It was felt that war would
plunge the Chinese and the Japanese peoples into a situation
from which it would be most difficult to extricate. Unfortunately, these words failed to stop the fanaticism of the
Japanese militarists.

On 26 July, Japan demanded the withdrawal of the
Chinese forces in suburban Peiping to the west of the
Yungting River. Our Government rejected the Japanese demand and ordered our forces to prepare for action. On 28
July, the Japanese poured one division and three brigades
into a general attack on the local Chinese forces in Peiping.
Scores of Japanese planes took turns in the bombing. As our
gallant defenders offered strong resistance and suffered heavy
casualties, Tung Lin-ke, deputy commander of the 29th
Corps and Chao Teng-yu, commander of the 132nd Division
were killed in action in Nanwan. Similarly, the Hopei militia
also suffered heavy losses. In the same night, as our forces
rose hastily in combat, the situation was already unfavorable.
The main force of the 29th Corps withdrew to the right bank
of the Yungting River leaving one division for the defense of
Tientsin and one brigade for the defense of Peiping. On 29
July, the puppet peace preservation units of Tung Hsien
destroyed the local puppets and defected. The 38th Division
which was charged with the defense of Tientsin attacked the
Japanese airfield at Tungchutzu and destroyed many Japanese
planes. On 30 July, the Japanese took Tientsin and looted

the city resulting in heavy damages. On 4 August, our forces withdrew from Peiping. With the fall of Peiping, the puppet organization came into being on 9 August.

Formulating Total War Strategy

On 7 August, 1937, our National Defense Council decided to fight a general War of Resistance adopting the sustained attrition strategy. On 20 August, Generalissimo Chiang divided the anticipated theater of war into five war areas. The 1st War Area covered Hopei and northern Shantung; the 2nd War Area Shansi, Chahar and Suiyuan; the 3rd War Area southern Kiangsu and Chekiang; the 4th War Area Kwangtung and Fukien; and the 5th War Area northern Kiangsu and southern Shantung. The operational guiding principle was to seek the initiative so as to control but not to be controlled by the enemy. The 1st War Area adopted disposition in depth with multiple-line defense so as to maintain sustained actions. It would timely shift its main force to the 2nd War Area. The 2nd War Area would take advantage of the critical terrain to guard Shansi and North China. The 3rd War Area would concentrate elite Government Forces for the attack of the enemy bases in Shanghai, hinder enemy bases in Shanghai, hinder enemy landings, consolidate the nation's capital, force the Japanese to disperse their strength in those unfavorable areas south of the Yangtze River, and grasp favorable development in the overall situation. The 4th and 5th War Areas would deploy minimum forces for coastal garrison duties.

Later developments proved that the resistance policy adopted by Generalissimo Chiang was quite correct. Despite eight long years of hardships and suffering, Generalissimo

Chiang's wise decision and outstanding leadership guided China to final victory.

Communists Faking Surrender

On 5 May, 1936, in compliance with the instructions of the Communist International the Chinese Communist sought surrender. They dispatched a cable requesting "cessation of hostilities and negotiations of peace[14] and accepting the following four principles of the National Government:

1. Abide by the Three People's Principles.
2. Obey Generalissimo Chiang Kai-shek's orders.
3. Abolish the "Red Army" and have it integrated into the National Army.
4. Abrogate the Soviets and have them reorganized into local governments.

On 22 August, 1937, subsequent to the outbreak of the War of Resistance, the National Military Council appointed Chu Teh and Peng Teh-huai Commander and deputy commander respectively of the former Communist troops now renamed the Eighth Route Army of the National Revolutionary Forces. This army, composed of three divisions with a total strength of 20,000 men, was assigned to the Second War Area in northern Shansi under the command of Yen

---

[14] Cessation of Hostilities and Negotiation of Peace:

As early as 1 August 1935, the Chinese Communist Party issued a statement in compliance with Stalin's decision of "united front" at the Seventh Congress of the Communist International. In it, the Chinese Communists brought forth the slogans of "anti-Japanese people's front," "anti-Japanese but not anti-Communist," and "Chinese not fighting Chinese" to talk the local Chinese forces into maintaining neutrality and undermining the Government's policy of "internal pacification as a pre-requisite to resisting foreign aggression." Later, they advanced the request for ceasefire agreement aiming to avoid destruction and seek development.

Hsi-shan.

Lin Tsu-han and Chang Kuo-tao were appointed chairman and vice chairman of the Shensi-Kansu-Ninghsia Border Area Government[15].

Later, the units formerly under Yeh Ting and Hsiang Ying scattered in areas south of the Yangtze River were reorganized into the New Fourth Corps assuming command over four columns the strength of which approximate that of a division. Yeh Ting and Hsiang Ying were appointed its commander and deputy commander respectively. The Corps became a unit in the order of battle of the 3rd War Area under the command of Ku Chu-tung for employment in the Nanking-Wuhu area.

After the outbreak of the Sino-Japanese War in the summer of 1937, the Communist Central Committee issued a declaration on 22 September, stating its readiness to cope jointly with the national crisis. This declaration contained the following four points:

(1) As the Three People's Principles can adequately meet the needs of China, the Chinese Communist Party will work for their full realization.

(2) The Chinese Communist Party will abolish its policy of armed uprising and its sovietization movement, and will abandon its program of dispossessing the landlords through violence.

(3) The Chinese Communist Party will liquidate the existing soviet regime and hereafter practice democracy in order that the administrative authority of the nation

---

[15] Shensi-Kansu-Ninghsia Border Area Government:
Faking repentence and surrender, Chinese Communists changed the so-called "Soviet Government" to "Special District Government" and later to "Shensi-Kansu-Ninghsia Border Area Government."

> may be unified.
>
> (4) The Chinese Communist Party will abolish both the name and designation of the Red Army, and agree to have them reorganized into the National Revolutionary Forces and placed under the National Military Council of the National Government, and to have them wait for orders to move against the Japanese.

On 23 September, in reply to this declaration, Generalissimo Chiang issued a statement in which he said in part:

"The Chinese Communist Party's declaration proves that national consciousness has triumphed after all. The points contained in the Communist declaration, such as the abandonment of the policy of armed uprising and of sovietization movement, and the liquidation of the soviet area and of the Red Army, are all necessary conditions for mobilizing the nation's strength against aggression. The reference to readiness of the Communists to work for the realization of the Three People's Principles further indicates that all of China's efforts can now be directed toward one goal.

"Now that the Chinese Communists have given up their prejudices and recognized the paramount importance of national independence and national interests, we hope that they will sincerely fulfill their pledges. Furthermore, we hope that, like everybody else in the country, they will contribute all their strength to the nation's war effort against aggression under unified command and help complete the task of National Revolution."

Subsequent to the reorganization, the Communist forces were ill-trained, of poor quality, loose discipline and weak combat effectiveness. Meanwhile, the Japanese forces were both conceited and well-trained. In order to conserve the strength of the Communist forces and not to incur heavy losses in the initial stage, the National Military Council did not assign to the Communist Forces missions which would call for heavy fighting. Instead, it was hoped to employ them in relatively minor engagements so as to gradually enhance their combat effectiveness. Little did the Government realize that the Communist forces, in complete disregard of their four promises, avoided combat and conserved their strength. They not only failed to carry out their assigned missions, but also exercised complete freedom of action by not fighting the enemy but by ambushing friendly forces so as to gain strength. This was the Communists' pre-determined policy. Gen. Albert C. Wedemeyer's report indicating Mao's secret instructions to his party followers and military forces in October, 1937 is quoted in part as follows:

Mao's secret instructions:[16]

"The Sino-Japanese War affords our party an excellent opportunity for expansion. Our fixed policy should be seventy per cent expansion, twenty per cent dealing with the Kuomintang, and ten per cent resisting Japan. There are three stages in carrying out this fixed policy: the first is a

---

[16] Mao's Secret Instructions:

In the autumn of 1937 when the Chinese Communist 8th Route Army were ready to set out from northern Shensi, Mao addressed his troop. The following is an enumeration of the key points in his address:

(1) The Sino-Japanese War affords an excellent opportunity for expansion. Our fixed policy should be 70% expansion, 20% dealing with the Kuomintang (National Government), and 10% resisting Japan.

(2) This policy should be carried out in three stages.
First stage: Compromise with Kuomintang to seek survival and development.
Second stage: Achieve balance of power and stalemate with Kuomintang.
Third stage: Penetrate into Central China to establish bases and stage counteroffensive against the Kuomintang.

compromising stage, in which self-sacrifice should be made to show our outward obedience to the Central Government and adherence to the Three Principles of the People (Nationality, Democracy, and Livelihood, as outlined by Dr. Sun Yat-sen), but in reality this will serve as comouflage for the existence and development of our party.

"The second is a contending stage, in which two or three years should be spent in laying the foundation of our party's political and military powers, and developing these until we can match and break the Kuomintang, and eliminate the influence of the latter north of the Yellow River. While waiting for an unusual turn of events, we should give the Japanese invader certain concessions.

"The third is an offensive stage, in which our forces should penetrate deeply into Central China, sever the communications of the Central Government troops in various sectors, isolate and disperse them until we are ready for the counter-offensive and wrest the leadership from the hands of the Kuomintang."

In addition, the Communists' Central Political Bureau, in a resolution on "The Future of the War of Resistance and the Chinese Communists' Line of Action," laid down the following programs:

(1) To expand and to strengthen the United Front by removing the veils covering secret Communist organizations and activities and by extending regional operations to a nation wide scale for the purpose of obtaining for the Communist Party a legal and equal competitive status.

(2) Force being the determining factor in China politics, emphasis should be put on expanding the Communist

Party's armed forces in the course of the War of Resistance to lay the foundation in the struggle for political power in the future.

The above were the Communists' lines of development in the course of the War of Resistance. Their actions in the eight years that came later followed these lines.

North China Operations

On 7 August, 1937, the National Defense Council decided to fight a general war against Japan. Generalissimo Chiang successively dispatched forces to reinforce Hopei. He also ordered Tang En-po's two corps to mass in Southern Chahar mountainous area to strike and check the Japanese forces.

On 15 August, Japan declared nation-wide mobilization. Two corps were moved to Peiping and Tientsin and two divisions were concentrated in Shanghai. These moves were designed to defeat the Government forces in Hopei, capture Shanghai, threaten the nation's capital and subdue China.

Meanwhile, our main force was committed in Shanghai. Units were deployed in the Hopei Plains to form a multiple-line defense by means of the river. Between August and November, Chinese forces at Chinghai, Machang, Tsang Hsien, Potou and Teh Hsien conducted piecemeal resistance. On 13 November, our forces fell back to defend the Yellow River. Similarly, our forces along the Peiping-Hankow Railroad conducted piecemeal resistance at Liuli River, Tsao River, Hoto River and Yuanshih. Crack units were pulled and shifted for deployment in Shansi to protect the critical terrain features in North China. Flanking positions were occupied in order to strike the enemy and threaten the enemy arriving in southern Hopei so that the enemy had to change his southward front to the west in an up-hill attack. Thus, the enemy's original plans of driving southward into the Wuhan soft belly was smashed. After inflicting heavy losses on the Japanese, Government forces along the Peiping-Suiyuan Railroad at Nanko conducted piecemeal resistance at Kalgan, Tienchen, Yangkao and Chining. By 15 September, our forces fell back to the line along the Great Wall inside the Yenmen Pass. In Shansi, the Chinese and the Japanese forces fought for the possession of Pinghsing Pass which changed hands eight times. The 2nd War Area ordered the 8th Route Army (18th Army Group) under Chu Teh to control Pinghsing Pass and cut off the Japanese lines of communications. However, the 8th Route Army refused to obey the order. On the one hand, it propagandized the "Victory in Ambushing the Japanese at Pinghsing Pass." On the other hand, it exercised complete freedom of action withdrawing toward the Wutai Shan area, the Shansi-Hopei-Chahar Border Area and Shansi-Hopei-Honan Border Area and entering into the Hopei-Shantung-Honan Plains to attack local militias as well as guerrilla units, re-organize and expand their own strength. As a result of the freedom of action of the 8th Route Army, the Japanese forces broke through the interior Great Wall lines. In mid-October, our forces defeated the Japanese at Hsinko and Niangtzu Kuan (Ladies' Pass) killing over 20,000 enemy troops. Subsequently, the enemy turned back from southern flank of the Niangtzu Kuan. On 9 November, the Japanese captured Taiyuan occupying the narrow corridors along the railroads. The enemy forces were bogged down, as they were widely scattered.

Battle of Shanghai

Since the outbreak of the Lukouchiao (Marco Polo Bridge)

Incident, Japan started a series of provocations in many cities throughout China, particularly in the economic center of Shanghai. On 13 August, 1937, the Japanese marines in Shanghai attacked the local peace preservation units. Later, two Japanese divisions were brought in as reinforcements. Knowing the political significance of Shanghai in the international eyes, and Shanghai's importance in safeguarding the security of the nation's capital, Generalissimo Chiang decided to commit more than fifty crack Chinese divisions and took the initiative to start the offensive. With initiative, he shifted the main battle ground from North China to Shanghai, forcing the enemy to change the historically favorable north-south axis of operations (such as Yuan and Ching Dynasties vs. Sung and Ming Dynasties) to the unfavorable east-west uphill offensive. Our forces took full advantage of the complicated swampy terrain to fight bloody battles in Wusung, Kiangwan and Liuho. For three months, our forces fought for every inch of ground forcing the enemy to gradually mobilize a total of 300,000 troops. Enemy casualties ran well over 60,000. On 14 August, our air force scored its first victory over Chienchiao, Hangchow and followed up with the destruction of the famous Japanese Shikaya and Kisarazu Squadrons. Our naval forces blocked the channels, laid mines, damaged the Japanese warship "Izumo" and a number of vessels.

On 26 October, the unfavorable situation necessitated a shifting of positions. 800 men of the 88th Division defending the Four-Bank Warehouse in Chapei refused to withdraw, became isolated and fought gallantly. Later, upon friendly British advice, these men withdrew into the International Settlement.

At the time, the foreign press considered the gallantry of the Chinese forces a miracle. They expressed admiration over the orderly withdrawal of the Chinese forces.

On 5 November, the Japanese 10th Corps landed in the vicinity of Chinshanwei on the north coast of Hangchow Bay, detoured Sungchiang to attack our right flank. On 9 November, with the strategic objective fulfilled, our main force withdrew to Chekiang-Anwhei-Kiangsi border. Meanwhile, the Japanese main force moved along the Nanking-Shanghai Railroad to threaten Nanking. A part of the Japanese forces entered the area south of the Tai Lake bypassing Wuhu. Along the Yangtze River, the Japanese fleet moved up from westward. On 7 December, the Japanese forces attacked the primary positions in the outskirts of Nanking. Our forces fought hard and suffered heavy losses. Among those killed in action was Chu Chih, a brigade commander. On 13 December, Nanking fell. Once again, the Japanese troops went into a rampage of looting, plundering, killing and raping. Over 100,000 people were killed. Despite the fact that Japan proposed peace through the German minister Trautemann, Generalissimo Chiang remained firm in his attitude. On 17 December, he made public his "Message to the People on the Withdrawal of the National Forces from Nanking," in which he reiterated China determination to fight to the end. At the Wuchang Conference held in January, 1938, he pointed out the Japanese slackened discipline, horrible atrocities and certain defeat in the end.

Adjusting Command Organizations and Determining Operational Guidance

The gallantry of the Chinese forces was displayed in the

Battle of Taiyuan and the Battle of Shanghai. As Generalissimo Chiang saw the situation clearly, his direction of the military operations was superb. On 17 January 1938, the Supreme Command underwent reorganization, as the organizational outline of the National Military Council was revised and the order of battle of the Chinese forces was promulgated. The 1st War Area covered the Peiping-Hankow Railroad, the 2nd War Area—Shansi, the 3rd War Area—Kiangsu and Chekiang, the 4th War Area—Kwangtung and Kwangsi, the 5th War Area—Tientsin-Pukow Railroad, the 8th War Area—Kansu, Ninghsia, Chinghai. In addition, the Wuhan Garrison General Headquarters, the Fukien Pacification Headquarters and the National Military Council direct subordinate army groups (three army groups and one field army) were established. Meanwhile, subsequent operational guidance was determined. Crack units were transferred and controlled in Wuhan and Honan-Anhwei border area; they were readily replenished. From North China and areas south of the Yangtze River, units were pulled out to reinforce central Shantung and areas south of the Huai River, consolidate Hsuchow, lure the enemy main force into the areas along the Tientsin-Pukow Railroad in order to delay the enemy's advance to the west along the Yangtze River. Meanwhile, efforts were made to defend northern Honan and southern Shansi on the north bank of the Yellow River, impede the enemy southward crossing of the Yellow River and prevent the enemy from driving to Wuhan. Additionally, extensive guerrilla warfare was waged to check and wear out the enemy.

Battle of Hsuchow

After the occupation of Nanking in the spring of 1938, the

Japanese forces crossed the Yangtze River and advanced north to the Huai River. The Japanese forces in North China separately advanced toward Linchi and Taierhchuang. Realizing that the Japanese forces lacked coordination, Generalissimo Chiang went to Hsuchow to direct the operations. He supervised the 5th War Area to adopt the essentials of interior lines operation and defeat the enemy in detail while the enemy was isolated. In early March, elements of the 5th War Area defended the areas west of the Huai River and attacked the flanks of the Japanese forces in the southern section of the Tientsin-Pukow Railroad from Hofei and Tingyuan. In mid-March, one Chinese corps was shifted to reinforce Linchi. In coordination with the defense forces there, this corps successfully defeated units of the Japanese 5th Division from 12-17 March. On 23 March, the main strength of the Japanese 5th Division came to the rescue and engaged our force north of Linchi. In anticipation, Generalissimo Chiang pulled out the 2nd Army Group and the 20th Army from southern Shansi and northern Anhwei for employment in the vicinity of Taierhchuang. From 24 March to 6 April, the Japanese 2nd Corps was defeated with more than 30,000 casualties. In pursuit, our forces committed the reserves to exploit success, strengthen the defense of eastern Honan and consolidate the rear areas. In mid and late April, Japanese forces on either end of the Tientsin-Pukow Railroad were moving troops. There were indications that the enemy might initiate a converging attack on Hsuchow. Located at the junction of the Tientsin-Pukow Railroad and the Lung-Hai Railroad, Hsuchow was a key strategic locality north of the Yangtze River and a protruding corner in China strategy at the time. In early May, the Japanese dispatched two and half divisions across the Huai River. A part of the forces moved along the Tientsin-Pukow Railroad toward Hsuchow, while the main force made a turning movement from the west of the Tientsin-Pukow Railroad to Tang Shan and Kueiteh along the Lung-Hai Railroad. Meanwhile, four Japanese divisions crossed the Yellow River and the Canal in North China to attack Lanfeng and Kueiteh. Three Japanese divisions at Hanchuang and Yi Hsien swung south to shift the offensive attempting to cut the Lung-Hai Railroad and cut off the line of retreat of our forces. In mid-May, Generalissimo Chiang went to Chengchow to direct the operations, he broke the Japanese 14th Division, recovered Lanfeng and Lowang Station, restored traffic of the Lung-Hai Railroad, and pulled back 42 trains. While keeping the enemy's main force at bay, he made use of the flooding of the Yellow River[17] to cover the withdrawal of our main force to the west. Thus, our main strength in the war was conserved and the overall situation was stabilized.

Battle of Wuhan

Having been stopped by the flooding of the Yellow River, the Japanese forces changed their axis of operation and moved along the Pu-Hsin Highway and the Yangtze River for an attack on Hankow. In the face of such powerful Japanese forces, Generalissimo Chiang adopted strategic sustained operations. In order to prevent the Japanese forces from bypassing Poyang Lake and massing in Chiuchiang, a

---

[17] Flooding of the Yellow River:
   On 8 June, 1938, the Yellow River was flooded at the mouth of Huayuan east of Chengchow. The mainstream followed Lulu River into the Huai River.

line of blockade was formed at Matang Shan in the lower reaches of the Yangtze River offering strong resistance and forcing the Japanese forces to deploy east of the Poyang Lake.

In early June, under the cover of naval gunfire, the Japanese fleet attacked Matang. For one week, the defenders withstood the onslaught resulting in over 10,000 casualties. Finally, the defense was broken and Huoko fell. In late July, the Japanese captured Chiuchiang. Meanwhile, the Japanese 2nd Corps moved from Kaifeng to Hofei.

In late August, the Japanese began the general offensive on both the northern and the southern banks of the Yangtze River. Making use of terrain obstacles of Lu Shan and Tapieh Shan as well as the hilly and swampy terrain on the banks of the Yangtze River, our Army, Navy and Air Force conducted sustained resistance. Hundreds of engagements took place in a period of three months ending in numerous Japanese casualties. The fightings at Wanchialing, Tienchiachen, Fuchin Shan and Lo Shan dealt heavy blows against the enemy. Over one hundred Japanese vessels were sunk, and over one hundred aircrafts were shot down. The objective of a war of attrition was achieved. As the people and the materiel in Wuhan had been withdrawn well in advance, our forces abandoned Wuhan on 25 October falling back along the line of Hsiu River-Hsin-chiang River-Shayang-Sui Hsien.

As their losses became heavier, their battlefields wider and their forces more scattered, the Japanese decided to blockade our ports. They switched to counter-attrition operations, stopping along the line of Hsinyang-Yuehyang-Hsui River. Forces were dispatched for the capture of Amoy and Canton.

On 31 October, Generalissimo Chiang issued his "Message to the Nation's Soldiers and People on the Withdrawal from Wuhan" in which he reiterated our determination to go through anything for the cause, and the faith in our people to seek the final victory.

Expeditions and Air Battles

During the one year and two month period before the Battle of Wuhan took place, most of the Chinese planes were purchased from Italy, the United States and Soviet Russia. By comparison with the Japanese, these planes were obsolete, however, the training and morale of our pilots were excellent. Hence, their performance was remarkable. The achievements they scored included the shooting down of Japanese planes on 14 August over Shanghai. Subsequently, Japan's planes of the crack Shikayo and Kisarazu naval air squadrons were downed over Nanking and Hangchow. Despite numerical inferiority, the Chinese Air Force piled up a most outstanding combat record. On one occasion, a plane flown by pilot Yen Hai-wen was hit. Yen parachuted by mistake into the Japanese position. Determined not to be captured, Yen shot and killed several Japanese soldiers and then committed suicide. In admiration the Japanese erected a tablet bearing the words "Tomb of a Chinese Air Force Warrior" in his memory. In the Air Battle of Taiyuan, Major Hirashi Miwa, Japan's ace fighter was captured. In the months of August, September and October, heavy air battles were fought resulting in heavy loss of planes. By November, a number of Russian fighters arrived. In December, the strength of the Chinese Air Force was increased. Again, excellent combat records were scored over Nanchang and

Hankow. In particular, the Air Battle of 29 April was most successful. In an effort to awaken the Japanese warlords and people, planes of the Chinese Air Force were flown over Nagasaki, Fukuoka, Kuruma, Saga, and Kyushu on 19 May to drop leaflets and to reconnoiter Japanese ports and airfields.

Guerilla Operations

Since the general war broke out, China adopted the strategy of attrition warfare. Guerilla warfare was conducted to supplement regular warfare. Training directives on guerilla warfare were promulgated to train guerilla cadres. A number of regular units and local militias were assigned to engage in guerilla warfare. Officials in combat areas were ordered to lead the local military forces and resist the enemy in their assigned areas. This correct policy enabled the war areas to control the vast space behind the enemy lines, lead the people, contain and wear out the enemy resulting in excellent combat records.

When the Japanese forces shifted their main strength from the area south of the Chang River to Shansi, Lu Cheng-tsao of the 53rd Corps was appointed the 1st Independent Guerilla Commander fighting the Japanese in Central Hopei Province. Li Fu-ho and Sun Kuei-yuan were named the 2nd Independent Guerilla Commander and Western Hopei Guerilla Commander respectively. In addition, the National Military Council appointed Chang Yin-wu commander-in-chief of the Hopei Militia Force. As Chang had a fine reputation in Hopei, many joined him. Lingchuan was chosen as the site to train the cadres. Units were rapidly activated and organized. In early November, 1937, the 1st War Area began its counteroffensive against the Japanese along the Peiping-

Hankow Railroad. The 52nd Corps and the units under Sun Kuei-yuan operated in Kantan and Tze Hsien and at one time penetrated the enemy airfield to destroy many planes. In the spring of 1938, Chang Yin-wu's units entered central Hopei and routed one Japanese regiment in Ankuo and Poyeh. Unfortunately, Lu Cheng-tsao's force was infiltrated and controlled by the Communists who appointed him commander of the Central Hopei Military District. Units under Ho Lung and Liu Po-cheng (formerly the 18th Army Group) which were elements of the 2nd War Area entered Hopei in conjunction with Lu Cheng-tsao's force compelling Chang Yin-wu's force to move southward. Thus, the 18th Army Group confiscated arms belonging to the civilians and annexed local forces. As they escaped the mop-up of the Japanese forces, moved but did not attack the enemy, they had no combat record to speak of. They forced landlords, rich farmers and dissident elements to flee to the major cities and seek shelter under the enemy. On the contrary, our guerilla forces fought for more than five years in the Shansi-Hopei-Honan border areas and key localities southeast of Taihsing Shan. They made valuable contributions, as they successfully stopped the Communists and checked the Japanese.

In September and October, 1937, when the 2nd War Area fought against the Japanese at the Great Wall Lines inside the Pinghsing Kuan and the Juyueh Ko, Generalissimo Chiang ordered the 18th Army Group (formerly the 8th Route Army) under Chu Teh which was subordinate to the 2nd War Area to operate in Pinghsing Kuan and to cut off the Japanese lines of communications in the rear. As the 18th Army Group had its main strength scattered in the vastness of Shansi-Hopei-Chahar border area busily constructing bases and fighting for control of certain localities, it actually did not carry out its assigned missions. Instead, it turned in false reports on its combat results. It was busily engaged in propaganda and misleading people at home and abroad. Between October and November, at the Battle of Taiyuan, Chinese forces fought fiercely against the Japanese for twenty days at Hsin Ko and Ladies' Pass ending in many Japanese reverses. Nevertheless, the main strength of the 18th Army Group sat-idle along both sides of the Tung-Pu Railroad and the remainder along the Cheng-Tai Railroad. They were preoccupied with the expansion of their bases and the propaganda on the combat results of the guerilla activities. Between February and March, 1938, the Japanese forces moved south along the Tung-Pu Railroad from Taiyuan. Another Japanese force moved west through Tungyang Pass and Poai along the Peiping-Hankow Railroad. The 2nd War Area counter-attacked from Hanhouling, Shihkouchen, Wenshui and Chiaocheng. For over ten days, fierce battles were fought and victories were won. At this time, Communist Liu Po-cheng's 129th Division opened the Tungyang Pass permitting the Japanese to move into the key rear area locality of Linfen. Thus, the situation took a turn for worse and past endeavors were wasted. Yet, the 129th Division had the audacity to claim that it destroyed several hundred vehicles in the Japanese trains at Tungyang Pass and tried to deceive peoples at home and abroad.

After the fall of Tsingtao in late December, 1937, the 5th War Area shifted the marines and local militia to Chucheng and Chishui to start guerilla warfare. These guerilla units, in conjunction with the defenders were able to recapture Monyin and hold the cities in eastern and southern Shantung.

In January, 1938, guerilla commander Liu Chen-tung gave his life to the country in the defense of Chishui. During the Japanese attack of Linchi, guerilla forces harassed their rear areas, contained the enemy and hindered the movement of supplies. They contributed greatly to the victory in the initial Battle of Linchi. Later, the Japanese were forced to abandon the Wei Hsien-Yentai (Chefoo) Highway supply route and shifted to the Chufu-Szeshui route for their supplies. Thus, the vast eastern and southern Shantung, particularly Chimon Shan area and the northwestern mountain area of Jihchao Hsien became excellent guerilla bases for six years in the hands of the Chinese forces. By mid-May, after the evacuation of Hsuchow, the 69th Corps was left in southern Shantung to wage guerilla warfare, the 24th Army Group in northern Kiangsu and eastern Anhwei and its 57th Corps moved to southern Shantung to reinforce the guerilla forces there. Meanwhile, the administrative commissioners in Shantung continued to lead the local militia in defense against the enemy. Guerilla warfare was waged throughout the Shantung province. Commissioner Fan Chu-hsien, in particular, successfully held the outer hsiens of Tungchang (Liao Cheng) and distinguished himself in combat. Later, Commissioner Fan was killed in action, but his name has lived.

In response to the operations of the 5th War Area, the 3rd War Area began guerilla activities in Hangchow, Hsuancheng, Nanking, Wuhu and Kueichih in late January, 1938. In February and March, after numerous engagements in which heavy blows were inflicted on the Japanese, Fuyang, Haining, Haiyen, Anchi, Liyang, Tangtu and Hsuancheng were captured. At one time, guerilla forces penetrated into the city of

Hangchow, forcing the Japanese to launch a five pronged attack on the Kiangsu-Chekiang-Anhwei border area in mid-March. With high mobility, Chinese forces avoided hitting the Japanese in places where they were the strongest. By mid-April, the Japanese were so exhausted that they decided to call off the attack.

In January, 1938, the Central Government took in some 5,000 Communist remnants in southern Kiangsi and Hupei-Anhwei border area reorganizing it into the New 4th Corps (having command over four columns.) This corps, under the 3rd War Area, was stationed in southern Anhwei in Tungling, Fanchang, Nanling, and Ching Hsien for guerilla operations in Kiangsu, Anhwei and areas south of the Yangtze River. In order to facilitate its operations, Tungling and Fanchang were designated as the boundaries with the boundary areas under its command. Using such slogans as anti-Japanese and united front, it proceeded to deceive the youths, expand Communist organizations, coerce the eligible males and develop its own military forces. It never undertook operations against the Japanese.

During the Battle of Wuhan, the 3rd War Area organized several moving artillery detachments which were equipped with small-caliber guns, anti-tank guns and attached with necessary infantry and engineer units. These detachments operated along the Yangtze River in southern Anhwei attacking Japanese craft. Consequently the Japanese suffered losses in personnel and craft, and their water transportation was hindered. As the Japanese 116th Division was tied down along the Yangtze River, the situation became more favorable in the Battle of Wuhan.

Meanwhile, the Japanese General Headquarters realized

that its forces were bogged down in China's interior. The deployment of 30 divisions, the bulk of their field forces, (excluding the Kuangtung Army) enabled them to occupy only major cities and the 10km strips along the lines of communications. They found themselves completely helpless. Since then, our guerilla forces had occupied vast areas harassing and wearing out the enemy.

The Program of Resistance and National Reconstruction and the People's Political Council

On 29 March, 1938, the Kuomintang Provisional Congress began a 10-day conference. Among the important resolutions, four were most outstanding.

(1) Formulation of the Program of Resistance and National Reconstruction as the guiding principle throughout the nation.

(2) Election of Generalissimo Chiang as the party's director-general who is clearly designated as the party's leader serving as the stabilizer in the revolutionary organization.

(3) Termination of the National Defense Advisory Council and the establishment of the People's Political Council as the highest wartime people's organization.

(4) Establishment of the Three People's Principles Youth Corps. As the political party in power, this party is responsible for training the nation's youths so that everyone believes in the Three People's Principles. The establishment of the Youth Corp abolishes the party member candidate system.

The Program of Resistance and National Reconstruction was the primary guiding principle in wartime diplomacy, military affairs, politics, economics, mass movement and education. It was also the basis for the combined employment of political strategy and military strategy. This program was supported by both the People's Political Council as well as the nation's people.

As the highest wartime people's organization, the People's Political Council was organized in April, 1938. Initially, there were 150 members; later, it was increased to 360. By the time constitutional rule ended in May, 1947, four conferences (13 meetings) had been called resulting in great contributions to the basic policy of resistance and national reconstruction. Members of the Young China Party, the National Socialist Party, the Communist Party and non-party prominent leaders all participated in the council. During the War of Resistance, members of the People's Political Council made many proposals, supported the Program of Resistance and National Reconstruction, stood firm in continuing the war, formulated laws on the establishment of democratic system, denounced traitor Wang Ching-wei, formulated the May 5 Chapter, impeached derelict officials and organized such agencies as the "Szechuan-Sikang Inspection Team," "Military Discipline Inspection Team," "Constitutional Government Association," and "Szechuan-Sikang Economic Reconstruction Association," which all contributed to the war effort. Under the major premise of fighting the Japanese and with the exception of the Chinese Communists who were working on their own plots, all other political parties aimed at the common objective with the Program of Resistance and National Reconstruction as their scope and the expulsion of the Japanese as their main duty. Despite Wang Ching-wei's betrayal and subsequent surrender to the enemy and Japan's creation of the puppet regime in Nanking, the United anti-Communist Front of the various political parties (excepting the Chinese Communists) stood firm. Their fortitude and perseverance enabled our people to win the final victory.

Meanwhile, the provincial and city provisional assemblies were established consecutively. Certain provinces even established hsien assemblies. In the guerilla area in North China, election of hsien magistrates, precinct chiefs and village chiefs were determined by popular vote.

Section 3
Second Phase Operations (See Map 11)

Characteristics of the Second Phase Operations

After the Battle of Wuhan in November, 1938, the Japanese frontline extended from Paotou, Fenglingtu, Kaifeng, Hsinyang, Yuehyang to Hangchow. Furthermore, they occupied Canton, controlled the estuary of the Pearl River, seized both banks of the Yangtze River and seized the narrow corridor within 10 km. from the major railroads in North and East China. As the Chinese main forces confronted the Japanese frontline armies, Generalissimo Chiang advanced the strategy of turning the enemy rear areas into frontline areas and left powerful forces in rear of the enemy to lead the people and to coordinate guerilla tactics with attrition strategy. Meanwhile, the Japanese had already committed 14 divisions and 2 air groups in Manchuria and Korea guarding against the Russians; and 7 divisions for garrison duty in Japan proper and Taiwan. There was no strategic reserve. Further advance would run counter to their national defense objective (the Japanese army considered Soviet Russia its primary objective). The strategic posture thus turned more and more unfavorable. The Chinese Government's flat refusal to negotiate peace, the Chinese soldiers' determined will to fight and die rather than captured, and the unfavorable international situation made things worse for the Japanese. On 1 July, 1938 the United States announced the embargo of strategic materials to Japan. On 6 November, based on the Nine Power Pact, the United States lodged a protest against Japan's so-called Greater East Asia New Order. In July and August, Soviet Russia started the Changkufeng Incident in which one Japanese division was defeated. The Japanese abandoned Changkufeng and sued for peace. All these events forced Japan to change her operational guidance, stop her offensive, concentrate her efforts in mopping up the guerrilla units in North and East China, help set up the puppet organizations, use Chinese against Chinese, squeeze all possible resources and continue the war by means of war. Meanwhile, the Japanese deployed mobile forces in Wuhan to weaken the Chinese forces by means of limited offensives. Furthermore, they cut off all the routes leading from China to foreign countries and conducted strategic bombings and counter-attrition warfare.

After the Battle of Wuhan, Generalissimo Chiang called separate military conferences at Nanyueh and Wukung to review the gains and losses in the first phase of the War of Resistance. Views from the officers and men on subsequent operations and reforms in military administration were solicited. He pointed out that the characteristics of the second phase operations lay in turning the defensive into an offensive and in turning defeat into victory. He emphasized the importance of political warfare, propaganda warfare and guerrilla warfare and urged a study on the spirit of Tseng Kuo-fan and Hu Lin-yi in perseverance, fortitude, loyalty, simplicity, harmony, sense of shame and determination to take revenge. He personally wrote an implementing outline of the Four Musts in the War of Resistance (1. Boosting morale 2. Winning people's hearts 3. Economizing materials 4. Looking after the wounded and sick). He also pointed out the essentials in the second phase war preparations and education.

Based on the above-mentioned review, command organizations were adjusted, and headquarters of field armies, armies, division-subordinate brigades were eliminated. The corps was considered as a strategic unit. The Generalissimo's Headquarters in Canton, Sian and Chungking were deactivated, while the Generalissimo's Headquarters in Kweilin and Tienshui were activated to unify the military operations in the southern and northern theaters. The Civil Affairs Military Government Committee was established and placed directly under the National Military Council. Sub-committees were established behind enemy lines to arouse the people into greater efforts for the total war, to destroy the puppet organizations and to thwart the enemy's political, economic and cultural aggressions. Those corps and divisions which had suffered prohibitive losses were rotated for replacement and training under the direct control of the National Military Council. Thus, they were able to restore their combat strength quickly and to return to combat. In accordance with the development of the overall situation, the second phase operational guidance was prepared and the battle of order changed.

Operational Guidance and Order of Battle of the Second Phase Operations

Successively, the Chinese forces launched limited offensives and counterattacks in order to check and wear out the enemy, respond to the guerilla forces behind the enemy lines, intensify control and harassment of the enemy rear areas, turn the enemy rear areas into frontline areas, force the enemy into defending points and lines, prevent the enemy from exercising general rule and the looting of materials and crush their attempt to check the Chinese with Chinese and to continue the war by means of war. In the meantime, units were pulled out on rotation for replenishment and training so as to enhance their combat effectiveness for the general offensive.

In order to adapt to the development of the overall situation and to step up guerilla operations behind the enemy lines, Generalissimo Chiang divided the nation into ten war areas. The 1st War Area covered Honan and a part of northern Anhwei. The 2nd War Area covered Shansi and a part of Shensi. The 3rd War Area covered southern Kiangsu, southern Anhwei, Chekiang and Fukien. The 4th War Area covered Kwangtung and Kwangsi. The 5th War Area covered western Anhwei, northern Hupei and southern Honan. The 8th War Area covered Kansu, Ninghsia, Chinghai and Suiyuan. The 9th War Area covered northwest Kiangsi, Hupei. Hunan and the area south of the Yangtze River. The 10th War Area covered Shensi. The Shantung-Kiangsu War Area covered northern Kiangsu and Shantung. The Hopei-Chahar War Area covered Hopei and Chahar.

Victory in the First Battle of Changsha

After the winter of 1938, the National Military Council ordered two corps into Shantung and Hopei to step up guerilla operations. Two offensives were launched in April and July, 1939 to respond to the guerilla operation there. At the same time, the Japanese initiated the Battle of Nanchang and the Battle of Suihsien-Tsaoyang[18] resulting in heavy losses on both sides. By early September, the Japanese set up the China Expeditionary Forces General Headquarters in Nanking with Juozo Nishio as the commander-in-chief to exercise unified command over the forces fighting in China Meanwhile, two Japanese divisions were massed in areas west of the Kan River, four divisions in northern Hunan, and the naval fleet was assembled in Yuehyang ready for an invasion of Changsha.

At this time, Soviet Russia and Germany signed a non-aggression pact and partitioned Poland. With the outbreak of the war in Europe, Soviet Russia and Japan signed the Normankan Treaty.[19] To pacify Japan, Britain closed the Yunnan-Burma Road[20] in order to concentrate her efforts

---

[18] Battle of Nanchang and Battle of Suihsien-Tsaoyang
The Battle of Nanchang took place in mid-February, 1939 and ended in early May of the same year. The Battle of Suihsien-Tsaoyang began in late April, 1939 and ended in mid May of the same year.

[19] Normankan Ceasefire Agreement:
On 28 May, 1939, the Japanese and the Russians fought bitterly at Normankan on the border of Manchuria and Mongolia. The fighting lasted until 15 September when a ceasefire agreement was signed.

[20] Closing of the Yunnan-Burma Road:
On 17 July, 1940, the British Government announced the stopping of transportation on the Yunnan-Burma Road for three months.

in Europe. In the light of the changing international situation and the possibility of the Japanese forces mounting an attack on Changsha, Generalissimo Chiang ordered the various war areas to mount the September offensive to tie down the enemy, and instructed the 9th War Area to crush the enemy's offensive in accordance with the pre-arranged mobile defense plans. (Meanwhile, Japan was alarmed over the U. S. abrogation of the U. S.—Japanese trade and navigation treaties. As Russia and Germany signed a non-aggression pact, Japan was on the alert for Russia and watched the situation hesitatingly and carefully. In accordance with established policy, Japan conducted anti-attrition war against China.)

The 9th War Area ordered a part of the forces under its command to stop the Japanese in northern Kiangsi, while the main forces offered piecemeal resistance along the Hsin-chiang River, Milo River, and Liuyang River and lured the enemy forces to the vicinity of Changsha where they were destroyed.

On 13 September, the Japanese forces in northern Kiangsi started the attack. Having engaged units of the 9th War Area for over 10 days they left a part of the forces there to undertake defense and moved the main force to Hsiushui to respond to the Japanese forces in northern Hunan. The Chinese forces in western Kiangsi immediately began the offensive throwing the Japanese back to their original positions with heavy losses. On 22 September, the Japanese forces in northern Hunan and southern Hupei began the attack employing a part of their forces in left turning movement to respond to the Japanese forces in northern Kiangsi, while their main forces headed toward Changsha.

In accordance with pre-arranged plans, the 9th War Area offered piecemeal resistance in previously constructed positions and conducted ambushes and flank attacks resulting in tremendous gains.

On 30 September, the leading elements of the Japanese forces entered the northeast section of Changsha. As their forces were widely scattered in the paddy fields and forests in Hunan, Hupei and Kiangsi, they were most vulnerable. Thus, the Chinese forces struck where the defenses were weak and wore out the Japanese. In time, the Chinese reinforcements in the vicinity of Changsha arrived. The offensives launched by the 5th and the 6th War Areas threatened the enemy rear areas. On 1 October, the Japanese forces in northern Hunan began to retreat. In pursuit, Chinese forces received much assistance from the local populace and killed many Japanese. On 16 October, all the original positions were recovered.

Battle of Southern Kwangsi

In January, 1939, upon request of the Japanese Navy, the Japanese General Headquarters decided to capture the Chinese air operation and blockade operation base. In February, Japanese forces landed on Hainan Island, took Haikow, and captured the port of Yulin in preparation for their southward advance. In September, as the war in Europe broke out, Britain and France were too pre-occupied to pay any attention to the east. In early November, in an attempt to cut off the road from Kwangsi to Indochina, the Japanese employed the 5th Division, the Taiwan Brigade, 50 vessels and over 100 aircraft in a forced landing at Chinchow Bay on 15 November. As they attacked toward Nanning, Chinese forces offered resistance. On 24 November, Nanning fell, followed by the fall of Kunlun Pass. In early December, Generalissimo Chiang massed 25 divisions totalling 150,000 men. The counteroffensive began on 16 December under the unified command of the Generalissimo's Headquarters in Kweilin. On 31 December, Chinese forces captured Kunlun Pass destroying one brigade of. the Japanese 5th Division. Later, Patang was also recovered. In January, 1940, the Japanese reinforced with one and half divisions from Kwangtung. A part of the Japanese forces attacked Pinyang, while the main force attacked Kunlun Pass. On 2 and 4 February, Pinyang and Kunlun Pass fell into Japanese respectively. Subsequently, Shanglin and Wuming were captured by the Japanese. As a result, Chinese forces were redeployed to take the offensive. On 24 February, Kunlun Pass, Chiutang, Patang, Liutang were recaptured by the Chinese forces with the Japanese falling back to defend Kaofenghuan and Nanning. In mid-June, the Japanese advanced westward along the Yenning-Lungchow Highway. On 2 July, Lungchow fell. On 12 October, the Chinese forces started the offensive recovering Lungchow and Nanning on 28 and 29 October respectively. Taking advantage of the French defeat, the Japanese 5th Division invaded Indo-China from Chennan Pass chasing the French out by 17 November.

In late February, 1940 when Chinese forces captured Kunlun Pass once again and the Japanese withdrew to Nanning. Generalissimo Chiang called a military conference at Liuchow to review the gains and losses in the operations and plan the future improvements. His instructions included the following essentials:

(1) Bearing in mind the spirit of the Japanese forces, our

officers should have a sense of self-awareness and vigilance.

(2) Description of the strength and weaknesses of the Japanese tactics.

    1. Strength of the Japanese tactics:

        a. Rapidity — The so-called "attacking the enemy where he is unprepared and appearing where you are not expected," and "at first, exhibit the coyness of a maiden and afterwards emulate the rapidity of a running hare."

        b. Toughness — Hold positions with fortitude and perseverance.

        c. Sharpness — Bold conical advance.

        d. Secrecy — Maintenance of secrecy to keep the enemy guessing.

    2. Weaknesses of the Japanese forces:

        a. Smallness — Capability to undertake only small unit invasion or harassment.

        b. Shortness — Capability to engage in limited combat only.

        c. Shallowness — Capability to launch shallow attacks only.

        d. Emptiness — No reserve strength; emptiness behind Japanese lines.

(3) Instructions on tactics to overcome the enemy and countermeasures:

    1. Tactics exploiting the Japanese weaknesses in order to achieve victory — Large units should be employed against small enemy units. Counter enemy attacks of short duration by grappling with the enemy for an extended period. Employ

disposition in depth against short-distance enemy attacks and harassment. Advance boldly to penetrate the enemy's lightly defended rear areas.

2. Tactics and countermeasures aiming at the strength of the Japanese forces:

   a. Control the enemy's "rapidity" with "stability."

   b. Overcome the enemy's "toughness" with "fortitude."

   c. Break the enemy's "sharpness" with "ambush."

   d. Counter the enemy's "secrecy" with "rigidity and vigilance."

(4) Announcing the present phase operational guidance — Seeking initiative with total effort and actively undertaking the offensive.

Immediately after the Liuchow Conference, Generalissimo Chiang called a nation-wide Chiefs of Staff Conference in early March. At this conference, he advanced his revolutionary tactics, the essentials of which are listed as follows:

(1) Strategically the operations would be sustained and fought hard. However tactically, the operations would be ended as soon as possible.

(2) In making the advance, boldness is the key. Disregard the flanks, front and rear to attain the objective with determination. Commanders at various levels should cultivate the knowledge and prowess of conical assault.

(3) Adhere to no past practices in the withdrawal and withdraw behind the enemy lines.

(4) Commanders at various levels must be equipped with

command ability so as to develop the power of the revolutionary forces in defeating a numerically superior enemy and to write glorious war history.

Winter Offensive

During the summer Battle of Suihsien-Tsaoyang and the first autumn Battle of Changsha in 1939, the Japanese forces retreated hastily without suffering fatal blows. However, it was quite obvious that they were bogged down. If they were not reinforced, they would not be able to launch a major offensive. However, as the Japanese were situated in the interior lines with adequate communications, it was possible for them to shift their forces, conduct local offensives, mop up our guerilla units and reduce our combat effectiveness. Hence, it was necessary that the Chinese forces seek the initiative, conduct multiple attacks, tie down the enemy so as to frustrate the enemy attempts in local offensives and to exploit the advantage of fighting on exterior lines.

In October, 1939 the Chinese forces completed the second phase reorganization and training. With greatly increased combat effectiveness, the Chinese forces began the winter offensive.

Generalissimo Chiang employed the reorganized and trained units directly under the National Military Council and units of the 2nd, 3rd, 5th and 9th War Areas as the main effort. Units of the 1st, 4th, 8th, Shantung-Kiangsu and Hopei-Chahar War Areas were employed for diversionary attacks.

On 1 December, the 1st War Area opened the offensive against the enemy and sabotaged the bridges and stations along the Lung-Hai Railroad, Tao-Ching Railroad and Peiping-

Hankow Railroad. With the disruptions in communications, the Lowang Station was captured, the enemy in Kaifeng City mopped up and depots burned. As Kweiteh was bypassed and Hsinyang taken, excellent combat results were reaped.

The disposition of the 2nd War Area aimed at a three-pronged attack to mop up the Japanese forces in the southern Shansi triangle with emphasis on Chufu and Houma. At dawn on 10 December, a general offensive began in southern and eastern Shansi. As the operation progressed smoothly, the Japanese were driven out of strong points suffering many casualties. By mid-January, 1940, the Japanese were largely routed. However, Chinese forces in western Shansi encountered difficulties, as the 18th Army Group conspired with the new army units in Shansi headed by Po I-po, Han Chun and Wu Sheng-wu in rebellious activities. Communist forces numbering over ten regiments raided the rear areas, confiscated food belonging to the people (food for the troops fighting the war) and prevented the people from selling food to the government forces. Hence, supply difficulties arose resulting in inability to furnish supplies in accordance with pre-arranged plans.

On 16 December, the 3rd War Area began the offensive by organizing advance columns to move toward the river banks and to attack enemy ships. In Chekiang, Chinese forces, in succession, attacked Hangchow, Fuyang, and Yu-hang killing many Japanese troops. Later, after being reinforced, the Japanese moved south to capture Hsiao Shan. Along the Kan River, Chinese plainclothes men entered Nanchang to play havoc inflicting heavy casualties on the Japanese.

In Kwangsi of the 4th War Area, the Japanese moved into

Nanning. Having suffered defeat in the winter offensive, the Japanese fought hard in the vicinity of Kunlun Pass and Kaofenghuan for two months (for details, see the Battle of Southern Kwangsi). In order to check Chinese forces and to break the siege of Nanning, the Japanese forces in Kwangtung invaded northern Kwangtung from Yinchanhuan under air cover on 8 December. Chinese force counterattacked. By 31 December, the Japanese moved into Wongyuan, Yingteh and Chingyuan. In time, our reinforcements arrived to start a counterattack to repel the invading Japanese. By 16 January, 1940 all the original positions were recaptured.

The 5th War Area divided its forces into the River North Army, the Right Army, the Left Army (the River East Army), the Southern Honan Army and the Eastern Hupei Guerilla Force. On 12 December, 1939, the offensive began resulting in the capture of many small Japanese strong points and in many casualties. On 28 December, the Northern Hupei Army was organized to operate in Huayuan and Kwangshui and to exploit success. By 22 January, 1940, the Japanese held their strong points and refused to fight in the open. Several thousand Japanese troops were killed by our forces.

In order to tie down the Japanese forces and to respond to the main effort operations, the 8th War Area attacked toward Paotou-Kweisui. On 18 December, 1939 an offensive was launched. At one time, Chinese forces entered the city of Paotou but later pulled out as Japanese reinforcements arrived. In late January, 1940, Japanese forces moved west for an invasion. In early February, Wuyuan and Linho fell. In early March, the Japanese at Wuyuan were surrounded.

On 1 April, Wuyuan was captured. Subsequently, all the Japanese forces within the Ordos bend of the Yellow River were wiped out.

With the main force of the army groups as the garrison forces, the 9th War Area conducted diversionary attacks against the enemy in its present posture. A part of the army groups was designated as the advanced army to attack the enemy. From 10 December, 1939 to 10 January 1940, railroads were sabotaged. Wires cut, strong points captured, and materiel siezed rendering the enemy isolated. In particular, the Nanchang-Chiuchiang Railraod never was operable. The Wuchang-Puhsin section of the Canton-Hankow Railroad was operable only once. The extent of the destruction could be imagined.

In the Hopei-Chahar War Area, communications were cut off, as the section south of Shihchiachuang along the Peiping-Hankow Railroad and the section between Tehchow and Tsanchow along the Tientsin-Pukow Railroad were sabotaged.

In the Shantung-Kiangsu War Area, the southern section of the Tientsin-Pukow Railroad was sabotaged to stop the enemy advance.

All in all, from 26 November, 1939 when the offensive began to the end of March, 1940, a total of 77,386 Japanese troops were killed, over 400 prisoners were captured and 2,743 rifles were seized. Although not all the war areas accomplished their pre-arranged missions and achieved the anticipated results, the objectives of wearing out and tying down the enemy were attained. However, during this period the 18th Army Group took advantage of this opportunity to attack the guerilla forces, engulf the local militia and expanded their occupied territories resulting in our heaviest losses in the winter offensive.

Fighting on Three Fronts

In the spring of 1940, the Japanese forces harassed, plundered and blockaded all the ports along the southeastern coast. Meanwhile, the puppet regime under Wang Ching-wei[21] came into being in the hope of reaping political benefits. Little did the Japanese realize that the establishment of Wang's regime only aroused greater common hatred of the Chinese people. Superior Chinese forces in the vicinity of Tahung Shan on the outskirts of Wuhan were ready to swoop down on Wuhan. In an attempt to remove this threat, the Japanese initiated the Battle of Tsaoyang-Ichang in May. In mid-June, Ichang which was controlling the water transportation of Szechuan, Hupei and Hunan fell into Japanese hands. Japanese massive bombings of the major cities in the rear areas posed a threat to Chungking. After reorganization and training in 1939, the Chinese Air Force grew in strength. Air battles were fought against the Japanese over Chungking, Liang Shan, Chengtu, and Pi Shan. The Chinese Air Force suffered heavy losses as its Russian planes were poor in performance. In late September, taking full advantage of the French debacle (In June, Germany swept the entire western Europe), Japanese forces occupied northern Indo-China thereby severing China's link with the outside. Meanwhile, Japan, Germany and Italy signed an

---

[21] Establishment of Wang Ching-wei's Puppet Regime:
On 18 December, 1938, Wang Ching-wei secretly flew to Kunming from Chungking and on 21 December to Hanoi. On 29 December, he issued a message advocating cessation of hostilities and peace negotiations with Japan. On 29 March, 1940, he set up the puppet regime in Nanking.

alliance attempting to threaten the United States and Britain, tie down Soviet Russia and isolate China so as to bring an end to the Sino-Japanese War.

In view of the above-mentioned situation, China revised her operational guidance. Efforts were made to intensify the sabotage of traffic communications in the various theaters, revamp the terrain, construct echeloned positions and assume mobile defense and fall-back offensive to crush the enemy offensive. Persistent guerilla operations behind enemy lines were conducted in order to tie down and wear out the enemy. In January, 1941, the insubordination of the New Fourth Corps in massing forces at will led to open rebellion and attack on Government forces. Orders were issued to deactivate the New Fourth Corps in order to nip the bud before it was too late. In February, the Japanese initiated the Battle of Southern Honan[22] and in March the Battle of Shangkao[23]. In compliance with the above-stated operational guidance, Chinese forces successfully defeated the enemy and reaped glorious combat results.

On 13 April, 1941, knowing that Germany was about to launch an invasion on her, Soviet Russia signed a nonaggression treaty with Japan in order to concentrate her efforts against Germany.

Soviet Russia exhorted Japan to move south, renew her offensive against China and facilitate the development of the 18th Army Group. On 19 April, the National Military

---

[22] Battle of Southern Honan:
  The Battle of Southern Honan began in late January, 1941 and ended in early February of the same year.

[23] Battle of Shangkao:
  The Battle of Shangkao began in mid-March, 1941 and ended in early April of the same year.

Council estimated that the Japanese Forces would dispatch reinforcements to launch local offensives, destroy our counteroffensive preparations and conserve their main strength for an opportunity to move south. Thus, our operational guidance was revised. Key localities were held; sustained actions, internal stability and foreign aid were sought. Military administration was streamlined and self-sufficiency was sought while awaiting the enemy's southward advance so as to undertake the offensive once again.

In May, the Japanese forces in North China massed six divisions and three brigades to launch the Battle of Chungyuan (i.e. the Battle of Southern Shansi) by laying a siege of Chungtiao Shan. Meanwhile, the Japanese forces in Central China massed three and half divisions from northern Hupei to respond to a northward advance. Fierce fighting lasted for more than a month with heavy casualties on both sides. Eventually, the Japanese forces in Central China withdrew to their former positions. Having occupied the various landing sites of the Yellow River on the southern side of the Chungtiao Shan, the Japanese forces in North China were able to weaken our guerilla strength north of the Yellow River. Thus, the 18th Army Group in North China ran havoc.

On 21 June, Germany attacked Russia thus giving Japan a golden opportunity to move north and south, and to attack China in force. However, after four long years of war, Japan was totally exhausted. The main strength of the Japanese army was bogged down in the China Theater, having been depleted of the strength to attack Russia. Japan lacked strategic materials, particularly petroleum. Thus, to continue her war effort, Japan had to look for resources in the south.

With limited potentials in shipbuilding and machinery manufacturing, Japan fell far behind the United States and Britain. Therefore, she had to think carefully in her advance to the south. Realizing China's determined effort to fight on and the gradual diplomatic development favoring China. In October, 1940, Britain reopened the Yunnan-Burma Road. In March, 1941, the United States announced that the Lend Lease Act was applicable to China. Furthermore, in April, Britain provided US$50 million as security assets for the Fahpi (Chinese currency), and Japan's confidence in ending the war by force wavered. Therefore, the so-called new national policy decided upon on 2 July was no more than speculation. Japan was undecided as to whether she should move north or south. In late July, Japanese forces occupied southern Indo-China in order to seize strategic materials and to establish bases for their southward advance. Immediately, the United States, Britain and the Netherlands froze all the Japanese assets. On 9 August, judging the Russo-German War would be an extended one, Japan actively made preparations for the southward advance and increase the pressure on China. Between August and September, Japan launched the Second Battle of Changsha[24] immediately after bombing China's cities and factories in the rear areas. Chinese forces repelled the Japanese attacks by undertaking fall-back offensive. The net result was that Japan's gains were overwhelmingly offset by her losses.

Mutiny of the New Fourth Corps

Since the New Fourth Corps moved into southern Anhwei

---

[24] Second Battle of Changsha:
The Second Battle of Changsha began in early September and ended in early October of the same year.

in the spring of 1938, it took advantage of the fact that the hard-pressed Government forces were locked in bitter fighting against the Japanese, and took upon itself to expand its forces, establish local administration, draft men, demand food and levy taxes. It went so far as to guide the Japanese in attacking Government forces. By the winter of 1940, its strength was increased to 35,000. Its various columns under Chen Yi, Tan Chen-lin and Chang Ting-cheng harassed Government forces in northern and southern Kiangsu. For fear that any action against them would prove detrimental to the war effort against Japan, the National Military Council was tolerant with the Communists. Operational areas were designated in order to prevent the Communists from harassing the rear areas and to exhort them into fighting the Japanese. The New Fourth Corps was ordered to assemble in Ching Hsien by 31 December, 1940 passing through the Government-controlled river crossing sites east of Wuhu to conduct operations north of the Yellow River. Unexpectedly, the New Fourth Corps refused to obey orders. Under the excuse of moving north, it massed all its forces in the vicinity of Maolin, Ching Hsien in early January, 1941 ready to attack the Government forces and then flee to the Kiangsu-Anhwei-Chekiang border area so as to control the Nanking-Shanghai-Hangchow triangle area. In the night of 5 January, it suddenly launched an attack on the Government's 40th Division at Sahchichen. Ku Chu-tung, commander of the 3rd War Area, therefore, took disciplinary actions against the New Fourth Corps. Between 6 and 14 January, the rebel force was disbanded. On 17 January, the National Military Council deactivated the New Fourth Corps and arrested Yeh Ting, the corps commander, for court martial. According to Yeh's confession, Mao Tse-tung pointed out that the Communist long-range program was divided into the following three phases.

Phase One — Communist units would advance from northwest Shansi in two columns. One column would move east, cross the Peiping-Hankow Railroad and enter central and eastern Hopei. Another column would enter southern Shansi, northern Honan, southern Hopei and western Shantung via the area south of the Taihsing Shan, cross the Tientsin-Pukow Railroad and enter northern and eastern Shantung. Thus, the traffic communications of the Government forces would be severed.

Phase Two — Establishment and consolidation of military and political bases, simultaneous with the wiping out of all Kuomintang influences north of the Yellow River.

Phase Three — Penetration into Central China, establishment of bases and severance of traffic communications of Government forces. Concurrent actions would be taken to sabotage Government forces and instigate rebellions in order to achieve the final victory of the Communist revolution.

These confessions coincided fully with the actions of the 18th Army Group since its entrance into Shansi.

Victory in the Third Battle of Changsha

On 7 December, 1941. Japanese forces attacked Pearl Harbor to begin the Pacific War. In consonance with the Allied forces to seek a common victory, the following day Generalissimo Chiang ordered all the war areas to conduct guerilla operations. Units were designated to attack and tie down the Japanese forces on a rotation basis. The 4th War Area was ordered to attack the Japanese in Canton in order to respond to the British operations in Hong Kong. Three corps were moved from Kwangsi and Szechuan to Yunnan ready to enter Burma. Additionally, two corps were ordered from Hunan to Kwangtung and Kwangsi as reinforcements.

In late December, in an attempt to prevent Chinese forces from reinforcing Hong Kong, Kowloon and Burma, the Japanese forces initiated the third Battle of Changsha. With a force of over 70,000, the Japanese crossed the Hsinchiang River in eight columns for a southward invasion. The Chinese forces employed a part of the forces to offer frontal piecemeal resistance, while the main force moved to the flanks. On 31 December, the Japanese forces reached the areas between the Laotao River and the Liuyang River fiercely attacking our positions in Changsha. The heavy fighting lasted until 4 January, 1942. As the Japanese offensive was frustrated, the Chinese forces, in accordance with prearranged plans, employed fourteen corps to surround and attack the Japanese from all sides. On 5 January, the Japanese took to their heels, and were ambushed suffering heavy casualties. One Japanese brigade which moved south to reinforce was surrounded by our forces. On 9 January, the routed Japanese forces heading north and their reinforcements linked up and retreated toward Milo with the Chinese forces in hot pursuit attacking fiercely, the Japanese suffered prohibitive losses. On 15 January, enemy remnants south of the Hsinchiang River were completely wiped out and everything returned to normal.

Distinguishing on Foreign Soil

Simultaneous with the starting of the Pacific War, the

Japanese made a surprise landing at Songkla (Singora) on the Malay Peninsula. In February, 1942, with the capture of the entire Malay Peninsula, Japanese forces landed in Rangoon to move north hoping to take the South China Peninsula, cut off the communications between China, Britain and the United States so as to suffocate China and realize their dream of effecting a link-up with the German forces in the Middle East.

Upon request of the Allied forces, the Chinese Government organized an expeditionary force ready to enter Burma. On 11 December, 1941, a part of the expeditionary force moved into Burma to take over the defense of the northern Thailand and Vietnam border areas. By 16 February, 1942, the situation in Rangoon was most critical. Repeatedly, Britain requested China to dispatch forces to Burma and assist in the operations there.

Upon entry into Burma, the Chinese forces defeated the Japanese at Toungoo and struck a heavy blow against the Japanese forces west of Yehta. On 17 and 18 April, in the Battle of Yenangyaung, the main strength of the Japanese 33rd Division was routed. As a result, some 7,000 British troops, over 1,000 horses and 500 British prisoners of war, American missionaries and reporters were rescued. A new record was established in the revolutionary history of the Chinese armed forces in which Chinese forces achieved distinction abroad. Shortly afterwards, the Japanese moved in strong forces to capture Lashio and to cut off Chinese lines of communications in the rear areas. A part of the Chinese forces having entered Burma crossed the Yehjen Shan to fall back into India for reorganization and training, while the main force withdrew to western Yunnan. The Japanese forces moved along the Yunnan-Burma Road to capture Tengchung and Lungling in western Yunnan. In June, 1942, entire Burma fell into Japanese hands.

Combined Operations

On 23 December, 1941, the military representatives of China, the United States and Britain met at a conference in Chungking in order to reach an agreement on military cooperation against aggression. In bidding the representatives farewell, Generalissimo Chiang said to the British representative: "China and Britain, neither must fail. If China should fail, Britain's India will be endangered." It was most regrettable that the British Government withheld and took the U. S. Lend-Lease aid materials which had arrived in Rangoon without even advising the Chinese Government in advance.

On 1 January, 1942, twenty-six nations including China, Britain and the United States announced an anti-aggression joint declaration in Washington in which the signatories indicated their determination to fight against the Axis powers and make no separate peace. This joint declaration centered around the four powers, namely, China, the United States, Britain and Soviet Russia. On 4 January, the Allied powers elected Generalissimo Chiang as the Supreme Commander of the 26-nation Allied forces in the China Theater. Vietnam and Thailand were also included in the China Theater with all the forces in that theater under his command. Thus, a strategic executive agency of the Allied powers in the East Asian continent was formally established. American and British public opinions spoke most highly of Generalissimo Chiang regarding him an unprecedented, fortitudinous and open-minded leader in the history of China.

Generalissimo Chiang Visiting India

After the outbreak of the Pacific War, Generalissimo Chiang expressed the hope that Britain would permit India self-rule so that she could join the anti-aggression front by contributing her manpower and material power. In January, 1942, Generalissimo Chiang asked Pres. Franklin D. Roosevelt to transmit his wishes to Prime Minister Winston Churchill. In reply, the British Government expressed its welcome and hoped that, upon his arrival in India, Generalissimo Chiang would issue a statement urging the Indian people to cooperate.

On 4 February, 1942, Generalissimo and Madame Chiang, accompanied by Wang Chung-hui and Chang Tao-fan, took off from Chungking, and on 9 February arrived in the Indian capital of New Dehli. In the morning of 11 February, he inspected troops at the plaza in front of the Viceroy's Residence. In the afternoon, he called on India's various maharajas and met the former chairman of the National Congress Jawaharlal Nehru as well as Abul Kalam Azad the then incumbent chairman. After visiting Generalissimo Chiang three times, Nehru publicly stated: "On behalf of my countrymen, I extend a hearty welcome to Generalissimo Chiang of China, India will not accept anyone's rule, be it Japanese or German. India accepts only the rule of India's masses . . . . . "

On 18 February, Generalissimo and Madame Chiang visited Mohandas Karamchand Gandhi in Calcutta. On 20 February, he again conferred with Nehru and advised him of the significance in the common struggle of the Chinese and the Indian peoples. Later, Nehru stated: "Generalissimo Chiang's visit to India has a historical significance. This visit marks the beginning of a new era in the Hindu-Chinese elationship. China's War of Resistance is a part of the big war in which the entire world seeks freedom. In many parts of the world some have achieved victory and others will achieve victory in the war to seek freedom."

On 21 February Generalissimo Chiang concluded his visit to India and sent a message to the Indian people in which he expressed the hope that China and India would work together to achieve freedom for mankind. His expectation of Britain to grant India political power left a new page in the annals of history.

Battle of Chekiang-Kiangsi

On 18 April, 1942, planes of American aircraft carriers landed in airfields in Chekiang after raiding Tokyo and Nagoya. Panic seized the Japanese people, as the society became tumultuous. In an attempt to stop the American planes from conducting shuttle bombings, the Japanese General Headquarters ordered the China Expeditionary Forces to occupy the airfields in Chekiang as soon as possible. Hence, the Battle of Chekiang-Kiangsi was fought. At this time, the Japanese forces had already captured the Philippines, Burma, Malaya and Dutch East Indies. As the Pacific War came to an end, the Japanese were free to shift forces from other areas for this campaign.

Fully aware of the overall situation, Generalissimo Chiang ordered the 3rd War Area to avoid decisive engagements and conduct sustained resistance. For more than three months, fierce fighting raged resulting in heavy Japanese losses

(Japanese suffered 17,000 casualties). Meanwhile, efforts were made to improve the garrison of the Szechuan-Shensi Highway, the Hanchung-Paiho Highways and both banks of the Yangtze River in order to consolidate the gateway to Szechuan.

Since the spring of 1942, the Japanese General Headquarters had plans to pull sixteen divisions and logistic units from Japan proper, Northeast and the South Seas to reinforce the China Expeditionary Forces preparatory to the employment of the main strength (ten divisions) from southern Shansi and of another force (six divisions) from Ichang to attack Szechuan in the spring of 1943. In June, Japan suffered a humiliating defeat in the Battle of Midway. In August, the U. S. forces began the counteroffensive against the Solomons by an assault landing on Guadalcanal. Despite gradual reinforcements, the Japanese suffered extremely heavy losses. In late September, the Japanese decided to postpone their preparations for the invasion of Szechuan. In November, when the Japanese forces on Guadalcanal were totally defeated, the war situation took a complete change. Japan lost the freedom to shift her forces. By the end of the year, preparations for the invasion of Szechuan were stopped.

Signing New Equal Treaties

After the merging of the eastern and the western theaters, China's greatest diplomatic achievement was the abrogation of unequal treaties and the signing of equal treaties. On 31 May, 1941, U. S. Secretary of State Cordell Hull announced that as soon as peace was restored in China, the United States would confer with the Chinese Government for the abrogation of extraterritoriality in China. On 4 July, British Ambassador Kerr transmitted a note to the Chinese Ministry of Foreign Affairs indicating the desire to coordinate the abrogation of consular rights, the return of the concessions and the revision of unequal treaties. After continued efforts of the Chinese Government, the U. S. and British Governments simultaneously issued formal statements relinquishing their extraterritoriality and related rights on China's national day on 10 October, 1942. On 11 January, 1943, the new Sino-U.S. and Sino-British Treaties were signed and went into effect on 20 May.

Subsequently, the Sino-Cuban Amity Treaty and Sino-Panamanian and Sino-Belgium Treaties were signed. Later, Holland, Norway, Venezuela, Mexico, Peru, Colombia and British Dominions of Canada, Australia and Union of South Africa relinquished the special rights and signed new treaties with China.

Chinese and U.S. Dignitaries Exchanging Visits

Subsequent to the outbreak of the war in the Pacific Roosevelt sent Republican leader Wendell Willkie to visit China in order to promote Sino-American relationships. Mr. Willkie received a rousing welcome upon arrival in Chungking on 2 October. In Generalissimo Chiang's conversation with Mr. Willkie, these were the following three points:

(1) Could there be a complete change of the past U.S. isolation policy and traditional concept.

(2) The attitude and the misunderstanding of the American civilian and military officials on China would lead to unfortunate stumbling blocks in the Sino-U.S. relationship.

(3) Should there be no special cooperation or alliance between China and the United States, the Pacific Ocean would lose the protection of a permanent peace. This would be the joint responsibility of Chinese and American statesmen.

On 6 October, further discussion was continued on the situation in the Pacific. It was noted that the four provinces in the Northeast (including Port Arthur and Dairen) and China's lost territory of Taiwan must be returned to China. However, Port Arthur could be jointly constructed and used by China and the United States. As China would be responsible for the defense of the port, the concept of a joint defense by China and the United States could perhaps be realized.

In the winter of 1942, Madame Chiang's visit to the United States received much attention in the American political circles. On 17 February, 1943, Madame Chiang visited the White House and was the honored guest of Pres. Roosevelt. On 18 February, she was invited to address the U.S. Congress. She first went to the Senate and later the House of Representatives. Her speech was broadcast by four major radio networks. Previously, only when something extremely important occurred, was a program broadcast in this manner.

Madame Chiang was the first Chinese who ever addressed the U.S. Congress. It was also the first time that the U.S. Congress invited a foreign guest visiting the United States in a private capacity to deliver an address. American public opinions considered Mme. Chiang representing a people whom the Americans loved and respected. Such respect was derived from China's heroic resistance against the Japanese during the past five years.

Mme. Chiang spent seven months in the United States

visiting New York, Chicago, San Franscisco, Los Angeles and her alma mater Wellesley. Finally, upon invitation of the Canadian Government, she visited Ottawa, Canada's capital, contributing greatly to China's prestige and diplomatic posture. The fact that the United States repealed the anti-Chinese act was indicative of the cooperation between the two nations.

Cairo Conference

In July, 1943, U.S. Pres. Roosevelt indicated his desire to meet Generalissimo Chiang before his conference with Stalin. In October, Pres. Roosevelt sent three messages to Generalissimo Chiang reiterating his desire. On 12 November, he sent Patrick Hurley as his personal representative to Chungking saying that he wished to listen to the views of the Chinese and British leaders on their own policies. He stated that he wished to mediate the differences between China and Britain. Generalissimo Chiang readily consented. As Chairman Lin Sen of the National Government passed away on 1 August and Generalissimo Chiang was chosen as his successor, he went to Cairo as the Chief of State of the Republic of China.

Cairo Conference began on 23 November and ended on 26 November. Generalissimo Chiang, was deeply impressed with Pres. Roosevelt's enthusiasm for China and fortitude. He was also impressed with Prime Minister Churchill's foresight and firmness in attitude. In his first broadcast upon his return to the United States, Pres. Roosevelt gave the following as his impressions of Generalissimo Chiang:

"Generalissimo Chiang is equipped with great foresight and fortitudinous spirit. His views on the present and future problems are penetrating."

Upon conclusion of the conference attended by the leaders of the three nations, the following joint declaration was made on 3 December 1943:

"The military leaders of the three nations have reached an unanimous agreement on the future operation plans against Japan. The three great allies are determined to apply relentless pressure — naval, ground and air — on the brutal enemy. This pressure has been increasing.

"The purpose of the three great allies in prosecuting this war is to check and punish Japan for her aggression. The three nations are determined not to seek selfish gains nor territorial expansion. The objective of the three nations is to deprive Japan of all the islands she has seized or occupied in the Pacific since the First World War in 1914 and to return to China all the Chinese territories that Japan has taken from China such as the four Northeast provinces, Taiwan and the Pescadores. Japan will be expelled from all the land that she has seized by force or greed. The three great allies, fully aware of the enslaved treatment received by the Korean people, are determined to provide freedom and independence to Korea in due time.

"Based on the above recognized objectives which are in full accord with the other objectives of the United Nations in the operations against Japan, the three great allies will engage in the significant and long war with perseverance so as to obtain Japan's unconditional surrender."

This declaration guaranteed the return of the four Northeast provinces, Taiwan, and the Pescadores to China when victory was achieved. Unfortunately, it was undermined at the Yalta Conference when Soviet Russia was permitted to occupy Port Arthur and Dairen, the two sinews guarding the Northeast.

At the Cairo Conference, Pres. Roosevelt asked Generalissimo Chiang's views on the type of government that Japan should have. Generalissimo Chiang said:

"The culprits in the war involving Japan are really their militarists. Let us first bring the downfall of the militarists. As to the type of government that Japan should have, I believe we should leave it to the Japanese people after the war. We must not create permanent errors among the peoples in this war."

Thus, the original statement in the declaration that "the Japanese monarchy system be abolished" was deleted.

Bitter Fighting

Since May, 1943, the Japanese forces initiated the Battle of Western Hupei in an attempt to seize control of Szechuan so as to bring an end to the war against China. However, they were defeated by the gallant National Revolutionary Forces. In their retreat, they were fiercely attacked by the Flying Tigers led by Gen. Claire L. Chennault and suffered numerous casualties. As a result, the Japanese lay in hiding for six months. By October, Chinese forces pulled seven corps for employment in Yunnan and India, preparatory to assisting the Allies in a counter offensive in Burma and to clearing the China-Burma Road. In the Pacific, under the attack of superior U.S. forces, the Japanese gradually withdrew. In the European theater, in early August, 1943, Italy sought a cessation of hostilities from the Allies, while the German forces fighting in the Ukraine were tottering. Beginning 23 October, the foreign ministers of the United

States, Britain and Soviet Russia held a conference in Moscow. It seemed certain that the Allied forces would fight to the end. Under these unfavorable circumstances, the Japanese launched the Battle of Changteh to prevent the shifting of Chinese forces to Yunnan and India, capture our communications between Szechuan, Hupei and Hunan and destroy our counteroffensive preparations.

After a 15-day drawn-out battle, Changteh City fell as a result of the Japanese gas attack. The gallant defenders held on tenaciously and gave their lives. The enraged Japanese set fire to the city and engaged in wanton killing. Seven days after the fall of Changteh, four corps of the 9th War Area raced to the scene of battle. In conjunction with a corps moving south from Santouping, these four corps conducted counter-envelopment operations to put the Japanese to rout. On 8 December, Chinese forces recaptured Changteh.

Since the spring of 1944, the Japanese forces suffered a series of reverses in the Pacific and their sea communications were greatly threatened. Meanwhile, Chinese and U.S. Air Forces grew steadily in strength and effectively interrupted Japanese rear area communications. In an attempt to sabotage our airfields, open up mainland lines of communications, maintain the land communications of the South China Peninsula and check our counteroffensive in Burma, beginning April, 1944, the Japanese successively initiated the Battle of Central Honan, the Battle of Changsha-Hengyang and the Battle of Kweilin-Liuchow (dubbed Operation No. 1 by the Japanese). Instigated by Soviet Russia, the 18th Army Group actively attacked Chinese government forces, undermined Government reputation, prepared for open rebellion and reaped the fruits of victory.

During the Battle of Central Honan, the Japanese forces were bent on seeking victory. On 8 May, they succeeded in clearing the Peiping-Hankow Railroad, but later the railroad was cut by Chinese forces. Despite the gallantry of the Chinese defenders, Loyang fell into the Japanese hands in the night of 25 May. The Japanese then moved west to attack Hanku Pass. On 11 June, Shouhsiang fell. The concerted attacks of the 1st, 5th and 8th War Areas led to the recapture of Lu Shan, Sung Hsien, Suiping, Lungpao, and Shouhsiang. When the plan for the counteroffensive of Loyang was being executed, Mao's forces in northern Shensi, took advantage of the weaknesses in the rear areas of the 8th War Area to expand to the south, loot materials and attack local militia. As the 8th War Area had to pull back elite forces to contain the Communists, the plan for the counteroffensive of Loyang fell through.

During the Battle of Changsha-Hengyang, the Japanese forces attempted to clear the Canton-Hankow Railroad thus dividing China into the eastern and western portions and isolating Chungking and the various supply points scattered in Kiangsi, Chekiang, Fukien and Hunan Provinces as well as the air bases constructed by the Allies. In the meantime, as a result of the Russo-Japanese Agreement, the Chinese Communist forces and the Japanese were no longer hostile to each other. Instead, Communist forces were used to harass the Hopei-Chahar War Area and the Shantung-Kiangsu War Area, establish the Central Honan Military District and flee to the border areas of Hunan, Kwangtung and Kiangsi resulting in heavy losses of Chinese military forces and civilians. Hence, the Japanese were able to shift ten divisions from the areas east of Shanhaikwan and North China to the Hunan front and encountered no disruptions from the Communist guerillas along the way.

In May, the Japanese forces staged a wide-front pincer penetration to the south from northern Kiangsi and southern Hupei. The enemy flanks at Kukang and Yiyang were defeated by forces of the 9th War Area, followed by heavy fighting in Changsha. On 19 June, Changsha fell. The National Military Council decided to engage the enemy in a decisive battle in the vicinity of Hengyang. The 10th Corps led by Fang Hsien-chueh defended Hengyang for 47 days. Unfortunately, poor coordination with the outside counterattack forces led to the fall of the city on 8 August.

The Battle of Kweilin-Liuchow took place after the fall of Hengyang with the Japanese employing a force of 150,000 to move along the Hunan-Kwangsi Railroad and the Hsi (West) River to Yung Hsien in a great arc for the invasion of Kweilin and Liuchow from the north, east and south. In mid-September, the Japanese broke through the Huangsha (Yellow Sand) River to occupy the Chuang Hsien. On 11 November, the Japanese occupied Kweilin and later Liuchow. On 22 November, Nanning fell. Powerful Japanese forces were dispatched along the Kweichow-Kwangsi Railroad for a northward invasion. At one time, the Japanese forces reached into Tu Shan in southern Kweichow seemingly heading for Kweiyang.

Meanwhile, Generalissimo Chiang had already pulled elite forces from the 1st, 6th, 7th and 8th War Areas as reinforcement. Consequently, Tu Shan was recovered on 5 December, followed by Liuchai. The Japanese forces fell back to Hochih to confront the Chinese forces.

In northern Burma, the counteroffensive operations were

decided at the Casablanca Conference,[25] the Washington Conference,[26] the Quebec Conference[27] and the Cairo Conference. Despite great difficulties, the Chinese Government gave first priority to the forces in India and the expeditionary forces by equipping them with all the U. S. aid weapons and ammunition in order to seek a common victory with the Allies in Burma. The other war areas had to suffer from lack of supplies. Stilwell had wanted to start the counteroffensive in Burma at an early date. Beginning in late October, 1943, Chinese forces in India, with the support of Allied air force and engineers crossed high mountains and covered difficult terrain to capture Maingkwan in early March, 1944, followed by the capture of Mogaung and Myitkyina. Meanwhile, Chinese expeditionary forces made a forced crossing of the Salween River to launch the western Yunnan offensive, respond to the operations of Chinese forces in India and capture such strongholds as Lungling and Tengchung while heading for Wanting. On 27 January, 1945 Chinese expeditionary forces and the Chinese forces in India effected a link-up at Mongyu to clear the China-India Road. To assist the Allied forces in the capture of northern Burma, Chinese forces continued to pursue the retreating enemy by taking in succession Lashio and Hsipaw. On 30 March, Chinese forces and the British forces linked up at

---

[25] Casablanca Conference:

At the Casablanca Conference in January, 1943, the Allies decided to restore the land communications to China and step up the airlift over the Hump.

[26] Washington Conference:

At the Washington Conference in May, 1943, the Allies decided to increase the airlift over the Hump to 10,000 tons each month and to launch the Burma offensive after the monsoon season was over.

[27] Quebec Conference:

At the Quebec Conference held in August, 1943, the Allies decided to clear the ground lines of communications to China.

Kyaukme to accomplish their strategic missions.

Order of Battle in the Winter of 1944

To facilitate the prosecution of war, in National Military Council readjusted the order of battle designating the 1st (Hu Tsung-nan acting), 2nd (Yen Hsi-shan), 3rd (Ku Chu-tung), 5th (Li Tsung-jen), 6th (Sun Lien-chung), 7th (Yu Han-mou), 8th (Chu Shao-liang), 9th (Hsueh Yueh), 10th (Li Pin-hsien), and Hopei-Chahar War Areas and the Chinese Forces in India. Later, to coordinate with the Allied forces and to shift the offensive, the Chinese Army General Head-quarters· was established in Kunming to be responsible for the unified direction, reorganization and training of the forces in the southwestern war areas. Chief of the General Staff Ho Ying-chin acted concurrently as its commander-in-chief having under his command the Chinese Expeditionary Forces, Kweichow-Kwangsi-Hunan Border Area General Headquarters, the 4th War Area, Yunnan-Indo-China Border Area General Headquarters, and the two army groups under Tu Yu-ming and Li Yu-tang. Meanwhile, the China-India Road (the Stilwell Road) was opened to facilitate the flow of large quantities of American weapons and war materials. It was anticipated that thirty-six infantry divisions could be equipped with American weapons to provide adequate firepower. Similarly, the logistics of the forces participating in the counteroffensive were greatly improved. Morale was magnificently boosted. To meet the combat requirements of the future counteroffensive, the forces were reorganized into the 1st through the 4th Front Armies and the Kunming defence forces.

Youths Joining the Services

The winter of 1943 was the most difficult period in the War of Resistance. College and high school students volunteered for services. Multitudes throughout the nation signed up to fight the enemy. On 10 January, 1944, Chairman Chiang delivered an address to the students in the military service in which he said:

"The voluntary enlistment of the nation's educated youths from the various schools has wiped out the weak and cowardly practices of our youths in the past as they now take up arms to fulfill the responsibility of citizens in defense of their country. This is indeed most gratifying in our War of Resistance."

In the meantime, the slogan of "An inch of ground, an inch of blood; 100,000 youths, a force of 100,000" was advanced to inspire high school and college students, government employees, and even the trainees of the World Buddhist School, the Han-Tibetan Theological School, and the Shih-chu Monks Training Class. By the spring of 1945, 86,000 had signed up. One tenth of them were assigned to the Chinese forces in India, while the remaining 76,000 were organized into nine divisions.[28] Their active participation in the military service had a tremendous political and sociological impact on the people in China leading eventually to the military counteroffensive and expediting the total victory of the Allies.

Decision to Fight Behind Enemy Lines

Subsequent to the Battle of Wuhan, the Japanese forces

---

[28] Activation of Nine Divisions:
Nine divisions ranging from Youth Corps 201st-209th divisions were activated.

advanced to Paotou, Fenglintu, Kafeng, Hsinyang, Yuehyang, Tatung, and Hangchow. Later, the Japanese captured Canton and blockaded Haikow. However, they were able to control only points and lines but not areas. As the international situation turned more and more against them, they stopped their advance and switched to counterattrition warfare. Meanwhile, they began their peace offensive by luring our wavering elements, enlarging the puppet organizations, seizing natural resources, seeking to check Chinese with Chinese and fighting a war by means of another war.

To cope with the Japanese strategy, Generalissimo Chiang gave the instructions that political efforts were more important than military efforts; guerilla warfare more important than regular warfare; enemy rear areas be turned into our frontline areas; and one third of our efforts be expanded in the enemy rear areas. The frontline areas of war areas were designated as guerilla areas with units assigned to undertake guerilla activities. In January, 1939, the Hopei-Chahar and Shantung-Kiangsu War Areas were organized with one corps moving into Shantung and three corps moving into Hopei to step up guerilla activities. In March, the Battlefield Party-Political Committee was organized with sub-committees and branch committees in the various war areas and guerilla areas so as to achieve unity in battlefield party-political-military efforts for the destruction of the enemy.

Operations behind Enemy Lines in Hopei-Chahar War Area

When the Hopei-Chahar War Area was organized in January, 1939, units of the 18th Army Group under Ho Lung and Liu Po-cheng took it upon themselves to move

into the Hopei Plains from Taihsing Shan. Our 1st Guerilla
Column under Lu Cheng-tsao was infiltrated by Communists
ending in Lu's defection to the Communists to become the
Communist commander of the Central Hopei Military
District. By May, Communist units under Ho Lung, Liu
Po-cheng and Lu Cheng-tsao, in a converging attack, broke
the Hopei militia forcing the latter to fall back to the south
from the Hutuo River in the north. Later, sandwiched
between the Japanese and the Communists, the Hopei militia
which had grown weak were transferred to Honan Province
for reorganization. The Western Hopei guerilla force under
Sun Kuei-yuan controlled the Hopei-Shansi-Honan border
areas and continued to fight the Japanese and the puppet
with distinction. Later, it was reorganized into the New
5th Corps. Unable to withstand the attacks and mopping-up
of the Japanese and the Communist 18th Army Group, the
local militia organized by the Hopei-Chahar General Headquarters found the situation in the Hopei Plains untenable.
The general headquarters, therefore, retreated to Lulo to
the west of Hsingtai. Indeed, the situation was most critical.
Generalissimo Chiang ordered the 69th Corps and the New
8th Corps to Central Hopei from southern Shantung via
northern Shantung. The 99th Corps raced to western
Hopei from northern Honan to provide the reinforcements.
In January, 1940 when the 69th and the New 8th Corps
were exhausted after long march behind enemy lines and
were not yet established, they were attacked by the 18th
Army Croup in succession at Nankung, Chingho, Wei Hsien
and Puyang and were cornered in southern Hopei. Eventually they were driven into the Hopei-Shantung-Honan
border area. The 99th Corps safely reached Lulo with the

18th Army Group in control of the areas south of Lulo disrupting supplies and provisions, it was most difficult for the 99th Corps to remain there. Consequently, the General Headquarters of the Hopei-Chahar War Area and the 99th Corps were forced out of the Hopei Province. Later, under the pressure of the 18th Army Group, Shih Yu-san defected and in time was executed. Sun Liang-cheng was appointed commander-in-chief of the 39th Army Group directing the 69th Corps and the New 8th Corps in guerilla operations in the Hopei-Shantung-Honan border area. Subsequently, Sun Liang-cheng was captured, and Lu Chung-lin was relieved of command. Kao Shu-hsun was appointed commander-in-chief of the Hopei-Chahar War Area and concurrently commander-in-chief of the 39th Army Group using Pu Hsien in western Shantung as the base to conduct guerilla operations. The Hopei-Chahar War Area existed only in name as the vast areas formerly under its control were occupied by the Communists. The Japanese forces lay in hiding along the important points and lines, as there was non-aggression between the Japanese and the Communists. In the fall of 1940, Japan signed the Axis alliance with Germany and Italy. Fearful of Japanese attacks, Soviet Russia instigated the Chinese Communist forces (18th Army Group) to launch the so-called "Battle of one hundred Regiments," at which the Japanese lines of communications were attacked. Meanwhile, through the Russian Military Mission, Chinese forces were requested to launch a counteroffensive of Ichang. Word was let out that the Chinese forces would soon launch a general offensive to tie down the Japanese forces. The results of the so-called "Battle of one hundred Regiments" were the destruction of the local militia, strikes at the government forces, plundering of war materials and the expansion of occupied areas. In the winter of the year, the Japanese forces initiated mopping up actions in central and western Hopei. However, their efforts were in vain, as the Communists excelled in evasive actions. In April, 1941, Soviet Russia and Japan signed a neutrality pact enabling the Japanese to move south. As there was a tacit agreement between the Chinese Communists and the Japanese, the Japanese were free to construct the Techow–Shihchiachuang Railroad and a highway net in hsiens and cities and to loot war materials. The Communists tightened their control of the people and completed the construction of the tunnel networks in the Hopei Plains to facilitate their evasion. No major combat took place in Hopei-Chahar until the end of the War of Resistance.

Operations behind Enemy Lines in the Shantung-Kiangsu War Area

In Shantung Province, there were stationed two Chinese corps and some local militia. In northern Kiangsu there were one Chinese corps and some local militia. Four Japanese divisions and three independent brigades were separately deployed along the Chiaochow-Tsinan Railroad, the Tientsin-Pukow Railroad and the Lung-Hai Railroad. The vast space in the interior was controlled by Chinese forces.

In early June, 1939, the Japanese massed sufficient strength and advanced along the Chiaochow-Tsinan Railroad, the Tientsin-Pukow Railroad and the Lung-Hai Railroad for an attack of the Chinese guerilla bases in southern Shantung. They were ambushed and attacked in flank by Chinese forces. Heavy fighting lasted until 9 June when the Japanese finally succeeded in capturing Chu Hsien, Chishui, and Mon-yin. Having suffered over 5,000 casualties and advanced into the interior, the Japanese were tied to the points and lines. It was difficult for them to look after everywhere. As the Chinese forces were spread out in Chi Shan, Fei Hsien and Jihchao mountain areas in close coordination with the local militia, they had control of the whole area. Utilizing planes and gap-penetrating ground supply, they maintained close liaison with the rear areas.

In 1939, elements of the Communist 115th and 129th Divisions infiltrated into Shantung from Hopei in order to create disunity among the Government forces. They were friendly toward the Japanese co-existing in an atmosphere of mutual non-aggression, while they isolated and destroyed the Government forces. Between 1939–1940, the militia of the various administrative districts were sandwiched between the Japanese and the Communists losing one half of their men. One militia division was forced to surrender to the enemy. In August, 1940, Lutsun, temporary seat of the Shantung Provincial Government, was captured by the Communists who had now become more boisterous than ever. On 4 August, 1942 the Communists instigated Wan Yi, a brigade commander of the Government forces, to stage a rebellion, coerce the division commander and surround the general headquarters of the war area. Fortunately, most of the officers and men of the Government knew what was right. The rebellion was soon quelled, but the casualties ran high. Meanwhile, Communist and Japanese forces joined hands to attack the Government's Temporary 12th Division at Laiyang.

In early May, 1943, the Japanese began a seige of Chimon

Shan. Chinese forces made use of terrain and prepared positions to meet the Japanese killing over 3,000 Japanese troops. The Japanese then retreated to their original positions. As the Communist forces occupied the Chimon Shan area, it was no longer possible for the general headquarters of the war area to remain in Shantung. In a night attack on the Government's command at Anchiu in southern Shantung, Chin Chi-yung, the local commander, was killed in action. Thus, the Provincial Government has only the Shoukuang Hsien under the protection of two regiments of militia until Japan's surrender.

In North Kiangsu, Hsinghua was the center around which a guerilla base was built. The guerillas controlled the canal and the Nantung-Haichow Road growing in strength and threatening the Japanese.

In early October, 1939, the Japanese attacked the Chinese guerilla base in northern Kiangsu in force. They succeeded in clearing the canal for navigation and the Nantung-Haichow Road. However, Chinese forces still controlled the vast areas on both sides to continue guerilla operations.

In 1939, units of the Communist New Fourth Corps led by Lo Ping-hui and Chang Ai-ping, using Sheng Tzu-ching, a commissioner of Sze Hsien in Anhwei Province as a cover, passed the boundary of the 3rd War Area, crossed the Yangtze River and infiltrated into eastern Anhwei. In the spring of 1940, Communists bought over the local forces, established bases in Hungtze Lake and branched out to northern Anhwei and northern Kiangsu. In the meantime, another column of the New Fourth Corps led by Chen Yi crossed the Yangtze River to lie in hiding in the north. In the spring of 1940, Chen Yi led nine Communist regiments in an attack on the Kiangsu militia at Huangchiao. The Government's 89th Corps was forced into action. For five days, the battle raged. In the end, corps commander Li Shou-wei and brigade commander Weng Ta were killed in action, as the entire corps suffered over 5,000 casualties, Chen Yi took advantage of this opportunity to expand. Communist eastward column led by Huang Ke-cheng advanced to the area between Huaiyin and Haichow. Meanwhile, the Communist New 4th Corps mutinied, and the Central Government abolished the designation of the New 4th Corps. At this time, Chen Yi appointed himself commander of the New 4th Corps with seven divisions under his command. Each division had over 20,000 troops. They then moved to northern Kiangsu and central Anhwei. On 4 December, Chen Yi led two divisions in an attack on the Government's 89th Corps at Tsaotien. After twenty days of heavy fighting, Chen Yi's forces were routed. Unfortunately, his forces were not totally destroyed, as the Japanese were in the way. Therefore, the Communists began to slow down. In March, 1941, the Japanese captured Hsinghua. As non-combattants and trains were moving toward Huaitung, they were intercepted by Communist Su Yu's forces suffering heavy losses. By February, 1943, the Japanese massed two divisions for an attack of the Chinese forces. For over one month, Chinese and Japanese forces fought bitterly resulting in heavy casualties on both sides. Finally, Communist forces committed over ten additional regiments led by Peng Hsueh-feng and Huang Ke-cheng. Unable to hold any longer, Government forces withdrew to Fuyang in mid-March. Thus, the entire northern Kiangsu fell into Communist hands.

Operations behind Enemy Lines in the First, Second and Eighth War Areas

Since the spring of 1938 when the Japanese forces captured Hsinhsiang and cleared the Tatung-Pucheng Railroad and the Peiping-Suiyuan Railroad, our 1st, 2nd and 8th War Areas began to use Taihsing Shan, Chungtiao Shan, Luliang Shan and Wuyuan Ordos bend of the Yellow River as operational bases from which they conducted guerilla activities on the far bank of the Yellow River forcing the Japanese to defend the narrow strips along the railroads, withstand the continued attacks of the Chinese forces and suffer heavy losses. By May, 1939, the Japanese invaded Tselu twice and Chungtiao eight times in an attempt to lessen the threat on them. As their strength was insufficient, the attacks were repulsed. Later in October, 1939, they surrounded Luliang Shan and were again driven back by the forces of the 2nd War Area. From April, 1940 to the spring of 1941, the Japanese laid siege to the Chinese bases in the mountain areas in southeastern Shansi. Apart from one or two strongholds such as Chingcheng, the rest of the key localities were still controlled by Chinese force. In March, 1941, the Japanese initiated the so-called Battle of Chung-yuan (Battle of Southern Shansi). After three months of hard fighting, the Chungtiao Shan base fell into Japanese hands.

To respond to the Battle of Southern Shansi, the 8th War Area began the attacks on the Japanese forces between Suiyuan and Paotuo resulting in heavy gains. In July, many sections of railroads and highways were sabotaged.

In Taihsing Shan, from December, 1941 to September, 1943, Chinese guerilla forces were besieged by the Japanese on several occasions, but were able to repulse the enemy attacks. Later, as the Chinese forces were transferred to Honan for replenishment and reorganization, they were depleted in strength. Sandwiched between the Japanese and the Communist forces led by Tang Tien-chi, commander-in-chief Pang Ping-hsun, corps commander Sun Kuei-yuan and division commander Chen Hsiao-chiang were wounded and captured. Having lost half of its forces and encountered supply difficulties, Chinese forces withdrew to Honan. Thus, the Taihsing Shan area was divided and occupied by the Japanese and Communist forces.

Operations behind Enemy Lines in the Third, Fifth, Sixth and Ninth War Areas

Since the Battle of Wuhan in 1938, guerilla based were established by the 3rd War Area along the coast of Fukien and Chekiang, the 5th War Area in Tapieh Shan, the 6th War Area in the Chianghan delta area, the 9th War Area in Lu Shan, Min Shan, Chiukung Shan and Tayun Shan. By 1945, the Japanese forces were attacked, railroads and highways were sabotaged, and pillboxes and bridges were destroyed ending in excellent combat results. The effect was tremendous as large Japanese forces were immobilized. During this period, the efforts of the 3rd War Area to capture Foochow were most outstanding.

Section 4
Counteroffensive and Japanese Surrender (See Map 12)

Victory in Western Hunan

With the completion of the China-India Road and the

availability of roads leading abroad, the equipment of the Chinese forces was greatly improved enabling the Chinese forces to make active preparations for the counteroffensive. To insure the traffic communications of the southern section of the Peiping-Hankow Railroads, the Hunan-Kwangsi Railroad and the Canton-Hankow Railroad, sabotage Chinese Air Force bases in western Honan, southern Shensi, northern Hupei and Chihchiang, Hunan and prevent the Chinese from making counteroffensive preparations, the Japanese started offensive actions in western Honan, northern Hupei and western Hunan in the spring of 1945. The four sieges laid by the forces of the 1st War Area led to the killing of many Japanese troops which had fled to Hsihsiako from western Honan. The Japanese were defeated first at Laohoko in western Hupei and later at Hsuehfeng Shan in western Hunan. As the Japanese were stopped at Ninghsiang and Yiyang, Chinese forces were able to move to Wuyang to attack their flanks. On 8 May, the Chinese Air Force rendered assistance in the counteroffensive which surrounded the enemy in a pincer movement. By 27 May, most of the enemy troops were annihilated with a small number in flight. 17 Japanese officers, 230 enlisted personnel, 347 horses, 24 guns of various calibers, 100 light and heavy machine gun, 1,333 rifles and 20 tons of supplies were captured.

Counteroffensive to Overcome the Enemy

During the Battle of Western Hunan, the Japanese forces already realized that their depleted combat effectiveness would not enable them to control China's vast areas. They, therefore, attempted to shorten their front lines, abandon secondary strong points and concentrate their forces so as to meet the counteroffensive of the Chinese forces. Seeing the morale of the Chinese forces had been boosted, that of the Japanese had deteriorated and that most of the Chinese forces had been equipped with U. S. weapons, the National Military Council ordered the 2nd Front Army to operate in the Tuyang Shan range for the capture of Nanning, a part of the 3rd Front Army advance along the Liuchow-Yishan Highway to take Liuchow and the main force of the 3rd Front Army to advance along the Canton-Kweilin Road and cross the Yuehcheng Shan range for the capture of Kweilin. As the Chinese forces recovered Nanning on 27 May, the Japanese realized that the situation was too far gone. On 29 June and 28 July Liuchow and Kweilin were recovered respectively. Within a period of three months, the Chinese forces covered 750 kilometers. After the Japanese forces in Kwangsi were mopped up, preparations were made for the strategic counteroffensive aiming at Canton and the wiping out of the Japanese in Kwangtung and Kwangsi. As the Chinese forces swung north, the Japanese knew the situation was hopeless. When Japan announced unconditional surrender on 10 August, the war finally came to an end.

Sino-U. S. Military Cooperation

In the spring of 1941, U. S. Congress passed the legislation on the Lend-Lease Act. In May, Lend Lease materials arrived from the Yunnan-Burma Road. By the end of November, the monthly tonnage rose from 4,000 to 15,000. On 1 August of the same year, the American Volunteer Group (AVG) was established to provide effective air defense to southwest China. In November, a military advisory group was sent to China to be in charge of equipping and training the new Chinese armed forces. By the time the Pacific War broke out, there were altogether twenty-six nations, known as the United Nations, fighting against the Germany-Italy-Japan Axis alliance. Generalissimo Chiang was appointed the supreme commander of the forces of the twenty-six nations in the China Theater (including Indo-China and Thailand). In March, 1942, the United States dispatched Gen. Joseph Stilwell to China to take command of all the U. S. forces and some Chinese forces in the China-Burma-India Theater. Gen. Stilwell was also appointed by Generalissimo Chiang as his chief of staff in the China Theater. In order to achieve closer coordination, the headquarters of the U. S. forces in the China Theater was situated in China's wartime capital Chungking. Each week, Gen. Stilwell or his representative participated in the conferences of the Chinese Supreme Command to review the weekly situation and the overall operation plans. Meanwhile, Gen. Chennault's Flying Tigers (AVG) was redesignated the U. S. 14th Air Force to continue fighting the Japanese from bases in China. Thus, the Sino-U. S. military cooperation became closer than ever.

In March, 1942 when the Japanese moved into Burma, the military situation in China became more difficult than ever. There was an acute shortage of war material, as the European Theater was given first priority on all the strategic war materials. China's communication with the outside world consisted of only one feeble air supply route over the Hump. The amount of materials that was brought in could only supply the 14th Air Force with the petroleum, bombs and ammunitions that it required. The materials so urgently needed by China could not be made available. This difficult situation remained until after January, 1943 when the air resupply over the Hump was stepped up.

In August, 1943, the Southeast Asia Allied Supreme Command was established with Admiral Sir Louis Mountbatten as the supreme commander and Gen. Joseph W. Stilwell his deputy. The military operations in the China Theater, however, remained under the command of Generalissimo Chiang. Gen. Stilwell continued to serve as the chief of staff directing the Chinese and the American forces in Burma. The R. A. F. and the U. S. A. F. in Burma were combined under the command of Gen. George Stratemeyer. In the China Theater, the Chinese-American Composite Wing was organized in Kweilin with Col. Morse. U. S. A. F. as the commander. The wing came under the unified direction of Gen. Chennault. Meanwhile, the monthly tonnage flown over the Hump rose to 20,000 tons. Additionally, air bases for the Flying Fortresses were constructed in Szechuan and Yunnan preparatory to the U. S. bombing of Japan proper.

In October, 1943, in accordance with the Allied pre-arranged plans, Chinese forces in India moved along the front section of the Ledo Road into the Hukawng Valley to link up with the U. S. Jungle Forces. Having crossed the hazardous jungle terrain, Chinese forces captured Mitkyina airfield. In the meantime, Chinese Expeditionary Forces crossed the Salween River from Pao Shan in Yunnan to take part in the northern Burma offensive.

A soldier of exceedingly strong will, Gen. Stilwell had a strong sense of responsibility. During his stay in China, he contributed greatly to the defeat of Japan. Unfortunately, he lacked a profound understanding of the Chinese Communists and was misled by the Communists and their fellow-travelers. In October, 1944, he was relieved of his command

by the U. S. Government and recalled. In order to facilitate
subsequent operations, the China-Burma-India Theater was
divided into the India-Burma Theater and the China Theater.
The India-Burma Theater was commanded by Gen. Saltan,
while the U. S. forces in the China Theater was commanded
by Gen. Wedemeyer. Gen. Wedemeyer arrived in China on
31 October, 1944 and succeeded Stilwell as Generalissimo
Chiang's chief of staff. Chinese and U.S. forces were deployed along the Chindwin River. The offensive began after
the monsoon season was over. On 27 January, 1945, they
linked up with the Chinese Expeditionary Forces at Mongyu
and cleared the China-India Road. On 30 March, a linkup
was effected with the British forces at Kyaukme.

In the winter of 1944, the Chinese Army General Headquarters in the China Theater was established to coordinate
with the Allied forces. Located in Kunming with four front
armies under its command, its missions were to organize,
train and command the U.S.-equipped forces and to fight
final decisive battles against the Japanese forces on the China
Mainland.

In January, 1945 when the Ledo Road was completed,
land transportation was increased. Pipelines moved 54,000
tons of petroleum each month. Thus, China was able to
equip rapidly thirty-five infantry divisions and a number of
special troops. According to Marshall's report, the materials
provided to China were worth US$500 million excluding
transportation charges. However, when compared with the
U. S. assistance to other countries, what China received was
not much. Indeed, China could take justifiable pride when
one considers her vast contributions in the long and bitter
war fought by the Allies in Asia.

Japanese Surrender (See Map 12)

In the summer of 1945, under the Chinese and American converging attack, the Japanese showed signs of collapse. On 26 July, the Chinese, American and British leaders issued the following declaration at Potsdam:

"An ultimatum is issued to Japan demanding her unconditional surrender; otherwise, we shall bring to bear the total strength of the armies, navies and air forces of the three countries for the final destruction of the Japanese military forces and Japan proper."

Meanwhile, an emergency conference was held in Japan. At one time, Japan attempted to refuse to surrender and stated, "The Japanese Government has decided to fight to the bitter end." Later, on 5 and 7 August, U. S. A. F. dropped atomic bombs on Hiroshima and Nagasaki. Plans were made to coordinate the Allied and the Chinese forces for a major counteroffensive in South China. On 9 August, Soviet Russia took advantage of the opportunity to declare war on Japan. Knowing her fate of final defeat was irrevocable, Japan again broadcasted requesting the United Nations for more lenient terms so that she could stop all hostilities. The Allies flatly refused Japan's request and reiterated the implications of an unconditional surrender. The so-called unconditional surrender did not imply the destruction nor the enslavement of the Japanese people.

On 10 August, the Japanese Government's surrender text was transmitted to the Allies through Switzerland and Sweden in which Japan expressed her willingness to accept the provisions of the Potsdam Declaration and to surrender unconditionally to the United Nations. Her only request was the retention of the emperor as the titular head. On

15 August, the Chinese Foreign Ministry formally received the Japanese surrender text. On the same day, Generalissimo Chiang cabled Neiji Okamura, Japanese supreme commander in China instructing him on the six surrender principles.[29] He also designated Gen. Ho Ying-chin, commander-in-chief of the Chinese Army, to receive the Japanese surrender in the name of the Supreme Commander of the China Theater. At the same time, he broadcasted to China and to the world expressing the hope that peoples throughout the world, regardless of their locality or color, unite as members of a family in order to develop the spirit of mutual understanding and mutual respect and to establish the relationship of mutual confidence and mutual trust so that this war might become the last world war. With regard to Japan, China would bear no past grievances, seek no revenge. She would employ the strength as she did in the war to engage

---

[29] Six Surrender Principles:

The six surrender principles were as follows:

(1) The Japanese Government has officially announced unconditional surrender.

(2) The Japanese commander will order Japanese forces to end all military actions and dispatch a representative to Yushan where he will receive his orders from General Ho Ying-chin, Commander-in-Chief of the Chinese Army.

(3) Upon termination of military actions, the Japanese forces may retain temporarily their weapons and equipment and may maintain their present status. They will maintain local order and traffic communications while awaiting the orders of General Ho Ying-chin, Commander-in-Chief of the Chinese Army.

(4) All the Japanese aircraft and ships and craft will remain in their present positions. However, Japanese ships and craft will assemble at Ichang and Shashih.

(5) No facilities or materiel will be destroyed.

(6) The Japanese commander and his subordinate commanders are held personally responsible for the execution of the abovementioned orders. He will also make an immediate reply to the above.

in the arduous post war tasks march onto the road of democracy and cooperation in order to maintain permanent peace in the world.

On 21 August, eight Japanese peace emissaries headed by Takeo Imai flew to Chihchiang, Hunan to make necessary arrangement with Hsiao Yi-su, the representative of Chinese Army Commander-in-Chief Ho Ying-chin who is responsible for the overall Japanese surrender.

On 3 September Japan formally surrendered to the Allies on board the U.S.S. Missouri in Tokyo Bay. On 9 September, Gen. Ho Ying-chin, on behalf of the Supreme Commander, officiated at the Japanese surrender ceremony of the China Theater in Nanking. Immediately after the signing of the surrender text, Gen. Ho handed the Supreme Commander's order No. 1 to Gen. Okamura stipulating that all the Japanese army, navy and air forces in the China Theater (including Taiwan, Penghu and area north of 16° lat. of Vietnam and excluding Manchuria) receive orders and surrender themselves to the designated Chinese commanders responsible for the acceptance of the surrender. At that time, the Japanese surrendered a force of 1,283,240. Meanwhile, to expedite the surrender arrangements, the entire nation was divided into 16 surrender zones. The senior local military commanders accepted the Japanese surrender.

Upon completion of the surrender plans, the Chinese Army General Headquarters ordered the various war areas and the front armies to advance to the strategic localities by air, land, water and foot. Upon arrival of the Chinese forces, the Japanese forces were assembled and disarmed.

From 11 September to mid-October, 1945, most of the Japanese forces were assembled and disarmed. The entire operation moved smoothly except in North China, Shantung, and northern Kiangsu where the Chinese Communists interrupted. The operation was not completed until February, 1946. The total number of Japanese and Korean officers, men and national stood at 2,129,826, assembled in various major cities awaiting transportation. From October, 1945 to June, 1946 all the Japanese in China were repatriated with the assistance of the United States Navy.

Chinese Communist Insubordination and Plunder

Upon receipt of Japan's declaration of surrender on 10 August, the National Military Council of the Chinese Government immediately instructed all armed forces in the country to wait for orders pertaining to the acceptance of surrender in accordance with Allied agreements. In an order to the 18th Army Group, the council specifically instructed the following:

"All its units were to remain where they were until further orders. Those committed to combat operations were to abide by orders of their respective war area commanders. Under no circumstances were they to make any unauthorized move."

But the Communists flatly disobeyed the council's order, and Chu Teh, in the name of the "Yenan Headquarters," issued the following "order".

"As Japan has declared her unconditional surrender, the Allies will, on the basis of the Potsdam Declaration, consult on the surrender measures. Hence, I issue the following order to all the armed forces in the 'liberated areas.'

"(1) In accordance with the provisions of the Potsdam Declaration, any armed force fighting the Japanese, may deliver an ultimatum to the enemy force and its command agency in the vicinity of cities and traffic communications centers giving the time at which they will turn over all their arms to the Chinese combat units concerned. Upon being disarmed, they will be protected in accordance with the regulations governing the treatment of prisoners of war.

"(2) Any armed force fighting the Japanese in the 'various liberated areas' may deliver an ultimatum to the puppet regime in its vicinity demanding its defection and acceptance of its reorganization or discharge before the signing of the Japanese surrender. After this time, they must turn in their arms.

"(3) In the event the Japanese or the puppet regime armed forces refuse to surrender and turn in their arms, all the armed forces fighting the Japanese in the 'various liberated areas' should destroy them with determination.

"(4) Our forces have the right to dispatch troops receive, and occupy any Japanese or puppet regime controlled cities, towns and traffic centers so as to exercise military control and maintain order. Further more, special commissioners will be appointed to take charge of the administration in the various areas. Any person engaged in sabotage or resistance will be dealt with in the same manner as a traitor."

On 11 August, the "Yenan Headquarters" again issued six orders directing the movement of the Communist forces as follows:

(1) For the sake of coordinating with the Soviet Red Army's entry into China:

1. Troops under Lu Cheng-tsao were to move from Shansi and Suiyuan into Chahar and Jehol.
2. Troops under Chang Hsueh-shih were to move from Hopei and Chahar into Jehol and Liaoning.
3. Troops under Wan Yi were to move from Shantung and Hopei into Liaoning.
4. Troops under Li Yun-chang were to move from Hopei and Jehol into Liaoning and Kirin.
5. Korean Communist troops were also to enter the Northeastern Provinces.

(2) For the sake of coordinating with the Outer Mongolian troop's entry into Inner Mongolia, Suiyuan, Chahar, and Jehol:

1. Troops under Ho Lung were to move northward from Suiyuan.
2. Troops under Nieh Yung-tseng were to move northward from Chahar and Jehol.

(3) All troops in Shansi were to be placed under Ho Lung's unified command and to occupy the areas along the Tatung-Pucheng Railroad and in the Fen River valley.

(4) In order to seize or sever all principal arteries of communication in the country, all Communist troops along the Peiping-Liaoning Railroad, the Peiping-Hankow Railroad, the Tatung-Puchow Railroad, the Chengting-Taiyuan Railroad, the Paitsing Railroad, the Taotsing Railroad, the Tientsin-Pukow Railroad, the Lungchow-Haichow Railroad, the Canton-Hankow Railroad, the Shanghai-Nanking Railroad, the Nanking-Wuhu Railroad, the Shanghai-Hangchow Railroad, the Canton-Kowloon Railroad, the Chaochow-

Swatow Railroad and on both sides of principal arteries of communication in other liberated areas were to go actively into attack.

On 14 August, Chu Teh and Peng Teh-huai cabled Generalissimo Chiang openly rejecting the order issued by the Supreme Command to the Communist 18th Army Group. On 15 August, Chu Teh, the self-styled commander-in-chief of the "Anti-Japanese Forces in the China Liberated Areas" cabled Okamura demanding the surrender of the Japanese forces to the "Red Army." However, his demand was rejected by Okamura. On 17 August, Chu Teh presented a set of six demands to the Government:

(1)　In accepting the surrender of Japanese and puppet forces and in concluding agreements or treaties for the purpose, the Government should consult first the Anti-Japanese People's Armed Forces in "liberated areas" in order to reach unanimity of views.

(2)　All Anti-Japanese People's Armed Forces in "liberated areas" and in occupied areas should have the right, under the terms of the Potsdam Declaration and the procedure as laid down by the Allies, to accept the surrender of Japanese and puppet troops and to take over their arms and supplies.

(3)　The Anti-Japanese People's Armed Forces in "liberated areas" and in occupied areas should have the right to send delegates to take part in accepting Japanese surrender and in administering local affairs after the surrender.

(4)　All Anti-Japanese People's Armed Forces in "liberated areas" should have the right to designate representatives to the peace conference and to United Nations meetings.

(5) Generalissimo Chiang should be asked to stop the civil war by assigning troops in "liberated areas" to accept the surrender of Japanese and puppet troops they have surrounded in their areas, and by assigning "Kuomintang troops" to accept the surrender of Japanese troops they have surrounded in their own areas.

(6) A multi-party conference, including also non-partisan representatives, should be called at once to form a democratic coalition government to effect democratic political and economic reforms.

The purpose behind Chu Teh's six demands is abundantly clear. Militarily, the Communists were to take unauthorized action to disarm the Japanese and the puppet troops, and to occupy and disrupt lines of communication, so as to extend their area of control and enable them to join forces with the Soviet and Outer Mongolian troops then pouring into the Northeastern Provinces and Jehol, Chahar and Suiyuan Provinces. Politically, by demanding the formation of a "coalition government," they were to support their military moves with political warfare and subversive activities against the Government.

Chinese Communist Obstruction in the Acceptance of Japanese Surrender

The 41-day negotiation in Chungking riveted the nation's attention and gave the Communist troops an opportunity to carry out their practical actions. According to an account in the October 17 issue of the Communist Hsinhua Daily News, the Communists seized as many as 200 cities and towns during the month from 11 September to 11 October, and brought under their control numerous points along the Tsingtao-Tsinan Railroad, the Tientsin-Pukow Railroad, the Lungchow-Haichow Railroad, the Peiping-Suiyuan Railroad, the Peiping-Liaoning Railroad, the Tehchow-Shihchiachuang Railroad and the Taotsing Railroad. They were thus able to disrupt the principal communication systems in North and Central China. They threatened shipping along the coast from Shanhaikwan in the north to Hangchow Bay in the south; along the Yellow River from Hwanchu to Wuchih; along the Yangtze River in Kiangsu and Anhwei Provinces; and also along the Grand Canal, which links up Tungchow east of Peiping in the north with Hangchow in the south.

It was under these circumstances that, on 11 September, Government troops began the acceptance of Japanese surrender in various parts of the country. Altogether 1,255,000 Japanese troops laid down their arms in 11 areas within 30 days. These were later all repatriated to Japan in accordance with stipulations of the Allied Headquarters. But the Chinese Communists detained nearly 30,000 Japanese troops they had disarmed in Chahar, Hopei, Shantung, and northern Kiangsu.

While obstructing the acceptance of Japanese surrender by Government troops, the Communists launched a vigorous anti-American campaign throughout the country.

Both the Chinese Government and the Chinese people had complete confidence in, and were greatly indebted to our American friends for their part in the combined operations against Japan during the war, and for helping us to accept the Japanese surrender after the war. But the Communists charged that by assisting the Government in its acceptance of

Japanese surrender in Tientsin, Chinhuangtao, Peitaiho, Tsingtao, and Yentai (Chefoo), the Americans were "interfering in China's internal affairs."

The Communists alleged that while Russian troops were being withdrawn from the Northeast Provinces, American troops were being landed in North China to help the Government carry out its "anti-democratic policies." One purpose of this propaganda was to arouse public opinion in the United States to force the American Government to withdraw its troops from the China Theater. Another purpose was to accept Japanese surrender, especially to stop Government troops from entering the Northeast Provinces to restore Chinese sovereignty there.

While the campaign praising the Chinese Communists to the skies was sweeping over the world, the Communists cut lines of communication, breached the Yellow River dykes, dynamited or dismantled many mines in Hopei, Shansi and Honan Provinces, burned or damaged factories, razed to the ground a large number of villages and rural towns, perpetrated massacres, forced able-bodied men into their armed forces, expanded their area of control, and issued and forced upon the people vast quantities of "Anti-Japanese Currency Notes" and "Border Area Currency Notes," thereby undermining the nation's monetary system. All these actions aimed to obstruct the acceptance of the Japanese surrender.

Victorious Return to the Nation's Capital

In order to expedite the completion of the turnover, the National Government ordered the mobilization all the available means of waters and air transportation, so as to move 80,000 well-trained and well-equipped crack Chinese units to the key localities in North China. By the end of 1945, important cities in North China such as Peiping, Tientsin, Paoting, Taiyuan and Chinan were all turned over to the Chinese forces.

On 30 April, 1946, the National Government formally promulgated an order for its return to the nation's capital in Nanking. On 4 May, Chairman Chiang arrived in Nanking by air. On 5 May, the National Government officially resumed its functions in Nanking.

CHAPTER SIX

Institution of Constitutional Government and Suppression of Chinese Communists

Section 1
Passive Military Operations under International Settlement

Soviet Intrigues

The Second World War came to an end when Germany and Japan surrendered unconditionally in 1945. Immediately, democratic nations began demobilization to meet the fervent desire of their peoples for peace. In order to realize their dream of "peaceful co-existence," they went so far as to yield to the demands of Soviet Russia. Geographically, they hoped to achieve a political buffer zone between the powers in Eurasia and Soviet Russia.

Little did they realize that the ultimate objective of the Communist bloc was the communization of the entire world. Taking full advantage of the post-war situation, the neutral strategy of "peaceful co-existence," and the lack of will to fight on the part of the democratic nations, Soviet Russia proceeded to divide Germany, subvert Poland and Czechoslovakia and the Balkan nations for the control of southeastern Europe. In the Orient, she created two Koreas and two Vietnams and actively engaged in infiltrating Indonesia,

Malaya and the Philippines. Of course, she did not relax
her grip on China, a nation on which she. had laid her eyes
in the past decades. Her policy had been based on Lenin's
statement that "the shortest route from Moscow to Paris
is from Peiping via Calcutta." Therefore, at the Teheran
Conference and the Yalta Conference, Soviet Russia created
opportunities to divide Outer Mongolia and dispatched
forces to Manchuria to set up the bases for large-scale rebellions. All these are their detour strategy to communize the
world. Their aggressive and intriguing designs on China were
most active and exposed.

The unconditional surrender of Germany and Japan did
not mean truly the end of the Second World War. On the
contrary, it meant crises on the East Asia Continent and
the Western Pacific. Starting with the Northeast Provinces,
Soviet Russia stepped up the development of the crises.

While refusing a "third party" to enter the Northeast
Provinces and hoping the Chinese Government would ask
Moscow directly to mediate so as to form a "coalition government" with the Communist Party as well as the other
parties participating, Soviet Russia's objective was to gradually turn China into her satellite and to achieve bloodless
control of entire China.

Therefore, Soviet Russia dispatched troops to the Northeast Provinces and delayed the withdrawal to provide cover
for the Chinese Communists so that the Chinese Communists could infiltrate Manchuria, occupy a favorable position,
and receive the equipment surrendered by the Japanese
forces to grow in strength. Such an intrigue had a geographical advantage. As the Northeast Provinces were con-
tiguous with Soviet Russia, the Chinese Communists and

the Russians worked closely with the latter providing direct support to the former. Speaking of the military operations in the Northeast, there were only two routes leading from interior China to the Northeast. The overland route started from Peiping through Chinhuangtao to Mukden. This railroad corridor was a narrow and long strip in the entire length vulnerable on both sides. The sea route extended from the landing on the port of Dairen at the foot of Liaotung Peninsula. Under pretext, Russian forces occupied Dairen and its vicinities closing the sea route to Mukden hinterland and refusing the landing of Government forces. Thus, the Government forces were compelled to travel over the narrow corridor on land in the operations in the Northeast exposing themselves in long distance marches along the railroads. On the one hand, they continued to fight war of attrition against the Communist forces. On the other hand, forces had to be drawn from the interior to maintain the rear area lines of communications. Thus, large bodies of troops were tied down and worn out in the rear areas. In order to keep up the military operations in the Northeast, sizeable forces had to be moved north through Shanhaikwan. Again, the military forces required for pacification purposes were reduced in strength. Communist remnants in the interior had a respite to grow in strength. Speaking of the overall situation, Chinese Government forces found themselves in an unfavorable geographical location which led to their collapse in the Northeast. As the operations in the Northeast met reverses, the overall situation took a sharp turn for worse. Russian entry into the Northeast, blockade of Dairen, cover for the Communist forces, and preventing Government forces from accepting the surrender played decisive roles.

Chinese Communist Full-Scale Rebellion to Interrupt Japanese Surrender

An account of the general rebellion of the Chinese Communists is given in the following sections. At the time of Japan's announcement of unconditional surrender, the Chinese Government, after eight long years of arduous war again Japan was making plans for the takeover. Communist Chu Teh issued seven rebellious orders completely discarding their commitment to obey the military chain of command and took independent actions. In Shansi Province, they rapidly occupied the areas from which the Japanese forces had withdrawn, and surrounded the narrow Taiyuan area under the jurisdiction of the Central Government. In Chahar Province, they took over from the Russians and occupied the provincial capital of Kalgan. In other areas, the Chinese Communists gradually expanded the scattered guerilla areas controlling many sectors in Shensi, Hopei, Shantung, Jehol and northern Kiangsu and harassing and attacking Government forces in order to obstruct the acceptance of Japanese surrender. Such actions spread like bush fire into full-scale rebellion. Directly the major cities of Peiping-Tientsin and Nanking-Shanghai were threatened as the fire went unchecked.

When the war was concluded, the Chinese Communists claimed to have 470,000 men under arms. But if the Government had successfully launched its program of demobilization, reconstruction, and rehabilitation, the people would have begun to live and work in peace again. Then even if the Communists should have resorted to violence, they would have been forsaken by the people and thus obliged to adopt instead lawful methods in pursuing their political activities. If, on the contrary, the Government had elected to suppress the Communist insurrection by forces, it could have won just as it had done during the fifth campaign ten years previously in southern Kiangsi.

Meanwhile, Chairman Chiang had the assurance and confidence to stabilize the overall situation. He, therefore, decided to meet the needs of the people and the nation. He had given much thought to formulating the policy of peace and reconstruction, and aimed at the establishment of an independent, sovereign, modern, democratic and unified nation. He sought world peace and stability. As he had in mind peace and reconstruction, he did all he could to accommodate the Communists. However, the Communists took advantage of this opportunity to grow in strength.

The Communists also knew if the Government had chosen either of the two alternatives of peace or war, it would have meant the destruction of the Communists. Under Moscow's instigation, the Communists used "peaceful coexistence" at home and abroad to cover up their armed insurrection which they used to help their political offensive. Meanwhile, they manufactured a preposterous logic abroad condemning any measures taken by the Central Government to prevent Communist armed insurrection as the match to ignite "civil war." They used such a logic to frighten the world, for "civil war" constituted a threat to world peace.

Under the influence of such a logic, the United States considered that the key to China's unification did not lie in military power to prevent Communist insurrection but in political compromise with the Communists to form a "coalition government."

In August, 1945, U.S. Ambassador Patrick Hurley made such efforts. After 41-days of political consultation, the following agreement was reached with the Communists:

"Concerted efforts were to be made—under the leadership of Chairman Chiang and on the basis of peace, democracy, solidarity, and unity—to ensure lasting cooperation; resolutely to avoid civil war, to build up China as an independent, free, rich, and strong nation, and fully to implement the Three People's Principles. As advocated by Chairman Chiang, the nationalization of the armed forces, political democratization, and equal and legal status for all political parties were to be the road to take toward peaceful national reconstruction."

However, on the military side, the Communists advanced the following strong demands:

(1) Communists and local autonomous armed organizations should participate in the National Government's National Military Council and all its affiliated agencies.

(2) After the reorganization, all the officers at various levels will continue to command their original units. The discharged officers will be given training by the Government.

(3) All the military units in the "liberated areas" will be reorganized into the local militia.

"The purpose of this request was not the nationalization of the armed forces but a measure to legalize Communist private military forces. Knowing this to be the stumbling block in the problem of national unification, Chairman Chiang considered that: "Within the territory of the Republic of China, there should be no private military forces. No political party should retain military forces. Only when armed forces are not commanded by individual interests or for individuals nor guided by the selfish desires of a political party, can the nation's unification be consolidated."

Politically, the Communists made the following demands:

(1) That the Government appoint the Communist nominees for provincial governors and members of the provincial governments of "Shensi-Kansu-Ninghsia Border Area," Jehol, Chahar, Hopei, Shantung and Shansi Provinces.

(2) That the Government appoint the Communist nominees for the lieutenant governors and members of the provincial governments of Suiyuan, Honan, Kiangsu, Anhwei, Hupei and Kwangtung Provinces.

(3) That the Government appoint the Communist nominees for deputy mayors of Peiping, Tientsin and Tsingtao.

(4) That the Government accept the Communist nominees to serve in the administrative organizations in the Northeast.

Obviously, the aim was not political democracy, but the legalized distribution of the Communist-controlled areas. Hence, forty-one days of laborious political consultation, in reality, was fruitless.

The 41-day negotiation riveted the nation's attention and gave the Communist troops an opportunity to screen the real actions in the Communist insurrection. From the time the political consultation began on 14 August to 11 October, the Communists seized as many as 200 cities and towns, and brought under their control numerous points along the

Tsingtao-Chinan Railroad, the Tientsin-Pukow Railroad, the Lungchow-Haichow Railroad, the Peiping-Suiyuan Railroad, the Peiping-Liaoning Railroad, the Tehchow-Shihchiachuang Railroad, the Peiping-Hankow Railroad, and the Taotsing Railroad. They cut lines of communication. They destroyed railroads in North China, not once but several hundred times. They breached the Yellow River dikes to inundate the surrounding country. In Honan Province alone, they flooded an area of several hundred square kilometers. They dynamited or dismantled many mines in Hopei, Shansi, and Honan Provinces. They put torch to or otherwise seriously damaged numerous factories. In Shansi Province alone, they destroyed more than 500 of them. They razed to the ground a large number of villages and rural towns in Kiangsu, Shantung and Honan Provinces. They perpetrated massacres, of which the most barbarous case occurred in Kalgan, north of Peiping. They forced able-bodied men into their armed forces and spared no one between 15 and 45 years of age. They issued and forced upon the people vast quantities of "Anti-Japanese Currency Notes" and "Border Area Currency Notes." In Chahar, Hopei, Shansi, Shantung and northern Kiangsu, they illegally surrounded and disarmed some 30,000 Japanese troops and refused to release them. They obstructed the acceptance of the Japanese surrender and the demobilization and return of millions of people and soldiers to their homes. They intercepted the Government Forces heading for North China and Central China resulting in the pacifying operations at Shangtang, Changho, Kweisui, Paotou and northern Kiangsu. The fighting at Changho, in particular, cost the Government forces heavy losses. It affected the Japanese surrender in Peiping and

Tientsin and led to the subsequent unfavorable situation that the Government forces found themselves in North China.

While the Chinese Communists staged insurrection on the one hand, they stepped up anti-U.S. propaganda on the other charging the U.S. assistance to the Government in its acceptance of Japanese surrender in Tientsin, Chinhuangtao, Peitaiho, Tsingtao, and Yentai, (Chefoo) as "interfering in China's internal affairs." The Communist alleged that while Russian troops were being withdrawn from the Northeast Provinces, American troops were being landed in North China to help the Government carry out its "anti-democratic policies." Their purpose was to arouse public opinion in the United States so that the United States had to withdraw its troops from the China Theater.

Marshall in China for Peace Settlement

As a result of his efforts in the political consultation, Gen. Hurley thoroughly understood the Communist intrigues and the mistakes of the American policy toward China. He realized that the efforts toward the formation of a "coalition government" would only help the Communist to undermine Chairman Chiang's power and deprive the United States of a stanch anti-Communist ally. Upon return to the United States, he strongly recommended that the United States Government change its policy. However, Pres. Truman decided to adopt the policy of "peaceful and democratic ways to achieve unification of China." Thus, Special Envoy George C. Marshall was sent to China on 15 December, 1945.

Overly believing in the Communist propaganda, Marshall regarded the Communists as "truly democratic, political workers" and "just agrarian reformers." Upon arrival in China, he proposed the following to the National Government:

(1)　That the National Government and the Chinese Communists cease hostilities.

(2)　That the Communist forces be integrated into the Government forces at a ratio in accordance with the relative strength.

(3)　That a nationwide conference be called including the Kuomintang, the Communist Party and the various independent parties in order to end the Kuomintang period of political tutelege and to form a coalition government.

Meanwhile, Chou En-lai who was dispatched by the Communists to Chungking, did his best to win Marshall's friendship and provide distorted views which favored the Communists. He even made use of "neutralism" by exploiting the so-called "Democratic Alliance" leaders such as Chang Lan and Lo Lung-chi. Thus, Marshall was further deceived. Later, Gen. Wedemeyer was recalled and Leighton J. Stuart substituted Hurley as the U.S. ambassador in China.

After six meetings, held between 7 and 10 January, 1946, A Committee of Three, composed of a Government delegate, a Communist delegate, and Marshall, agreed on a cease-fire order. On 10 January, both the Government and the Communists issued the order to their respective commanders in the field. The order became effective at noon, 13 January. An Executive Headquarters was established in Peiping dispatching teams to the various areas to carry out cease-fire order.

The Political Consultative Conference was convened the

day the cease-fire order was issued. In his opening address, Chairman Chiang stated with all sincerity.

"The Government is prepared to accept any resolution that may be reached at this conference so long as it helps the nation's reconstruction, promotes the people's welfare, and aids the progress of democracy."

At the same time Chairman Chiang announced that the Government had decided to take adequate measures to safeguard people's freedom, to respect the legal status of political parties, to implement the program of local self-government, to hold general elections, and to release political prisoners.

The Government delegate was the first to propose the broadening of the Government's base. He announced that before the convocation of the National Assembly, the Government would appoint members of other political parties and non-partisan leaders to serve together with Kuomintang members in the State Council and the Executive Yuan (Cabinet) as preparatory steps toward constitutional rule.

After 21 days of deliberation, the Political Consultative Conference reached five agreements.

On Government reorganization, it was decided that a transition stage coalition government be adopted before the convocation of the National Assembly. Government functions would be decided by the 40 members of the State Council who were represented by the various political parties.

On the program of peaceful national reconstruction, the Three People's Principles should be observed as the supreme guide in the nation's reconstruction. The entire nation should unite under Chairman Chiang and work for the realization of a united, free, democratic New China. Chairman Chiang's views on political democratization, the nationalization of all armed forces, and an equal and legal status for all political parties, should be regarded as indispensable steps toward peaceful national reconstruction. Political means should be used to resolve political disputes in order to ensure peaceful development of the nation as a whole.

On military affairs the important points were that the armed forces should belong to the State, no political party or faction should be allowed to engage in activities, overt or covert, among the armed forces. The National Military Council should be reorganized into a Ministry of National Defense under the Executive Yuan. In this ministry, there should be set up a Military Planning and Development Committee to be composed of representative from various relevent groups in the country. All the nation's armed forces, including Central (Government) forces and Communist forces, should be unified and reorganized into from 50 to at most 60 divisions in all.

On the National Assembly, it would be convened on 5 May, 1946, and the function of the first National Assembly would be to adopt a national constitution. The number of regional and vocational delegates would remain at 1,200 as previously suggested. The number of delegates from political parties and of prominent civil leaders would be increased to 700. 150 additional regional and vocational delegates would be allocated to Taiwan and the Northeast Provinces.

On the proposed revision to the draft constitution, the Political Consultative Conference proposed 12 principles for revising the Draft Constitution. The conference also decided that a Draft Constitution Re-examination Committee should be formed to prepare a new text in accordance with the proposed principles of revision, and that views from various quarters should be taken into consideration during the revision.

On the surface, the Communists seemed to cooperate. Marshall, too, thought that the first phase of his mission had come to a successful end. Soon afterwards, he returned to Washington on 13 March to report to the State Department.

Reorganization of Chinese Armed Forces and Communist Breach of Truce Agreement

In reality, after Marshall's return to the United States, the Communists no longer honored the cease-fire order refusing to carry out all the agreements.

The central military organizations, on the other hand, seriously carried out the above agreements, 17 independent agencies under the National Military Council and the Ministry of War were reorganized into the Ministry of National Defense in June 1946. After reorganization, the strength of the Ministry itself, the General Staff, and the General Headquarters of the Army, Navy, Air Force and Combined Service Forces was reduced from 24,000 to 9,000 officers and 5,000 enlisted men. Armed Forces began to undergo reorganization. 38 Army Groups were reduced to 24; 7 Army Groups were reorganized into 7 reorganized corps. 89 corps and 242 divisions (of which 3 were Communist divisions) were reduced to 36 corps and 108 divisions (of which 6 corps and 18 divisions were Communist units) in three stages, 55 corps and 143 divisions were reorganized into 55 reorganized divisions and 143 reorganized brigades. 4 corps and 7 divisions were deactivated. The Youth Corps which had 3 corps and 9 divisions were reorganized into 6 divisions. The nation's advance forces totalling 700,000 men were integrated into local militia and reorganized divisions, 1 replacement group and 22 replacement regiments. 600,000 puppet forces which were integrated were discharged or reorganized. The remaining 135,000 were organized into 10 columns and 10 independent groups. Of the 210,000 puppet forces in the Northeast and 80,000 "self-awakening" forces, 100,000 were integrated into the Government and the remainder was integrated into the provincial militia in the Northeast. Additionally, 180,000 officers were organized into 29 officers' group and 3 direct subordinate battalions ready to be discharged, resettled and transferred. The strength of the armed forces was reduced from 6 million to 4 million. On the contrary, the Communists did not carry out the reorganization. Instead, they expanded their forces from 500,000 to 800,000. Furthermore they organized 400,000 militia and enticed the discharged Government officers and men and members of the puppet forces to join them.

On the other hand, Russia was merely exploiting the American mediation to further her own schemes of "neutral tactics." In the first place, even though she had turned over the arms of more than a million Japanese and puppet troops to the Chinese Communists, the latter would need more than a year to replenish their numbers and to complete their training before they could be ready for an all-out rebellion. Russia, therefore, sought to take advantage of American mediation to gain the needed time for the Chinese Communists. In the second place, she not only tried to rupture Sino-American relations, but actually kept an even larger objective in mind, i. e. eventually to strangle the mediation altogether.

When Soviet troops evacuated from Changchun on 23 January, 1946, Chinese Communist troops immediately moved in. When the Communists attacked Government troops, the latter, being bound by the cease-fire order, could not resist, much less counterattack, and had to move away to avoid clashes. By this time, the Chinese Communists, with the support of Soviet forces, had further extended their rebellion over wider areas in the Northeast Provinces, making it impossible for the cease-fire teams to operate.

The Communists concentrated their troops at Szepingchieh to block Government troops moving northward from Mukden on take-over duties and brought on a fierce battle which raged for a week. The Communist troops under Lin Piao, said to number 300,000 were routed by Government forces. More than half of the Communist effectives became casualties. The rest fled in disorder toward Harbin and Suifenho in the north. Government forces moved up from Szepingchieh and entered Changchun on 23 May. Government troops, ordered to push on along the Chinese Eastern Railway with Harbin as their objective, met with practically no resistance. This was the most decisive battle since the Government's fifth campaign in southern Kiangsi in 1934. On 21 May, Chairman Chiang flew to Mukden to receive the frontline reports. It was believed that the Communists were practically vanquished once and for all after the terrific beating they received barring international complications.

Second Marshalls visit in China to Mediate

Meanwhile, Special Envoy Marshall rushed to China on 18 April, 1946 to make renewed efforts in mediation.

Honoring the mediation of a friendly nation and giving the Communists a chance to awaken, the National Government issued a second cease-fire order on 6 June, in compliance with Marshall's suggestion. Government pursuit units which had already crossed the Little Sungari River and were deployed near Shuangcheng were ordered to withdraw to the south bank of the Sungari River to assume the defensive. Meanwhile, Chairman Chiang announced: "I have just issued an order to all Government troops in the Northeast Provinces to cease attack, advance, or pursuit as from noon of 7 June for a period of 15 days so as to give the Chinese Communists another chance to fulfill their obligations under the various agreements thus far concluded. This does not prejudice the Government's right to re-establish Chinese authority in these provinces in accordance with the Sino-Soviet Treaty."

During the 10 days in question, repeated discussions on the basis of Marshall's proposals for the termination of hostilities in the Northeast Provinces were held between the Government, the American, and the Chinese Communist delegates. No decision, however, was reached. On 21 June, Chairman Chiang extended by eight days, i. e., until noon 30 June, his earlier order for the Government troops to withhold advance or attack. The Chinese Communists, however, made even stiffer demands, thus making it impossible for the delegates to reach any agreement.

Since the issuance of the second cease-fire order on 7 June, the military actions of the Chinese Communist forces not only defied the order but, on the contrary, greatly intensified their activities as the Government forces observed the cease-fire. They launched attacks and expanded their areas of control. In areas outside the Northeast Provinces, they launched co-ordinated offensive actions.

On the Jehol-Chahar front, despite the first cease-fire order, Communist troops entered Chihfeng. Again, despite the second cease-fire order, the Communists entered Chengteh. Yielding to Communist pressure, even the Executive Headquarters' cease-fire team itself at Kalgan had to withdraw on 20 September.

On the Shantung front, the Communists seized Tsaochuang on 9 June. The following day they occupied Tehchow, Taian, Kaomi, Chiaohsien Nanchuan, and Lantsun. In the meantime, they concentrated 50,000 troops on the outskirts of Tsingtao and 100,000 troops around Chinan.

On the Northern Kiangsu front, the Communists threw a force of 16 regiments against the city of Taihsing on 30 June and inflicted heavy losses on the Government troops there. After taking Taihsing, the Communists pushed on toward other towns on the north bank of the Yangtze River in Kiangsu to threaten the nation's capital Nanking. Government troops were forced to fight back in what was known as the Battle of Northern Kiangsu.

On the Shansi-Suiyuan front, despite the first cease-fire order, the Communists stormed and occupied Houma and Tsining. Even after the second cease-fire order, they seized 22 more counties including Wenshan, Su Hsien, Hsinchiang, Yutzu and Chiehsiu, steadily completing their encirclement of Tatung and Taiyuan. They provoked the Battle of Southern Shansi and the Battle of Tatung.

To prevent further extension of the scope of the conflict, the Government ordered the Communists to evacuate Chengteh in Jehol in order to protect Peiping and Tientsin, to evacuate the Tientsin-Pukow Railroad in order to restore the north-south main artery of communication, and to evacuate northern Kiangsu in order to safeguard Nanking, the national capital. But the Communists were obdurate and the Marshall mediation was rendered impotent.

The second cease-fire order turned out to be the Government forces' debacle in the Northeast. If the Government units near Shangcheng (less than 100 km. from Harbin) had not been halted but had pressed on forward toward Harbin, a city of considerable strategic military importance on the Chinese Eastern Railway, the Communist remnants in the northern part of the Northeast Provinces would have been liquidated. However, with the issuance of the second cease-fire order, the morale of Government troops in these provinces began to suffer as a result of the negative position in which they had been placed. With the drop in morale, our military initiative was also affected. The Communist forces took advantage of this respite to rest and replenish and receive Russian equipment. They turned from an inferior to a superior position. Thus, the die for the defeat of the Government forces in the Northeast provinces in the winter of 1948 was cast.

As the Executive Headquarters issued orders on 5 July, 1946 to the executive teams in various places to supervise the execution of the cease-fire, the Communists made an announcement on 7 July, 1946 denouncing U.S. policy toward China. Communist troops under Tsao Chih-fu called an anti-American mass meeting at Anping in Hopei Province. On 28 July, Communist forces southeast of Anping cordoned off the area. The following day, a U.S. Marine Corps convoy comprising 30 officers and men on their way from Tientsin to Peiping was ambushed by Communists. This resulted in killing 3 and wounding 17 of Americans.

On 3 September, 1946, Chairman Chiang accepted Marshall's suggestion of creating a Political Subcommittee of Five to discuss the questions concerning the Government's reorganization and the National Assembly. The Committee of Three would continue in the meantime its mediation effort in the military field. This was a great concession on the part of the Government, as it all along had been maintaining that military problems should be solved first. Under pretext of the Kalgan question, Communists reversed their position saying that if the Government did not cease its military action against the Communist troops in Kalgan and in its environs, the Communists would regard it as the declaration of an over-all rupture. Shortly afterwards, Chou En-lai left Nanking for Shanghai to avoid further discussion.

Chinese Armed Forces Recapturing Kalgan

Ever since Kalgan was turned over by the Russians to the Chinese Communists, the latter stayed in Kalgan to conspire closely with the former. Since the issuance of the second cease-fire order, the Communists became more arrogant than ever. In an effort to stabilize the situation in Peiping-Tientsin and North China and to avoid being threatened, the National Government ordered the 11th and the 12th War Areas to launch a converging attack on Kalgan via the eastern and western sections of the Peiping-Suiyuan Railroad. A part of the Northeastern Army was ordered to operate in the vicinity of Chihfeng, Weichang and Tushihko to respond to the attack on Kalgan.

On 29 September, the 11th War Area dispatched one corps to Yungning from Huaijou and two corps to advance along the Peiping-Suiyuan Railroad. On 30 September, Kangchuang was recovered. On 1 October, the forces moved to the right bank of the Wei River east of Huailai tying down the 50,000 main strength of the Communist forces under Nieh Yung-tseng. Heavy fighting lasted for 10 days, meanwhile, the 12th War Area assigned one brigade to stage a divisionary attack from Liangcheng toward Yuyu to hold the main force of Ho Lung. Two cavalry corps were concentrated in the attack and moved right in. On 8 October, Changpei in the rear of Kalgan was captured. On 11 October, an attack from the front and the rear with air support resulted in the capture of Kalgan. The Northeastern Army attacked and advanced from Lingyuan. On 14 October, units of the 11th and the 12th War Areas linked up at Hsuanhua. The Northeastern Army captured Yungning on 11 November to effect a linkup with the 11th War Area. Communist forces in Chahar were largely mopped up and the Russians were dealt heavy blows.

Failure of International Mediation

Hoping to end the stalemate, Marshall called on Chou En-lai on 9 October and asked him to return to Nanking to continue the negotiations. In reply, Chou presented the following demands:

(1) The Government should call off indefinitely its projected attack on Kalgan.

(2) The Chinese Communists and the Democratic League should have veto power in the State Council.

(3) The date of convocation of National Assembly and the number of delegates to the Assembly should be settled by the General Committee of the Political Consultative Conference.

Actually, the Chinese Communists gained all the time they needed for preparing their all-out insurrection; consequently their tactical smile to American mediation need no longer be worn.

Chou stated to Marshall in an accusing tone that the Chinese Communists could not agree to the American Government aiding the National Government (which Chou maliciously referred to as the Kuomintang Government) at a time of civil war, and that they were particularly opposed to the failure of American forces to withdraw from China as promised. Chou added that he had noticed that every time Marshall and Stuart issued any statement, it was invariably after the Communists had rejected some Government terms and never after the Government had rejected any Communist terms. Though Chou admitted that these American statements contained no obvious censure of the Communists, their timing, he asserted, had caused misunderstanding on the part of the general public. This signified the virtual termination of the peace talks and military mediation centered around Marshall.

In early October, when the Government forces were heading satisfactorily toward Kalgan, Marshall knew well enough that Kalgan was a Communist key locality. To ease the tension which was unfavorable to the political consultation, Marshall requested the Government forces for a cease-fire. Once again, Chairman Chiang accepted Marshall's suggestion and ordered a 10-day cease-fire. As the Chinese Communists showed no willingness to resume the negotiations after the expiry of the 10-day extension, Government troops retook Kalgan. This enraged Marshall who took actions to stop the delivery of all military supplies to the Chinese Government in the following eight months.

On 7 January, 1947, Marshall was named the U.S. Secretary of State. Before departure, he issued a statement saying that although his experiences ran counter to his ideals, he still felt that "there are liberal groups on the Chinese Communist side who regarded the Chinese people's interests more important than those of the Chinese Communists." Therefore, he was still of the opinion that the Chinese Government must resolve the Communist problems with political consultation.

The fact was after two years of experiments, political consultation met complete failure. The Chinese Government found itself in a most precarious position—restricted by domestic political consultations on the one hand and tied down by international mediation on the other. It not only abandoned the best opportunity to destroy the Chinese Communists but also suffered in morale as its will-to-fight was adversely affected by the on again and off again fighting. People's anti-Communist inclination wavered. Conversely, the Chinese Communists took full advantage of this opportunity to have a respite and to replenish their supplies. In their political strategy, they realized their intrigue of "economy affecting politics; politics undermining military operations." Militarily, they grew in strength, as they received Russian equipment and training in the Northeast Provinces. Under the cover of peace talks, they ambushed government forces and occupied territories. The overall situation became increasingly serious.

Constitutional Rule of the National Government

In the midst of Chinese Communist expansion and the

failure of Marshall's mediation, the Chinese Government scored an accomplishment of historical importance. It was the implementation of constitutional rule in China in 1947.

On 15 November, 1946, the National Assembly was convened. Despite Communist refusal to participate, the Presidium kept 9 seats for the Communist Party and the Democratic League. After 41-days of conference, the Constitution of the Republic of China was passed. It was resolved that the Constitution be promulgated on New Year's Day, 1947.

With the drafting of the Constitution completed, a coalition government was formed in conjunction with the Democratic Socialist Party and the Young China Party. With the implementation of the Constitution, delegates to the National Assembly were elected. The first nationwide election in the history of China was held. The National Assembly met in Nanking on 19 March, 1948 to elect a president and a vice president. Chairman Chiang made known his desire not to seek the presidency and expressed the hope that someone other than member of the Kuomintang be elected the nation's chief of state so as to present a new look of China to the world. However, the nation was unanimous in drafting him to serve as the president.

In spite of the fact that the nation was becoming engulfed by Communism, it elected an outstanding President to steer the nation onto the road of constitutional rule and to strive for the building of a New China.

Section 2
Full-Scale Communist Suppression Operations

Recovery of Yenan

In the spring of 1947 when the international mediation was brought to an end, the Chinese Communists greatly expanded their rebellious activities. The spread of Communism became more rampant. By 4 July, the Government issued orders for mobilization and full-scale Communist suppression.

The original operational guidance of the Supreme Command was for the Government Forces to assume defense first so as to destroy the Communists within the Shanhaikwan and restore the traffic communication of the Tientsin-Pukow Railroad, since the Communist forces have grown strong after their receipt of Russian equipment. It was hoped to consolidate North China and stabilize the areas south of the Yangtze River before shifting the forces to the Northeast Provinces. The operational objectives of the Government forces within the Shanhaikwan were directed at the Communist bases in Yenan, Shensi and Nanma, Shantung in order to deprive the Communist forces of their nerve centers and to demoralize them.

In early January, 1947, Chinese Communists massed their forces in northern Shensi in the northwest before the convocation of the Four Ministers' Conference in Moscow saying that they would launch the so-called "Northwest Spring Offensive." To gain the initiative, the Supreme Command employed three reorganized divisions on 18 February to mop up the scattered Communist forces in the pocket areas in northern Shensi, prepare for the attack on Yenan, destroy the nerve center of the insurrection, and mop up the Communist forces west of the Yellow River.

Subsequent to the mop up of the scattered Communists in early March, the Government forces organized many guerilla columns and conducted harassing attacks in conjunction with the local forces two days before the actual attack took place. These columns bore false designations which greatly exaggerated the actual strength, and conducted feint attacks so as to mislead the enemy.

By 14 March, two reorganized corps, organized as the left and right task forces staged a strategic coordinated attack with the support of powerful air on the Communist Shensi-Kansu-Ninghsia Border Area with Yenan as the enemy's nucleus. A decisive mop-up offensive was launched. The left task forces struck the primary position of the Communist constructed so-called "Northern Shensi Maginot Line" in a frontal attack. The right task forces avoided the Communists' frontal prepared positions and in an eastward turning movement headed for Yenan.

On 15 March, with air support, the right task forces penetrated through gaps and took Yenan on 19 March. Meanwhile, the left task forces also captured frontal positions and pushed toward Yenan in a converging attack. Communist remnants fled toward Shansi. Thus, Yenan, where the Communists had lived for 13 years, finally fell into the hands of Government forces. 16,000 Communist troops were killed or wounded and 10,000 were captured. Subsequently, key localities in northern Shensi were captured.

Victory of Nanma

On the Shantung front, Chang Shao-wu, commander of

the Communist Huaiyang Column, defected on 22 January. On 27 January, Ho Peng-chu surrendered with a force of 20,000. Their defections rapidly changed the situation in Kiangsu and Shantung. In one stroke, Government forces took key localities in central Shantung. Communist Liu Po-cheng's forces were driven to eastern Honan. Continued mop-up operations resulted in the restoration of the northern and southern sections of the Tientsin-Pukow Railroad and the eastern and western sections of the Chiaochow-Chinan Railroad. Thus, Communist Chen Yi's remnants were surrounded in the Chimon Shan area.

By early May Government forces continued to mop up Communist remnants in the Chimon Shan area in central Shantung. Unfortunately, our 74th Division in the deep advance was surrounded by the Communists in Menglianku. After three days of heavy fighting, the entire division from its commander Chang Ling-fu down gave their lives to the nation.

After the reverse at Memglianku, Government forces made a thorough review and re-deployed the forces. On 27 June, the Supreme Command decided to employ an overwhelmingly superior force, avoiding the overlapping terrain barriers of Chimon Shan and using the west-east lateral corridor as the axis of operations, in a steam-roller and conical attack on the Communist forces, Communist base of Nanma in central Shantung laden with war materials was captured. Subsequent actions were taken to mop up the Communist remnants.

On 27 September, Government forces landed at Lungko, Yentai, Penglai, and Weihaiwei to tighten the control of Chiaochow-Chinan Railroad. Thus, the situation in Shantung was stabilized

Victory of Szeping

On the Northeast front, ever since the Government forces took the defense, three attempts by Lin Piao's forces to cross the Sungari River in southward invasion between November, 1946 and February, 1947 were repulsed. On 7 March, Communist Lin Piao's forces again crossed the Sungari River on a wide front in a southward invasion.

By 21 May, Communist forces surrounded Szepingchieh. The defenders fought hard while awaiting reinforcements. On 11 June, when the Communists entered the city, street fighting began. Every inch of ground was fought and every house changed hands. The fighting lasted 19 days resulting in 50,000 Communist casualties. On 24 June, Government reinforcements arrived. In a converging attack and with the support of the air force, violent attacks were made against the Communist positions. In the end, Communist lines wavered. In the night of 30 June, as the Communist forces withdrew, the siege was lifted. After action inspections of the Communist positions revealed that all the Communist battlefield communications were destroyed, having been subjected to repeated attacks of our air force. The bodies and equipment left on the battlefield were countless.

War of Annihilation in Yellow River Flood Area

To turn the tide of battle after their loss of Yenan and Nanma and the defeat at Szepingchieh, Liu Po-cheng's forces fled east to the Lungchow-Haichow Railroad to harass western Shantung and responded to the operations of Chen Yi's remnants in central Shantung. Communist remnants fleeing into Shansi from northern Shensi also joined the local Communist forces to encircle Tatung and Taiyuan. Hence, the Supreme Command decided to mass the main strength to engage in mobile war of destruction against the 300,000 troops under Chen Yi and Liu Po-cheng in the Yellow River Flood Area. By 7 July, Communists, having suffered over 100,000 casualties, collapsed.

Soviet Incursion of Peita Shan in Sinkiang

To respond to the Chinese Communist insurrection and to draw the attention of the government forces so as to rescue the Chinese Communists from a difficult situation, Soviet Russia, after the Yining Incident massed tens of thousands of Russian and Mongolian troops to invade Peita Shan in Sinkiang on 22 May under the cover of five Russian aircraft. 7,000 troops of the Government's 55th Division and 3,000 peace preservation cavalry troops led by Othman rose to offer resistance. After 15 days of bloody battle, division commander Kuo Chi was fatally wounded and the Government forces suffered heavy losses. Familiar with the terrain and mobile in movement, Othman led his forces to break the siege. On 8 June, he staged a counterattack which resulted in the destruction of 2,000 Russian and Mongolian troops. The Communists were pursued all the way to the border of Khobdo. On 28 June, the Russians instigated the "Uigur Cultural Promotion Association" to mass the riffraffs to start troubles and extensively staged the "East Turkestan Movement" to create disturbances and to attack Government positions. Sinkiang had been troubled by turbulence and terror until the mainland was lost to the

Communists.

Chinese Communist Political Offensive

Militarily speaking, Government forces scored a series of victories since the beginning of the Communist suppression. However, many serious political difficulties were encountered.

Since the participation in the military negotiations, the Chinese Communists had no real intention of seeking peace. They had anticipated that sooner or later peace talks would rupture and that the Government would undertake Communist suppression. Furthermore, Communist intrigues placed primary importance on economy and politics, and secondary importance on military activities. They, therefore, had always emphasized the fostering of "economy affecting politics; politics undermining military operations," so as to create social disorder.

On the surface, there were a few obvious cases. In Taiwan they made use of Communist spy Hsieh Hsueh-hung to instigate the hostility of the Taiwanese against the mainlanders. Thus, the "February 28 Incident" resulted. The incident was not pacified until 17 March, 1947, when the Government sent personnel over to quiet things down.

On the domestic side, under the pretext of the so-called "Shen Tsung Incident[1]" in which a Chinese girl student was supposed to have been criminally assaulted by an American soldier in Peiping on 24 December, 1946, the Communist

---

[1] Shen Tsung Incident:
On 24 December, 1946. Shen Tsung, a girl student in Peiping was raped by an American soldier. The Chinese Communists took advantage of such an individual act to start a full-scale anti-American riot.

stirred up anti-American movement and students in Peiping led strikes, parades and demonstrations. In January of the following year, students in Tientsin and Hankow followed suit demanding the withdrawal of American forces from China. Although the student strikes later subsided the Chinese Communists had professional students penetrating the nation's various schools while they maneuvered from behind the scene. By mid-May, Communist instigations caused the eruptions of student strikes in various places. On 17 May, students of the five colleges in Nanking led the student strikes, responded by the students in Shanghai, Peiping and Tientsin. Using the increase of supplementary food and subsidies as an excuse, the students staged the "eat-up movement.[2]" Later, this development led to the demand on the Government to conclude the "civil war," and restoration of peace negotiations with the Communists. Thus, social order and people's feelings were greatly affected.

As a result of changing situations in war, large numbers of refugees poured into the cities creating problems in employment. Communist sabotage of lines of communication and looting of materials led to inflation and depreciation of fah-pi (Chinese currency). To carry Communist suppression, the Government had to increase the budget for military expenses and relief. In time, the Government found itself in great financial difficulties. It was estimated that in early 1947, the total issuance of fah-pi stood at 3,500

---

[2] "Eat-Up Movement":
   On 12 May, 1947, the Chinese Communists instigated the students of the five colleges including the Central University and College of Drama to stage an "Eat-Up Movement" by going on strike under the pretext of improving nutrition.

billion. By July of the same year, it was 10,000 billion.

Concerned over the increasingly deteriorating situation in China, Pres. Truman sent Gen. Wedemeyer to China again on 11 July to make a fact-finding investigation of China's political, economic, psychological and military situation. Upon conclusion of his investigation, Gen. Wedemeyer made a departure statement saying that "In order to obtain and retain the people's faith, the Chinese Government must undertake timely, drastic and extensive economic reforms." Four years later, when he heard Gen. Douglas MacArthur's report at the Senate Military Affairs and Foreign Relations Committees, he himself admitted that he had been mistaken in the comments he made at the time. However, his comments had already influenced the feelings of the Chinese people and the U.S. policy toward China at the time. They proved damaging to the anti-Communist efforts of the National Government.

Government and Communist Military Disparity

In the beginning of 1948, Government forces in the various theaters totalled 2.7 million. The Communists' regular forces stood at 1.5 million in addition to militia, and were divided into the five "Liberation Armies" of the Northwest China, Central China, East China, North China, and Northeast China. The Communist forces in the Northeast were eager to seize China's heartland and to consolidate the international corridor leading to Russia. In response to the rebellion in the Northeast, the Communist forces in North China covered the rear areas of the Communist forces operating in Central China. Using central Shantung and southeastern Shansi as the bases, Communist forces under

Chen Yi and Liu Po-cheng operated in the Kiangsu-Shantung-Honan-Anhwei-Hupei border areas using bandit tactics to realize their objective of "seeking soldiers and food where they are supporting war by means of war." Communist forces in the Northwest moved to Shensi-Kansu to immobilize Government forces under Hu Tsung-nan. Thus, Hu's forces could not be shifted, while Communist forces were used to respond to the harassing operation of the Communist forces under Chen Yi and Liu Po-cheng.

The vastness of the defense areas made it only possible for the Government forces to defend key localities. Due to political reasons, many such localities could not be abandoned. As a result, defenses were set up in too many places constituting many weaknesses. Government forces, tied down by the Communists, could not be shifted to respond to the operations in these areas where they were most needed. Hence, the operations went from active offense to passive defense. Having gained the initiative, Communist forces moved at will, concentrated on the offensive and struck the vulnerable areas. Thus, Communist forces gained superiority, while Government forces suffered from inferiority.

The Government forces were compelled to defend the Northeastern Provinces. As the Communists engaged in extensive sabotage of the railroads in North China, Government forces in Kirin, Changchun and Mukden had to be supplied from the air. Yet, the air lift capability of the Air Forces could not meet the requirements. Supply difficulties, communication bottle neck, and the necessity to mass forces before mopping up the Communist made it necessary to evacuate the Northeast Provinces.

With the fall of the Northeastern Provinces, large-scale

military operations soon came to North China. To begin with, there were not sufficient forces in North China. The operations in the Northeastern Provinces placed further drain on manpower. Consequently, two years of bitter fighting failed to produce decisive results. By the time Communist Lin Piao's 300,000 troops moved south, Peiping and Tientsin were besieged. On 14 January, 1948, Tientsin fell. Later, entire North China was engulfed by the Red tide.

In North China, another Communist objective was Taiyuan in Shansi Province which had been surrounded by the Communists since July, 1948. On 22 July, at great personal risk, Pres. Chiang flew to Taiyuan to confer with Yen Hsi-shan. Of the three airfields in Taiyuan at the time, only one was still in hands of the Government forces. The city was completely cut off from the outside world and depended on air drop. However, the defenders were determined in their efforts to repel the attackers. Successively they beat back seven Communist offensives. On 24 April, 400,000 Communist troops, supported by 4,000 guns succeeded in taking the city. 40,000 Government troops and civilians in the city was killed or wounded. Acting Governor Liang Hua-wen and 500 officers committed suicide en masse and wrote an epic story in the anti-Communist war.

Battle of Hsuchow and Pangpu

As far back as 1946, Pres. Chiang, in his foresight and appraisal of the overall situation, had anticipated that the Yellow River and Huai River plains were the areas in which decisive battles of the Communist suppression campaign would be fought. In order to insure the security of the Yellow River and Huai River plains and the hilly grounds in Shantung, control the battlefields in Central China, and take advantage of the favorable overall situation, he instructed the Ministry of National Defense to organize the local populace, construct "peace preservation forts" (in line with the pillbox policy during the fifth campaign in Kiangsi) and implement the "integration of villages into forts" so as to calm the people and prevent the fleeing of Communist in the areas east of the Peiping-Hankow Railroad, west of the Tientsin-Pukow Railroad and on either side of the Lungchow-Haichow Railroad. It was hoped powerful armies be employed to trap the main strength of the forces under Chen Yi and Liu Po-cheng in the "operational areas" so well scattered with pillboxes and forts. Local militia were coordinated to open mop-up actions and destroy the Communist in a decisive battle.

Regretfully, at the time of the constitutional rule, discussions leading to the removal of people from their homes met with obstacles, as it was believed that such a move would violate the spirit of the constitution which guaranteed the freedom of people to live wherever they chose. The deteriorating situation in North China soon took the war to Hsuchow. At this time, the total strength of the Government forces was reduced to one million, while the Communist forces were increased to 1,620,000. 400,000 Government troops and 550,000 Communist troops were employed on the Hsuchow battlefield.

In November, 1948, the Battle of Hsuchow was unveiled. On the eastern front, 70,000 Government troops under Huang Po-tao guarded Chanchuang east of Hsuchow. 200,000 Communist troops were massed in repeated attacks on Huang's forces. In spite of numerical inferiority, Government forces began fighting fiercely from 7 November and defeated 7 invading columns killing nearly 100,000 Communist troops.

On the western front. Government forces under Chiu Ching-chuan destroyed 50,000 Communist troops in three victories. Beginning 18 November, Communist front started to waver.

Taking a big chance, Communists began to pour in reinforcements employing human sea tactics and thrust desperately against the Government forces on the eastern front. Fierce and bloody battles were fought. By 22 November, Huang's forces were tightly surrounded by the Communist. Chen Chang, commander of the 62nd Corps was killed in action. Huang's forces fought on gallantly despite prohibitive losses. In the end, Huang gave his life to the nation by committing suicide.

The reverses of the Government forces on the eastern front led to the southward retreat of the forces of Chiu Ching-chuan, Li Mi, and Sung Yuan-liang under the overall command of Tu Yu-ming. These forces encountered the Communist forces at Su Hsien and Pangpu. Government forces under Huang Wei rushing from Wuhan as reinforcements met the Communist forces at Shungtuichi. Communist forces established defense in every village and set up strong ambush position to stop the advance of Government forces. Surrounded by superior Communist forces, Government forces fought hard for a month. When ammunition and provisions were totally exhausted, Hsiung Chou-chun committed suicide. Only a small number of officers and men escaped alive. Government forces under Chiu Ching-chuan fought over the possession of every village with the Communists. Fighting was most bitter. By early January, 1949, Communists poured in large reinforcements. On 5 January, Communist forces launched violent attacks on Government positions. In one day, over 10,000 rounds of artillery landed destroying all houses. Gen. Chiu Ching-chuan sacrificed his life for the nation. Over half of his forces were killed or wounded. Only few escaped unhurt.

President Chiang's Forced Retirement

Despite reverses in the Battle of Hsuchow-Pangpu, the Government still retained a number of crack units and had assurance for victory. On New Year's Day, 1949, Pres. Chiang· issued a message in which he stated: "If the Communists persist in their armed insurrection and have no desire for peace, the Government, in fulfilling its duties to save the nation and the people, has no choice but to fight the Communists to the end. In particular, Nanking-Shanghai, being the political center of the nation, must be guarded at all costs. I believe the Government has the assurance of a decisive victory. What is more, the key to saving the nation and turning misfortune into fortune for our people will depend on the outcome of this decisive battle. Our compatriots must know that only when our servicemen and people are united, stand firm in self-defense and seek victory in the decisive battle will we be able to achieve genuine peace. Only when we are able to suffer pain and sacrifices, will we be able to avoid the life of hell behind the Iron Curtain."

However, the propaganda of the Chinese Communists and their fellow travelers spread many absurd comments detrimental to the Government, consequently, many people were tired of war and longed for peace even temporary peace.

Defeatism prevailed at home and abroad. In the United States, there were open discussions on the question of whether or not "Mao would become the Tito of China." Domestically, a number of short-sighted people openly favored peace negotiations with the Communists and absurdly stated: "If Pres. Chiang does not retire, the Chinese Communists would not discuss peace, and American aid would not be forthcoming." Under such circumstances, Pres. Chiang resolutely withdrew from public life in the hope that peace would be restored. On 21 January, 1949, he turned over the presidency to Vice Pres. Li Tsung-jen in accordance with the Constitution. At 4:00 P.M. on the same day he left Nanking for Hangchow to return to his home at Hsiko. Thereafter, the anti-Communist efforts seemed to have lost balance. Lacking a real leader in military and political affairs, people throughout the nation became restless and morale sagged. As the anti-Communist ideology collapsed completely, the overall situation was too far gone to be saved.

Section 3
Overall Situation Deteriorating
after President Chiang's Retirement

Defense of Yangtze River

After the military reverses at the Battle of Hsuchow and Pangpu, if the nation had united and concentrated on war preparations, defended the Yangtze River and the southwest against the Red onslaught, retained the wealth of South China to meet military requirements, gained time to step up combat readiness and improve foreign relations, the deteriorating situation could have been saved. However a number of short-sighted people, willing to sue for peace at any price, favored peace negotiations. As a result of the negotiations, Chinese Communists brought forth the following stiff demands:

(1) Punish "war criminals."
(2) Abrogate the Constitution.
(3) Abolish the name of the Republic of China.
(4) Reorganize the armed forces in accordance with "democratic" principles.
(5) Confiscate "bureaucratic capital."
(6) Revise land policy.
(7) Abrogate traitorous treaties.
(8) Convene Political Consultative Conference, denying participation of "reactionary elements;" establish "coalition government," and take over the Nanking Government.

These eight harsh demands were advanced with the stipulation that regardless of war or peace, Communist forces would cross the Yangtze River.

By this time, those who had favored peace, realized that they were deceived by the Chinese Communists.

At the end of March, 1949, Communist forces were massed on the north bank of the Yangtze River. On 8 April, as peace negotiations ruptured, Communist forces crossed the Yangtze River. On the western front, Communist forces under Liu Po-cheng and Chen Keng crossed the Yangtze River at Wuhu and Tikang. On the eastern front, Communist forces under Chen Yi rushed to take Chiangyin fortress. Communist forces under Lin Piao and Peng Teh-huai launched offensive toward Wuhan and Sian to tie down Government forces and respond to their own forces.

In the midst of these increasingly worsening situations, Pres. Chiang, in his retirement, suggested to Li Tsung-jen that he consolidate the defense of Shanghai and Hunan, insure the safety of Canton and Chungking, concentrate Government forces in the southwest for reorganization to save a most critical situation. Unfortunately, Li failed to take note and acted in panic. Without central leadership, the armed forces fought separately. Gradually, the overall situation became more and more hopeless.

On 20 April, Communist forces crossed the Yangtze River in a southward invasion. On 23 April Nanking fell. On 26 April, they took Wuhsing, later Changhsing, Yihsing and Nanchang. They continued to push toward to Hunan and Shanghai. On 27 April, Pres. Chiang issued a message in his home town calling on the Chinese people to fight on despite the futility of peace negotiations. He pointed out that "The Communist suppression operations today are a people's war against aggression. It is a social war in which every citizen and every family fight for our free way of life. It is also a cultural war in which we fight to protect our long history, cultural heritage, peace, kindness, love and moral virtues. The final outcome of this war will determine the survival or destruction of our entire nation, the life or death and the fortune or misfortune of every citizen and every family. If this war should fail, our national independence, sovereignty and people's free way of life will perish. Our future will then be widespread poverty, bleak starvation and world war. If this anti-aggression and anti-Communist war succeeds, our nation will become an independent nation, our people free people contributing gloriously to world peace and security." Later Pres. Chiang left Hsiko and boarded C. N. S. Tai-kang to inspect Shanghai. The following day, he left for Amoy. On 6 May, he left Shanghai on C. N. S. Chiang Ching for Chushan Archipelago to check on the dispositions of Government forces there.

Battle of Shanghai and Withdrawal from Canton

On 14 May, Chinese Communists massed over 400,000 troops for the attack of Shanghai. Despite his retirement, Pres. Chiang, compelled by moral obligations and sense of responsibility, went to Shanghai to direct the military operations. The battle was fought for 14 days resulting in 60,000 Communist casualties. Hundred thousands of Government troops along the Nanking-Shanghai Railroad and US$20 million worth of materials were safely evacuated. Thus, some resources for the later counteroffensive and national recovery by the Government forces were saved.

Meanwhile, subsequent to the fall of Nanking, the National Government was moved to Canton. Pres. Chiang suggested that Li Tsung-jen insure the safety of Canton and consolidate the Southwest. However, Li made no such plans. After abandoning Wuhan on 15 May, he ordered the main strength of the Government forces withdrawn to Kwangsi to protect his home province. He had hoped to use these forces as his last asset to conduct "partial peace negotiations" with the Chinese Communists.

As the Government forces in Central China were withdrawn, the Communist forces rapidly moved in. Fortunately, the National Government had appointed Huang Chieh governor of Hunan Province. Huang led Government forces to attack the Communist flanks from western Hunan. On 17 May, Government forces captured Chingshuping after inflicting over 10,000 casualties on the Communists. Later, Hsianghsiang and Hsiangtan were recovered. For a while the situation was stabilized.

In the Northwest, the defense areas of the Government forces under Hu Tsung-nan in the midst of the drastically changing situation were too exposed. Hence, Government forces abandoned Sian on 20 May and withdrew to southern Shensi. 300,000 troops were concentrated in the defense of Chinling Shan to guard the entrance to Chungking, Szechuan Province.

Politically and strategically speaking, the fall of Canton proved damaging to the National Government. As the Government forces from Central China moved into Kwangsi, the road to Canton was wide open. Having concentrated their forces in breaking the strong resistance of the Government forces under Huang Chieh in the vicinity of Hengyang, Communists made great advances. On 15 October, they entered Canton. With the exception of Foochow and Amoy, the entire China coast fell into Communist hands. The Government once again moved to Chungking; the removal greatly affected the morale of the people and the servicemen. As all the foreign embassies had already moved to Canton, they no longer wished to go to Chungking with the Government, and foreign relations with the international world became a vacuum. Britain rapidly extended diplomatic recognition to the Communist puppet regime. For the sake of her own interests, particularly when Hong Kong lies so close to Canton, Britain made such a move.

Battle of Chungking

The continued operation of the National Government after its removal to Chungking depended largely on the successful defense of the northeastern and southeastern gateways to Szechuan. In the Szechuan-Shensi border area on the northeastern front, Government forces under Hu Tsung-nan were still holding Chinling blocking the Communist passage. The terrain there is such that it favors the defenders. On the southeastern front, the defense depended largely on the possession of the critical terrain of Kweichow.

The fate of Chungking was sealed, as there was no one to provide Central leadership. As a result, Government forces fought separately. Soon, Kweichow fell into Communist hands. With the establishment of a regional autonomous state in mind, Li Tsung-jen refused to shift to Kweichow the 200,000 troops from Central China which he had ordered to Kwangsi. In the face of imminent Communist invasion, there was only the 89th Corps commanded by Liu Po-lung. Thus, Kweichow was lost. This unfortunate loss greatly endangered Chungking. Kwangsi was completely isolated resulting later in the defection of Lu Han in Yunnan.

In view of the situation, Li Tsung-jen cabled Pres. Chiang asking the latter to join him in a conference in Chungking. Knowing this to be a revolutionary duty which he could not shirk, Pres. Chiang resolutely went to Chungking on 14 November, 1949 despite great risk. However, Li left Nanning faking stomach trouble on 20 November and flew to the United States via Hong Kong deserting a most confused and chaotic situation.

Meanwhile, the situation in Chungking was one of utter

chaos. Communist agents were everywhere spreading rumours. On 2 September, they set fire in the city destroying thousands of houses. Over 1,000 people were burned to death and 100,000 were rendered homeless. Upon arrival in Chungking, Pres. Chiang took charge in his capacity as chairman of the Kuomintang Emergency Committee. He remained in Chungking until the last minute despite great personal danger. He had hoped that Chungking would be held a little longer so that Hu Tsung-nan's forces could have ample time to withdraw to Chengtu and Hsichang where a second line defense could be established.

On 24 November, Chichiang was lost. Communist forces crossed the Yangtze River at Chianching in an attempt to isolate the Paishihyi Airfield. On 28 November, they pushed to South Spring. It was not until the morning of 30 November that Pres. Chiang left Chungking for Chengtu. Meanwhile, 30,000 Communist troops had poured into Chungking.

For 11 days Pres. Chiang remained in Chengtu directing the final defense operations in Szechuan. However, local warlords conspired with the Communists. Thus, the situation in Chengtu was hopeless. On 8 December, the Government decided to move from Chengtu to Taipei. The General Headquarters which directed the operations against the Communists on the mainland was moved to Hsichang under the command of Hu Tsung-nan from where guerilla operations were continued.

On 10 December, Pres. Chiang flew to Taipei from Chengtu. On 27 March, 1950, Hu Tsung-nan's forces, after successfully attacking the Communist forces at Ningnan, Huili and Kangting withdrew from Hsichang. At the end of the year, Communist forces invaded Tibet. Thus, with the fall of the mainland, the Chinese people were shut behind the Iron Curtain. The entire mainland was bathed in Communist liquidation, persecution, and tyranny.

Despite military reverses on the mainland, the Republic of China continued its struggle in the free world against Communism to check the spread of the Red tide. Between 1945 and 1949, the Red onslaught had already made its inroads in Europe, Asia, the Middle East and the Far East. Hence, wars in Greece, Kashmir, between Israel and Egypt, Vietnam, Malaya, the Philippines and Korea took place. The situation in Southeast Asia was unstable. On 10 July, 1949, upon invitation of Pres. Elpidio Quirino of the Philippines, Pres. Chiang, in his capacity as director-general of the Kuomintang, flew to Baguio. The next day, a joint Sino-Filipino communique was issued calling on the nations in the Far East to form an alliance in order to thwart the threat of Communism.

On 6 August of the same year, upon invitation of Pres. Syngman Rhee of the Republic of Korea, Pres. Chiang arrived in the port of Chinhai in Korea. The next day, a joint Sino-Korean communique was issued reiterating the common desire of the two nations to stop the spread of Communism. Since then, the Republics of China, the Philippines and Korea have been closely united forming the anti-Communist front in Asia and maintaining peace in the world.

CHAPTER SEVEN
Armed Forces Reorganization and National Recovery

Section 1
Turning the Tide of Battle

Victories of Kinmen and Tengpu

On 17 October, 1949 Amoy was abandoned. In the night of 25 October, Chinese Communists massed 15,000 troops in 200 some junks and made a forced landing near Kuningtuo on Kinmen under the cover of shore batteries. They succeeded in taking several villages. The defenders fought resolutely under the support of naval gunfire. Later, tanks spearheaded the attack on the Communist positions. Bitter hand-to-hand fighting took place. By 27 October, all the invaders were either destroyed or captured. The victory amazed the world. As morale was boosted, the situation became stabilized. Communist attempts on Taiwan and Penghu were crushed.

Subsequent to their defeat in Kinmen, the Communist began an invasion of Chushan Archipelago in the hope of removing the blockade on the water and land communication in the Nanking-Shanghai-Hangchow area. On 3 November, 7,000 Communist troops landed on Taohua Island preparatory to an attack on Tengpu Island. Our defenders counterattacked violently with the support of air and naval forces. A see-saw battle was fought. By the morning of 7 November, most of the Communist invaders were annihilated, and remnants fled to Communist-occupied islands.

Thereafter, Government forces stepped up naval and air blockade and bombing of the mainland coast. Mainland guerilla activities and coastal raids were conducted successively to wear out the enemy. Thus, time was gained for war preparations in the Taiwan Straits.

President Chiang's Resumption of Office

Chinese Navy and Chinese Air Force which were evacuated to Taiwan were relatively intact. However, Army units scattered on the various islands were depleted in personnel and equipment. The strength on Taiwan proper was weak. On 5 January, 1950, the United States announced that she would no longer provide military aid to China. After the two heavy blows on Kinmen and Tengpu, the Communists withheld military activities for a while. However, as they stepped up the political offensive, military preparations became active. 300,000 troops were massed on the southeastern coast. With aircraft and submarines provided by Russia, Communists attempted to invade Taiwan and Penghu. Meanwhile, the people and servicemen on Taiwan were uneasy. Chinese people in all walks of life at home and abroad demanded Pres. Chiang's resumption of office. In compliance with the people's unanimous desire, Pres. Chiang resumed office on 1 March.

At the time of his resumption of office, Pres. Chiang issued a message in which he stated:

"For more than 40 years, I have devoted myself to the cause of the revolution. I have long paid no heed to life or death nor personal glory or humiliation. As a citizen, I bow to the desire of public opinion. At a critical time such as this, it is not possible to shirk my responsibility. Accordingly, I resume office on 1 March to exercise the authority of President. It has been less than 5 years since V-J Day, yet the situation has deteriorated so rapidly. I blame myself for my lack of leadership. I vouch to do my best, compensate my past failure, and plan future endeavors. I, therefore, call on all patriotic citizens, at home and abroad, to unite in sincerity; officers and men in the armed forces to work hard; and Government officials at all levels to do their utmost in order to restore the territorial sovereignty of the Republic of China, save the lives and freedom of our compatriots in the Communist-occupied areas, and maintain peace and security of the world. I urge all of you to combine your efforts and to fight to the end. We must wipe out the Communists, recover the mainland and reestablish the Republic of China into a nation of the people, for the people, and by the people."

Military Reorganization and Self Awakening

When Pres. Chiang first resumed office, he strongly felt that China's destiny hinged on the bastion of Taiwan. He, therefore, instituted party, political, economic and military reforms. Some of these reforms are briefly stated as follows:

On the party front: Pres. Chiang said: ' We must turn Taiwan into a bastion of national recovery, the vanguard of the free peoples of Asia in their struggle and a fighter for world peace. To realize this aim, we must thoroughly revamp our party. When we reorganize revolutionary organizations, we shall then restore our revolutionary spirit." Thus, the

Central Reform Committee and the Central Advisory Committee were established to spearhead the reform[1] of the party. By the autumn of 1952, the revolutionary line-up presented a completely new look.

On the political front, "Outline for the Implementation of Local Autonomy in the Various Hsiens and Cities in Taiwan" was promulgated in the spring of 1950. In April, general elections of hsien and city assembly men, "lin" chiefs, "li" chiefs, village (town) chiefs and hsien magistrates and city mayors were held. Such open-minded measures were most comforting to the people of Taiwan who have now rejoined our fatherland.

On the economic front, the 37.5% Farm Rent Reduction Program[2] was implemented, followed by the sale of public farm land,[3] and assistance to the owner farmers. On 26 January, 1953 "Regulations Governing Land to the Tiller"[4]

---

[1] Party Reform:
With regard to party reform, Pres. Chiang stated at an ad hoc meeting of the KMT Central Standing Committee in Taipei on 22 July that the reform aimed to restore revolutionary spirit, and intensify the cooperation of the people at home and abroad so as to enlarge the revolutionary line-up.

[2] 37.5% Farm Rent Reduction Program:
The purpose of the farm rental reduction was to improve the livelihood of the farmers and further prepare for the implementation of the "land to the tiller" policy. The program set a definite rate which must not exceed 37.5% of the total annual yield of crops. The program began in April, 1949 and was completed by the end of July in the same year.

[3] Sale of Public Farm Land:
To take the lead and to set an example in the implementation of "land to the tiller" policy, the Government gradually turned over the titles of national and provincial land to the farmers. During the period from 1951–1961, a total of 165,443 farmers became owners-farmers and 96,000 hectares were sold. Crop yield was increased by 1,500,000 kg.

[4] Land to the Tiller:
The purpose in the promotion of land to the tiller policy was to implement the farm and policy of the Principle of Livelihood which enabled the farmers

were promulgated so as to improve the livelihood of farmers and increase agricultural production. The establishment of land system, in particular, was fair and reasonable.

On the military front, since his resumption of office, Pres. Chiang proceeded to formulate three major guidance in re-establishing revolutionary forces. They are enumerated as follows:

(1) Restoration of revolutionary spirit and reawakening of the national soul: Such revolutionary spirit is the spirit of "sacrifice, solidarity and responsibility"[5] at the time of the armed forces build-up in Whampoa.[6] "Sacrifice" means the wholehearted devotion struggling for the nation and following footsteps of past martyrs despite personal danger. "Solidarity" implies united effort to practice the Whampoa motto "Love and Sincerity." Responsibility aims to realize the objective of "vanguards ye are, hold fast your aim, by sun and star, be earnest and brave, your country to save. One heart, one soul, one mind one goal." (passages from the Chinese national anthem) Based on the above, the Revolutionary Pragmatism Research Institute on Yangmingshan and

---

to own, till and profit from the land. It was mild and gradual. Excess land belonging to landlords was taken over and sold to the farmers presently tilling the land. Later, the Government made loans to the tillers so that they could purchase the land. The program began early in 1953 and was completed by mid-October of the same year.

[5] "Sacrifice, Solidarity, and Responsibility":
"Sacrifice, Solidarity, and Responsibility" was the Whampoa spirit. Despite subsequent changings of designations finally leading to the "Central Military Academy," the traditional Whampoa spirit remained and continued to grow.

[6] Armed Forces Build-Up in Whampoa:
For details, see Chapter One.

the Officers' Training Corps at Yuan Shan were established under the personal supervision of Pres. Chiang. Pres. Chiang's selected speechs such as the "Soldier's Soul,"[7] "Revolutionary Soul"[8] and "National Righteousness"[9] taught the trainees to stand firm in their determination to take revenge and eliminate disgrace. On the one hand, experiences and lessons drawn from past failure on the mainland were reviewed. On the other hand, studies were made on the program of national recovery. Members of the armed forces were imbued with the determination that people helped those who helped themselves and that everything started at the bottom. The will to succeed or perish formed the impetus in the defense of Taiwan. Foreign aid was welcome, as the nation marched forward to eliminate disgrace and recover lost territories. Our own performance finally led to the dispatch of the Military Assistance Advisory Group (MAAG) to Taiwan on 1 May, 1951. Military aid was soon followed by economic aid.

(2) Tightening organizations at various levels and esta-

---

[7] "Soldier's Soul":

A speech delivered by Pres. Chiang to the cadres of the armed forces at Yangmingshan on 16 April, 1950. The speech stressed the significance of "do or die" spirit for revolutionary soldiers.

[8] "Revolutionary Soul":

A speech delivered by Pres. Chiang to the cadres of the armed forces at Yangmingshan on 17 April, 1950. The speech stressed the importance of revolutionary soldiers to be determined and to succeed.

[9] "National Righteousness":

A speech delivered by Pres. Chiang to the cadres of the armed forces at Yangmingshan on 1 May, 1950. It emphasized the importance of revolutionary soldiers to have strong will power and sense of shame. It also amplified that "righteousness" was derived from "reasons" and "right."

blishing various systems: When the defense establishment was first reorganized, Pres. Chiang directed that the armed forces be built up and that systems and science be given primary importance. In compliance with Pres. Chiang's instruction, the Ministry of National Defense reorganized the army, navy, air force and service units, improved organization and equipment, reduced and integrated excess units, and eliminated the old and the weak in order to intensify training, strengthen combat effectiveness, and improve operations. Meanwhile, an excellent personnel system was established emphasizing fairness and reasonableness in award and punishment, promotion and demotion, and personnel assignment. A good quartermaster system was established to insure the correct accounting of personnel and stop the waste of public funds. A political system was established to enable all officers and men to realize the nature of the anti-Communist war and to uplift morale. At the same time, the four open policies of award and punishment, personnel, expression of views and quartermaster were successfully implemented. With past practice of lethargy on the mainland gone, the spirit of seeking improvement and strong will-to-fight were cultivated.

(3) Concentrating forces on the off-shore islands and consolidating the bastions of Taiwan and Penghu: For sometime, Government forces were scattered on the various distant islands and could easily be overwhelmed by the Communists. The Government, therefore, took the initiative to withdraw the forces on Hainan

Island and Chushan Archipelago in order to concentrate them on Taiwan. Such a move caught the Communists by surprise. Over 200,000 combat troops were thus added in Taiwan thereby consolidating the bastion of counteroffensive and national recovery.

Raiding Nanjih and Tungshan Islands

In June, 1950, under the instigations of the Chinese and Russian Communists, North Korean Communists invaded South Korea. The United States immediately dispatched naval and air forces to support South Korea and declared that she would send the Seventh Fleet to help defend Taiwan and prevent Chinese Government forces from conducting operations against the China mainland. Meanwhile, the United Nations resolved to send military forces to repel the North Korean invasion. Nevertheless, the Chinese Communists, in complete disregard of public opinion, launched the "Resist America and Support Korea" movement. On 5 November, they sent 300,000 troops to help the Korean Communists. The Government of the Republic of China time and again indicated its willingness to respond to the call of the United Nations by sending military forces to assist Korea or by undertaking counteroffensive on the mainland. It was hoped that such moves would help stop Chinese Communist aggression in Korea, but the proposal was never accepted. In an effort to coordinate with the operations of the United Nations forces against North Korea and North Vietnam so as to immobilize the Chinese Communist forces, and to provide actual combat experience to the Government forces which had already received amphibious landing and joint operation training, small amphibious raid units were organized on Kinmen to conduct surprise landings on the islands and ports along the coast of Chekiang, Fukien and Kwangtung and to deal heavy blows against the Chinese Communists. Among them, the raids against Nanjih and Tungshan were the largest in size and the lessons and experiences gained the greatest.

(1) Battle of Nanjih:

4,500 Government troops sailed successively from Kinmen for Nanjih on 10 Oct., 1952. Due to heavy sea, the ships were not moored until 0630, 11 October. The element of surprise was gone. At 0730, under naval gunfire support, Government forces made forced landings at three places despite a rough sea and heavy fire. At 1800, the entire island was captured. Over 1,000 Communist troops staged a counterattack. The coordinated efforts of our army and naval forces in three days and nights of bloody fighting resulted in the killing of over 1,000 Communist troops and the capture of 700 prisoners of war. When the objective of demoralizing the Communists was achieved, our forces withdrew safely.

(2) Battle of Tungshan:

Government forces organized amphibious landing forces in conjunction with airborne assault against Tungshan. Ships sailed from Kinmen on 15 July. At 0600, 16 July, airborne units landed on the objective area and immediately cut off Communist reinforcements and responded to the landing operations. Meanwhile, our surface assault units landed at three different places. Communists forces along the coast were crushed, as our \forces steadily advanced to capture Tungshan City. Later, Communist reinforcements arrived and launched counterattacks. Heavy fighting lasted until

0300, 18 July. With missions successfully accomplished, our assault units pulled out and sailed back·to the home base in the afternoon.

Return of Anti-Communist Fighters from Korea

In early July, 1953, Government forces and refugees who had been detained in South Vietnam for four years, were repatriated to Taiwan with the assistance of our friendly ally. In late September, aircraft of the Burmese Air Force bombed our anti-Communists guerillas in the Yunnan-Burma border area. With the assistance of the United States and Thailand, our guerillas were evacuated to Taiwan in two groups.

The return of these anti-Communist fighters greatly enhanced the anti-Communist strength of our Government forces. Furthermore, it demonstrated the indomitable fighting spirit of the Chinese Armed Forces.

On 20 January, 1954, 14,209 ex-POW's of Chinese nationality, carrying Chinese national flags and singing anti-Communist songs, stepped out of prisoner stockade in Korea. Trying desparately to persuade these anti-Communist fighters to return to the mainland, the Chinese Communists broadcast sweet talks. However, none of them fell into the Communist trap this time. On the contrary, they marched gallantly to freedom by boarding ships which took them back to their fatherland in Taiwan. On 27 January, they arrived safely at their destination. On 1 April, they requested enlistment in the armed forces and were duly integrated. They submitted a petition to Pres. Chiang reiterating their determination to fight Communism. All these indicate that Pres. Chiang's appeal to the servicemen and people under Communist control is overwhelming.

Section 2
Consolidating Anti-Communist Bastion

Air Battles and Artillery Shellings

On 11 May, 1954, an air battle took place over Chekiang Province. One of our propeller-driven aircraft shot down a Chinese Communist MIG-15. This proved that the Chinese Communists were equipped with the latest Soviet aircraft. Time and again, Government forces attacked Chinese Communist ships, aircraft and positions in the air, at sea, and on the ground. On 3 September, the Chinese Communist conducted large-scale shelling on Kinmen. The strong fortifications built by the defenders for five years took effect. In the end, the Chinese Communists wasted but a tremendous amount of ammunition. Later, they changed tactics and conducted sporadic shelling and air raids against Kinmen.

Meanwhile, the Chinese Air Force had been equipped with powerful jet aircraft. To insure air supremacy and sea supremacy, Chinese Air Force dispatched a number of aircraft over Amoy a few days after the September 3 shelling in a coordinated attack with naval and ground forces against the enemy. Thus, a series of coordinated counterattacks against the Chinese Communists began.

Sino-U.S. Joint Defense

In early December, 1954, the Republic of China and the United States signed a mutual defense treaty to prevent the Chinese and the Russian Communists from further aggression. In explaining the procedure of the "Sino-U.S. Mutual Defense Treaty," the U.S. Secretary of State stated that the U.S.

President could take drastic actions to meet crises created by Communist aggression. The Chinese Government also indicated that the signing of the treaty contributed to world peace. In early March, 1955, this treaty was ratified by both Governments and made effective. Thus, the Chinese armed forces and those of our closest ally, the United States, have jointly shouldered the safeguarding of the Pacific.

Courageous Battle of Yichiangshan

Since the September 3 shelling[10] , the defenders of the off-shore islands had maintained close surveillance over the Chinese Communist forces for possible sneak attacks. Chinese Communist forces in the southeast, though restless, failed to make any headway due to the coordinated efforts of our army, navy and air force. The joint attacks of our guerillas and the three services resulted in heavy Communist losses.

In an attempt to remove the near sea threat and further to invade Taiwan and Penghu at the opportune time, the Chinese Communists wanted to grab the off-shore islands first. On 18 January, 1955, they employed two army divisions, 154 ships and craft and 230 sorties of airplanes to attack Yichiangshan in the vicinity of Tachen. 1,030 of our raiders defending the island, though poorly equipped, were imbued with strong fighting spirit and destroyed countless invaders. Subsequently, Communist followup convoys were landed. Fighting raged on the entire island. Despite overwhelming odds, the gallant defenders held the nucleus strong points

---

[10] September 3 Shelling:
For details, see 1st Paragraph, Sec. 2, Chapter 7 of this book, "Air Battles and Artillery Shellings."

fighting tenaciously against superior Communist forces for three days. Having inflicted over 3,000 casualties on the enemy and destroyed 5 aircraft and many ships, all the defenders gave their lives to the nation. Such manifestation of revolutionary spirit won the highest admirations of peoples throughout the world.

Concentrating Military Forces and Consolidating Bases

In February, 1955, based on strategic requirement, the Government decided to redeploy the forces on the off-shore islands. Hence, the garrison forces on Tachen, Nanchi, Yushan and Peishan were withdrawn. Forces were concentrated to reinforce Kinmen and Matsu. These moves insured the security of Kinmen and Matsu outposts and consolidated the bastions of Taiwan and Penghu.

Prior to the Chinese Government's decision to withdraw the forces from Tachen, the President of the United States ordered the U.S. Seventh Fleet to render assistance and be prepared to accept the Communist challenge. On 7 February, powerful Sino-U.S. fleets passed through the Taiwan Straits to arrive at Tachen. 14,000 inhabitants of Tachen expressed the desire to come to Taiwan. On 10 February, ships brought them to Keelung. Again, this was evidence of the people's rejection of Communism. The Government forces which were withdrawn from Tachen arrived safely at their destinations on 13 February.

Achievements in Control of Kinmen and Matsu

Taiwan and Penghu form the bases for the Chinese Armed Forces to undertake counteroffensive and national recovery, Kinmen and Matsu form the outposts in the defense of Taiwan and Penghu. To consolidate Taiwan and Penghu, it is necessary to insure the security of Kinmen and Matsu. Kinmen and Matsu, therefore, constitute the pivoting points in our future counteroffensive on the mainland. In reality, our victory in the Battle of Kinmen which took place in October, 1949 paved the road to victory in our future counteroffensive. Such a victory demonstrates the powerful combat effectiveness of the Chinese Armed Forces and gave much confidence and hope to our compatriots at home and abroad. Former defense minister of West Germany commented during his visit to Kinmen: "In this anti-Communist war, the position of Berlin is comparable to Kinmen. If one does not see it for himself, he cannot realize the strategic importance of Kinmen nor why the Republic of China must defend this island."

As a result of the firmness of our Government to defend Kinmen and Matsu, U.S. Pres. Dwight D. Eisenhower announced at the end of March, 1955 that "in order not to damage the morale of Free China and to strangle their hope the United States has decided to assist in the defense of Kinmen and Matsu." Meanwhile, our continued efforts to seek improvements with our own resources and the over-coming-difficulty spirit of our armed forces gradually led to the scheduled completion of a tightly knit defense system.

Two Masterpieces Bringing Happiness to Mankind

In November, 1953, Pres. Chiang's "Two Supplementary Chapters on Physical Education and Recreation to Lectures on the Principle of People's Livelihood" appeared to further amplify the social policy on clothing, food, housing, transportation, physical education and recreation in Dr. Sun Yat-sen's Principle of Livelihood. Indeed, the Three People's Principles meets the requirements of the world trend. Its soundness and effect can be seen in the prosperity and well-being of the people of Taiwan.

To awaken the world so as to achieve solidarity and initiative in the anti-Communist endeavor, Pres. Chiang, fully aware of the peace offensives of the Chinese and Russian Communists, pointed out openly the objectives in their intrigues and the basic approach to end the Red tide. In "Soviet Russia in China" which he wrote in 1956, he unmasked the entire account of the Chinese Communist and Russian aggressions of China together with their treacheries and provided his 30-yr. experiences and findings in his struggle against Communism. This masterpiece became the only guidance in the world's war against Communism to-day.

Since "Soviet Russia in China" was published, many countries printed copies in different languages. Knowing the Chinese Communist strategem and intrigues, democratic nations became more aware of the danger. This book has enabled the democratic nations to combine their efforts in fighting Communism and has made invaluable contributions to the world by helping it to fight Communism and to seek peace.

August 23 Shelling

In July, 1958, Nikita Khrushchev opened the Middle East front by means of indirect aggression. In August, the Chinese Communists were told to open the Far Eastern front. The Chinese Communist Jen Min Jih Pao reiterated that "the Middle East and the Far East are different directions in a common struggle. Our struggle here and their struggle there are but the same struggle against a common enemy. That enemy is the American imperialists." This indicates that the Chinese Communists and the Russians shoulder combat missions in the east and the west with a common objective.

To carry out the Russian instigations, the Chinese Communists, on 7 August, massed 180,000 army troops (including 3 artillery divisions and 2 anti-aircraft divisions), 262 ships and craft and 298 various types of aircraft to begin attacks on our aircraft and ships on patrol. It was quite obvious that the Chinese Communists had the intention to invade the Taiwan Straits.

Since the victory at the Battle of Kuningtou in October, 1949, our defenders on Kinmen underwent nine years of reorganization and training. The defense works had changed from field fortifications to permanent fortress-type underground, systematized fortifications. The defenses had formed a Great Wall on the sea capable of meeting any exacting combat requirements. In conjunction with the Russian global strategy, the Chinese Communists were getting restless. Pres. Chiang had already anticipated such moves on the part of the enemy and directed the forces on Kinmen in early August to go into combat alert status.

On 23 August, Chinese Communists massed 342 guns to begin fanatical, carpet shelling against Kinmen Complex. The shelling which began at 1800 hours, lobbed 57,500 rounds on Kinmen in two hours. On 24 August, Chinese Communist naval and air forces took part in the actions. However, they were all repulsed by our anti-craft and naval gunfire. Beginning 25 August, the Chinese Communists switched to blockade tactics attempting to cut off our resupply to Kinmen and to isolate the defenders. Our artillery units conducted counterbattery to break the Communist blockade. Subsequently, neutralization and destruction fires were conducted inflicting heavy casualties on the enemy. By 6 October, the Chinese Communists had fired 474,910 rounds. Subsequently, in the 10 air battles and 4 sea battles that ensued, the Communists were defeated. The combined efforts of our army, naval and air forces destroyed many Chinese Communist gun positions, tank farms, ammunition depot, broadcasting stations. 215 fortifications and 131 guns were destroyed; 107 ships and craft were damaged or sunk; and 33 aircraft were damaged or destroyed. In particular, the Sea Battle at Liaolo Bay and the Air Battles over the Taiwan Straits reflected the spirit of the Chinese Navy and the Chinese Air Force in defeating an overwhelmingly superior enemy. Incapable of blockading our sea and air resupply to Kinmen and short of ammunition to fight on, the Chinese Communists shamelessly issued a cease fire in order to pull back and replenish.

The intensity of the shelling was unprecedented, so were the fortitude and gallantry of the Chinese Armed Forces. During the 44 days of bitter fighting, the Chinese Armed Forces scored a major victory in the first round despite great difficulties.

On the Double Ten National Day 1958, Pres. Chiang pointed out in his message the following:

"Due to the unique battlefield and marvelous combat records, this battle has broken precedence and has reflected the indomitable spirit of the Chinese people which can never be subjugated by despotism and violence. This is something that the Chinese and Russian Communists had never dreamed of. The iron will of the members of our armed forces in the anti-Communist revolution, their determination to take revenge and their epic are earth-shaking. The most obvious effect of this anti-Communist battle has not only established a basis for the renaissance of the Chinese people, but has also restricted the armed aggression of the Communist bloc to the border area of the China mainland. In fact, a first line defense has been established in the Pacific rendering the Chinese Communists incapable of moving into the Taiwan Straits. Indeed, they find themselves in a situation in which they cannot move forward nor give up. Communist imperialists consider that they are in control of the heartland of Asia and are matchless on the Eurasian continent. Therefore, they seek to grab the keys to the western gateway in the Pacific—Kinmen, Matsu, Taiwan, and Penghu. Their objective is to turn the Western Pacific into an interior lake monopolized by the Communist empire. That is to say, they want to realize their aggressive ambition of controlling the Eastern Hemisphere. Be it a combination of military and political efforts or peaceful and violent efforts, all the measures are designed to help them realize this objective. Hereafter, we must be on the lookout for still greater Communist military activities to expand the war. The present military situation between the enemy and us is such that we are only fearful that they will not come. If they really are intent on expanding the war, they will encounter the joint actions and the blows of the free world's anti-aggression front which will expedite their own destruction.

Section 3
Awaiting Opportunity to Launch Counteroffensive

President Chiang's Instructions on Counteroffensive strategy

On New Year's Day, 1959, Pres. Chiang issued a message[11] to the nation's servicemen and people in which he stated the following:

". . . . . Our strategy in the counteroffensive and national recovery has always considered politics of primary importance and military operations of secondary importance; our ideology the vanguard, and military might the support; and the mainalnd the main battlefield and Taiwan Straits the secondary battlefield. The effectiveness of military power must be aligned with the mainland revolutionary movement and military actions in the Taiwan Straits. Such has always been our guiding principle." This strategic guiding principle has been faithfully observed by our people and has frightened the Chinese Communists.

On New Year's Day, 1961, Pres. Chiang in his message to the nation explained the contrast in the situation between the Chinese Communists and us which would decide victory or defeat. He said: ". . . . . Revolutionary war has always depended on the inclination of the people, but not on the size of the territory or the number of people. It is built on the conscience of the revolutionaries themselves, but not on external conditions. Therefere, revolutionaries must maintain faith in the cause and national spirit—indomitable and determined. Within our bastions on Taiwan,

---

[11] Pres. Chiang's New Year Message:
Pres. Chiang's message which was broadcast to the nation and the world.

Penghu, Kinmen and Matsu, we have been able to combine our political, economic, cultural and social efforts into one entity in the past ten years. We have instituted basic reforms and full-scale reconstruction. Such efforts have not only provided a happy and free life to our people on the anti-Communist bastions, but have also furnished new guarantees in our future national recovery and national reconstruction."

These above efforts are in complete accord with our anti-Communist and resist Russia strategic guidance since the removal of our Government to Taiwan. They form the only strategic decisions which will be incomparably correct in achieving victory, be it the recovery of the mainland, liberation of our suffering compatriots, or peace and security of the world.

Anti-Communist Uprisings and Guerilla Operations

In early 1950, numerous anti-Communist people on the mainland joined hands with the remaining Government forces and local militia. For some time the movement gathered momentum as this force developed and expanded. Raids, attrition actions, surprise attacks and sabotage were conducted. In order to step up guerilla operations on the mainland, units were landed on the mainland in batches to go deep into enemy rear areas. The landings were successful with the response and cover provided by our compatriots on the mainland. They were able to remain for an extended period of time to establish bases and guerilla corridors. They continued to grow among the mainland masses and to develop in combat. These reflect the real feelings of the people on the mainland and the awakening of the Chinese

Communist officers and men.

Upon establishment of the Chinese Communist puppet regime in 1949, the anti-Communist uprisings on the mainland continued to erupt. According to the statistics published by the Chinese Communist Public Security Ministry, 716,503 anti-Communist cases were recorded during the period from June, 1955 to Dec., 1956. Of course, the number of anti-Communist uprisings prior to and after this period was astronomical.

Due to the successful landings of Government guerilla units, it is anticipated that future anti-Communist uprisings will grow in number and in intensity. Eventually, they will threaten the Chinese Communist puppet regime to such an extent that the regime will totter and fall apart in the face of powerful Government forces.

Destroying Red Tide and Establishing Permanent Peace

For more than two decade, Chinese Armed Forces have adhered to the guide line of "Consolidating Taiwan and realizing the recovery of the mainland" and the policy of "stabilizing the frontline, controlling the Straits, strengthening combat readiness, and awaiting the time for the counter-offensive." Efforts, therefore, were made to systematize, scientifize, and organize the armed forces, establish various systems, strengthen military organizations, enforce military discipline, augment troop equipment, step up troop training and improve livelihood of officers and men. Assistance from our ally has helped our combat strength to grow along the lines of the modern forces of our ally. Our will-to-fight and combat experiences are some of the things that other nations are lacking. Actions such as the Battle of Nanjih,

Battle of Tungshan, Battle of Yichiangshan and numerous engagements in the Taiwan Straits, especially the August 23 shelling all testified to the high morale and the gallantry of the Chinese Armed Forces which are capable of defending the Pacific and thwarting Communist ambition of world conquest.

The excellent state of combat readiness of the Chinese National Revolutionary Forces at present will not only enable us to directly shoulder the task of national recovery and national reconstruction but will also have an important bearing on the security of Asia and the entire world. The objective development of the situation in our anti-Communist endeavor indicates that events are turning in our favor. The time for our national recovery will soon arrive. Our officers and men are readying themselves for the signal to put an end to Mao's bloody regime, restore our beautiful land and accomplish the sacred missions in the third phase of our national revolution.

Index

MAPS

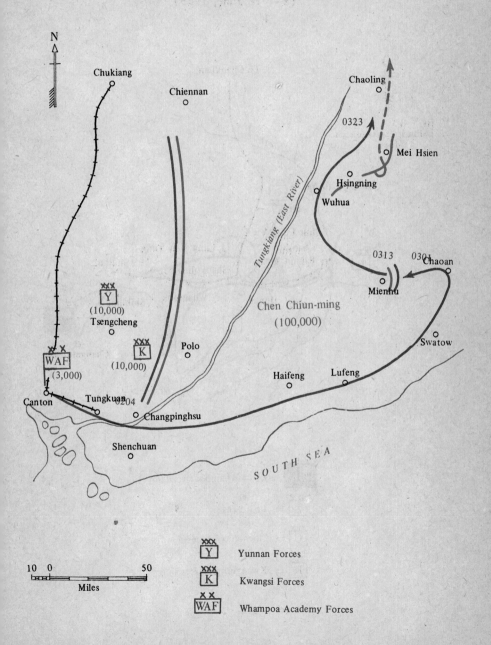

MAP 1
FIRST EASTWARD EXPEDITION
(Early January, 1925 — 23 March, 1925)

N

Chukiang

Chiennan

Chaoling

0323

Mei Hsien

Hsingning

Wuhua

Tungkiang (East River)

0313   0301   Chaoan

Mienhu

Chen Chiun-ming
(100,000)

Swatow

XXX
Y
(10,000)
Tsengcheng

Polo

Haifeng   Lufeng

XXX
K
(10,000)

WAF
(3,000)

Canton   Tungkuan
0204   Changpinghsu

Shenchuan

SOUTH SEA

10 0   50
Miles

XXX
Y   Yunnan Forces

XXX
K   Kwangsi Forces

XX
WAF   Whampoa Academy Forces

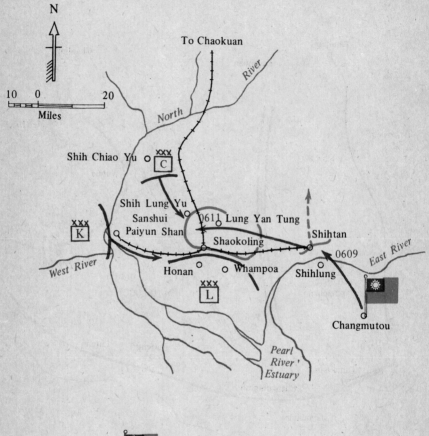

MAP 2
THE PROCEDURE OF THE RETURNING TO SUPPRESS
THE REBELLION OPERATION
(8 — 12 June, 1925)

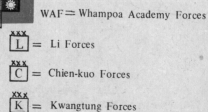

WAF = Whampoa Academy Forces

L = Li Forces

C = Chien-kuo Forces

K = Kwangtung Forces

MAP 3
SECOND EASTWARD EXPEDITION
(28 September — 7 November, 1925)

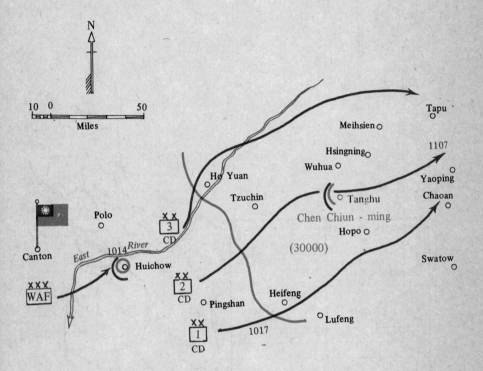

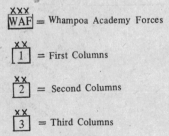

XXX
WAF = Whampoa Academy Forces

XX
1 = First Columns

XX
2 = Second Columns

XX
3 = Third Columns

MAP 4

THE SITUATION BEFORE NORTHWARD EXPEDITION

(July, 1926)

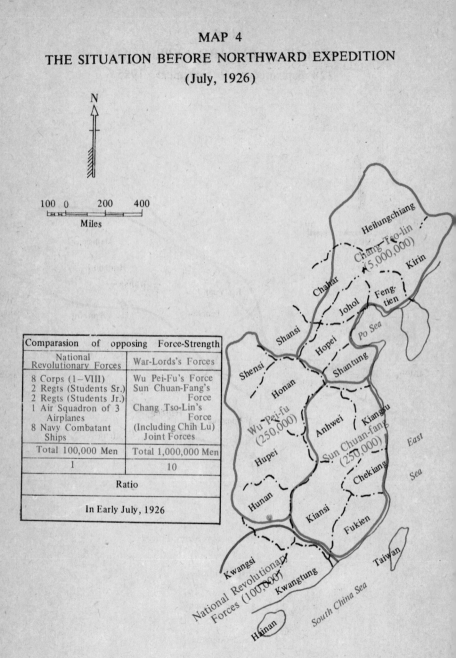

Comparasion of opposing Force-Strength	
National Revolutionary Forces	War-Lords's Forces
8 Corps (1–VIII) 2 Regts (Students Sr.) 2 Regts (Students Jr.) 1 Air Squadron of 3 Airplanes 8 Navy Combatant Ships	Wu Pei-Fu's Force Sun Chuan-Fang's Force Chang Tso-Lin's Force (Including Chih Lu) Joint Forces
Total 100,000 Men	Total 1,000,000 Men
1	10
Ratio	
In Early July, 1926	

N

100 0   200   400
Miles

Heilungchiang
Chang-Tso-lin (5,000,000)
Kirin
Chahar
Johol
Feng-tien
Shansi
Hopei
Po Sea
Shensi
Shantung
Honan
Wu Pei-fu (250,000)
Anhwei
Kiangsu
Sun Chuan-fang (250,000)
East
Hupei
Chekiang
Sea
Hunan
Kiansi
Fukien
Taiwan
Kwangsi
National Revolutionary Forces (100,000)
Kwangtung
Hainan
South China Sea

MAP 5

THE PROCESS OF NORTHWARD EXPEDITION

(5 June, 1926 — 29 December, 1928)

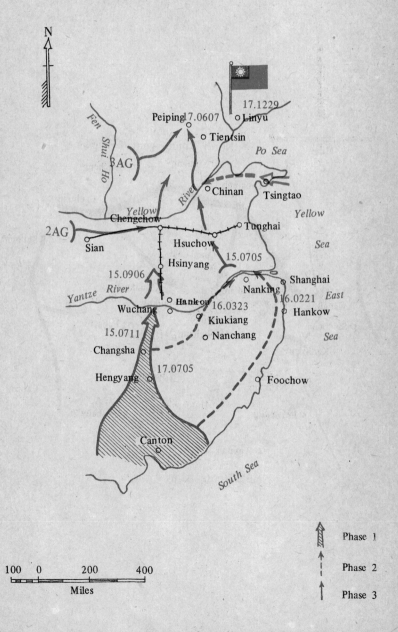

N

17.1229

Peiping 17.0607 Linyu

Tientsin

Fen Shui Ho

3AG

Po Sea

River

Chinan Tsingtao

Yellow Chengchow

Yellow

2AG Tunghai

Sian Hsuchow

Sea

Hsinyang 15.0705

15.0906

Yantze River Shanghai

Nanking

16.0221 East

Hankow 16.0323 Hankow

Wuchang Kiukiang

15.0711 Nanchang Sea

Changsha

17.0705

Hengyang Foochow

Canton

South Sea

100	0	200	400

Miles

➤ Phase 1

↑ Phase 2

↑ Phase 3

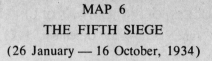

MAP 6

THE FIFTH SIEGE

(26 January — 16 October, 1934)

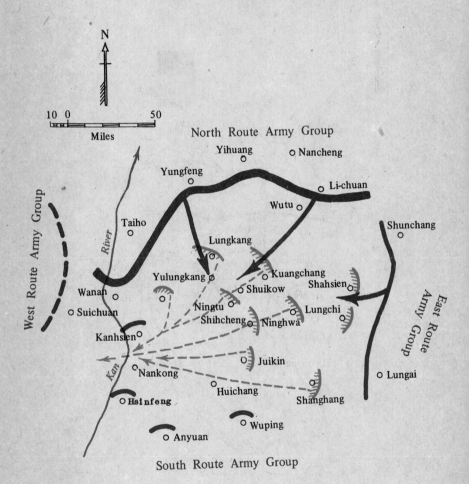

N

10 0   50

Miles

North Route Army Group

West Route Army Group

East Route Army Group

South Route Army Group

River

Kan

Yihuang

Nancheng

Yungfeng

Li-chuan

Wutu

Shunchang

Taiho

Lungkang

Yulungkang

Kuangchang

Shahsien

Shuikow

Wanan

Ningtu

Lungchi

Suichuan

Shihcheng

Ninghwa

Kanhsien

Nankong

Juikin

Lungai

Huichang

Hsinfeng

Shanghang

Wuping

Anyuan

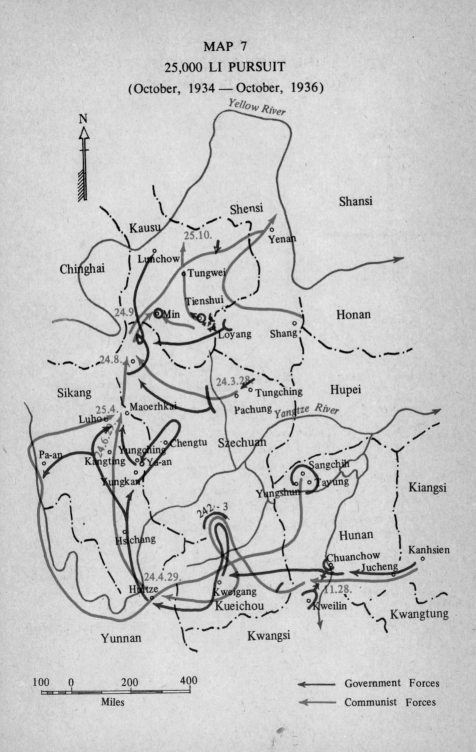

MAP 7

25,000 LI PURSUIT

(October, 1934 — October, 1936)

N

Yellow River

Shansi

Shensi

Kausu

Yenan

25.10.

Chinghai

Lunchow

Tungwei

Tienshui

24.9.

Min

Loyang

Shang

Honan

24.8.

Sikang

24.3.28.

Hupei

25.4.

Maoerhkai

Pachung

Yangtze River

Luhou

Chengtu

Szechuan

24.6.2.

Pa-an

Yungching

Sangchih

Kangting

Ya-an

Tayung

Kiangsi

Yungkan

Yungshun

242 - 3

Hunan

Hsichang

Chuanchow

Kanhsien

Jucheng

24.4.29.

Hutze

Kweigang

11.28.

Kueichou

Kweilin

Kwangtung

Yunnan

Kwangsi

100   0   200   400

Miles

⟵ Government Forces

⟵ Communist Forces

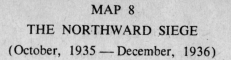

MAP 8
THE NORTHWARD SIEGE
(October, 1935 — December, 1936)

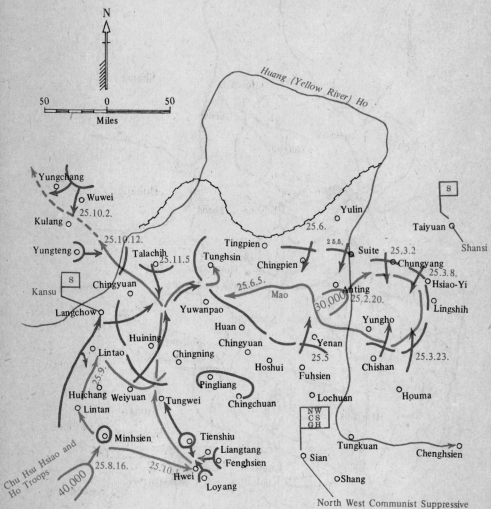

North West Communist Suppressive
General Headquarters

MAP 9
THE CHINA SITUATION BEFORE JULY 7 INCIDENT 1937

Before July 7 Incident Japanese Occupied Area
Communist Troops Occupied Area

100 0   200   400
Miles

MAP 10

AT THE END OF 1938 THE SITUATION AFTER CHINA RESISTANCE WAR FIRST PHASE OPERATION

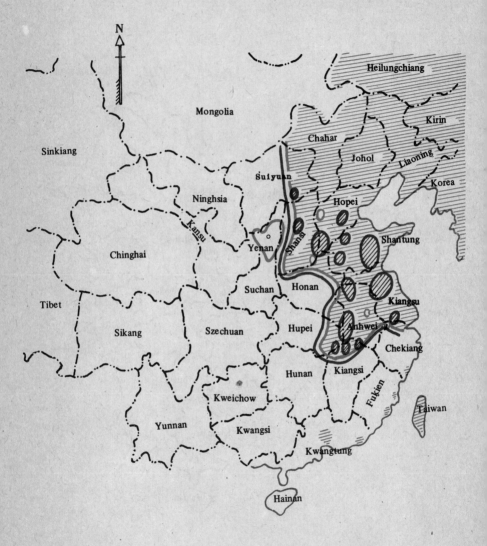

National Forces Guerilla Area
Communist Forces Extensive Area
Japanese Forces Occupied Area

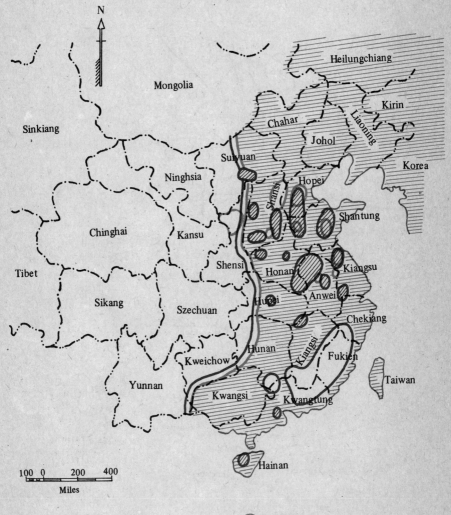

MAP 11
THE SITUATION AFTER CHINA RESISTANCE WAR
SECOND PHASE OPERATION
(During Spring)

N

Mongolia

Sinkiang

Heilungchiang

Kirin

Chahar

Liaoning

Johol

Korea

Suiyuan

Ninghsia

Hopei

Shansi

Shantung

Chinghai

Kansu

Shensi

Honan

Kiangsu

Tibet

Honan

Sikang

Szechuan

Hupei

Anwei

Chekiang

Hunan

Kiangsi

Fukien

Kweichow

Taiwan

Yunnan

Kwangsi

Kwangtung

Hainan

100 0   200   400

Miles

Japanese Forces Occupied Area

National Forces Guerilla Area

Communist Forces Extensive Area

Communist Troops invade
National Forces Guerilla Area

National Forces Post Area

MAP 12
THE SITUATION OF JAPANESE SURRENDER
(13 September, 1945)

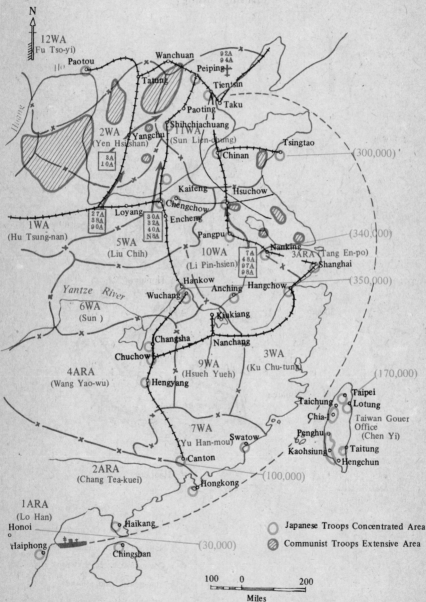

N

12WA
(Fu Tso-yi)

Paotou
Wanchuan
92A
94A
Peiping
Taitung
Tientsin
Taku
Paoting
Shihchiachuang
2WA
(Yen Hsi-shan)
Yangchu
11WA
(Sun Lien-chung)
Chinan
Tsingtao
(300,000)
8A
10A

Kaifeng
Hsuchow
1WA
(Hu Tsung-nan)
27A
38A
90A
Loyang
Chengchow
Encheng
30A
32A
40A
N8A
(340,000)
5WA
(Liu Chih)
Pangpu
10WA
(Li Pin-hsien)
7A
48A
97A
98A
Nanking
3ARA (Tang En-po)
Shanghai
Hankow
Anching
Hangchow
(350,000)
Yantze River
Wuchang
6WA
(Sun)
Kiukiang
Changsha
Nanchang
Chuchow
9WA
(Hsueh Yueh)
3WA
(Ku Chu-tung)
(170,000)
4ARA
(Wang Yao-wu)
Hengyang
Taichung
Taipei
Lotung
Chia-I
Taiwan Gouer
Office
(Chen Yi)
Penghu
7WA
(Yu Han-mou)
Swatow
Kaohsiung
Taitung
Canton
Hengchun
2ARA
(Chang Tea-kuei)
Hongkong
(100,000)
1ARA
(Lo Han)
Honoi
Haikang
Haiphong
(30,000)
Chingsban

○ Japanese Troops Concentrated Area
◑ Communist Troops Extensive Area

100   0   200
Miles

MAP 13

NATIONAL FORCES COMMUNIST SUPPRESSION OPERATION IN THE AREA OF SOUTH BANK OF THE SUNGARI RIVER

(From 19, May to 6, June, 1946)

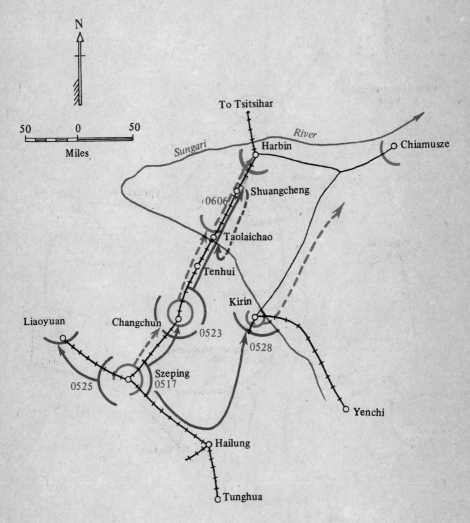

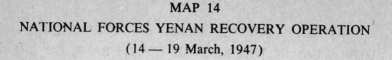

MAP 14
NATIONAL FORCES YENAN RECOVERY OPERATION
(14 — 19 March, 1947)

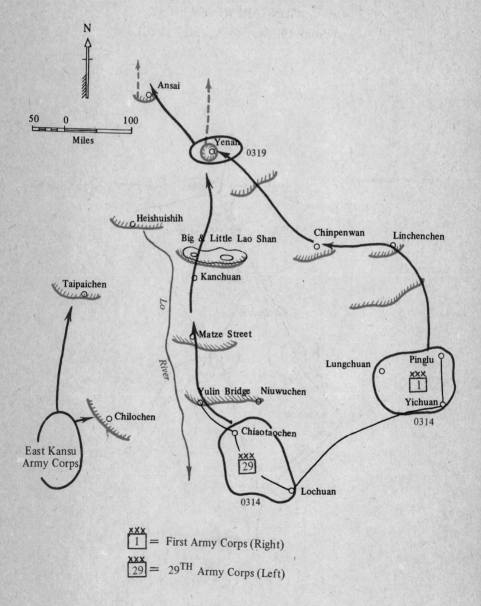

N

50   0   100
Miles

Ansai

Yenan   0319

Heishuishih

Big & Little Lao Shan

Chinpenwan   Linchenchen

Kanchuan

Taipaichen

Lo

River

Matze Street

Lungchuan   Pinglu

xxx
1

Yulin Bridge   Niuwuchen

Yichuan

0314

Chilochen

East Kansu
Army Corps

Chiaotaochen

xxx
29

Lochuan

0314

xxx
1   = First Army Corps (Right)

xxx
29   = 29TH Army Corps (Left)

MAP 15
NATIONAL FORCES NANMA OPERATION
(27 — 30 June, 1947)

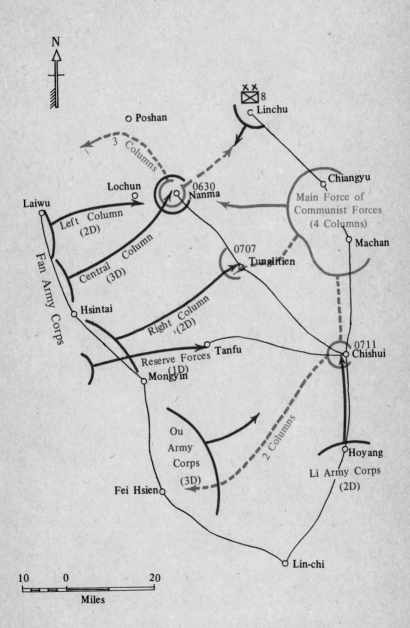

N

Poshan

⊠ 8
Linchu

3 Columns

Chiangyu

Lochun

0630
Nanma

Main Force of
Communist Forces
(4 Columns)

Laiwu

Left Column
(2D)

Machan

Central Column
(3D)

0707
Tunglitien

Fan Army Corps

Hsintai

Right Column
(2D)

0711
Chishui

Reserve Forces
(1D)

Tanfu

Mongyin

Ou
Army
Corps
(3D)

2 Columns

Hoyang

Li Army Corps
(2D)

Fei Hsien

Lin-chi

10   0   20
Miles